Battered Women, Their Children, and International Law

The Northeastern Series on Gender, Crime, and Law
   Editor: Claire Renzetti

For a complete list of books available in this series, please visit www.upne.com

The Unintended
Consequences
of the
Hague Child
Abduction
Convention

Battered Women,
Their Children,
and International Law

Taryn Lindhorst
Jeffrey L. Edleson

Northeastern University Press | BOSTON

Northeastern University Press
An imprint of University Press of New England
www.upne.com
© 2012 Northeastern University
All rights reserved
Manufactured in the United States of America
Typeset in Minion by Integrated Publishing Solutions

University Press of New England is a member of the Green Press Initiative. The paper used in this book meets their minimum requirement for recycled paper.

For permission to reproduce any of the material in this book, contact Permissions, University Press of New England, One Court Street, Suite 250, Lebanon NH 03766; or visit www.upne.com

Portions of chapter 7 appeared previously in W. Vesneski, T. Lindhorst, and J. Edleson, "U.S. Judicial Implementation of the Hague Convention in Cases Alleging Domestic Violence," *Juvenile and Family Court Journal* 62 (2011), 1–21.

The citation for the full report prepared for the National Institute of Justice, on which this book is based, is: J. L. Edleson and T. Lindhorst, *Multiple Perspectives on Battered Mothers and Their Children Fleeing to the United States for Safety: A Study of Hague Convention Cases* (Washington, D.C.: National Institute of Justice, 2010) (NCJRS Document No. 232624).

Library of Congress Cataloging-in-Publication Data

Lindhorst, Taryn.
Battered women, their children, and international law: the unintended consequences of the Hague Child Abduction Convention / Taryn Lindhorst and Jeffrey L. Edleson.
    p. cm.—(Northeastern series on gender, crime, and law)
Includes bibliographical references and index.
ISBN 978-1-55553-802-6 (cloth: alk. paper)—ISBN 978-1-55553-803-3 (pbk.: alk. paper)—ISBN 978-1-55553-804-0 (ebook: alk. paper)
1. Convention on the Civil Aspects of International Child Abduction (1980) 2. Parental kidnapping. 3. Abused women. 4. Family violence. 5. Custody of children. I. Edleson, Jeffrey L. II. Title.
K707.L56   2012
344.03'28297—dc23   2012023809

5 4 3 2 1

To Cindy, Maya and Cheryl—family in the truest sense of the word.
And to Sudha—visionary, steadfast advocate, and partner extraordinaire.

Contents

Foreword

When battered mothers cross international borders with their children, they are often seeking safety with relatives in their home country. But when they cross borders, they also run a risk that the left-behind fathers may petition the court for the return of their children. The 1980 Hague Convention on the Civil Aspects of International Child Abduction (the Hague Convention) provides a lightning-quick remedy for the left-behind parent. Under the Convention, courts in the United States commonly return children to the country from which they were taken in order for custody arrangements to be settled by that other country's courts. We expect the same from judges in the over 70 countries and territories that have partnered with us by signing this Convention and entering into an agreement with our government.

As happens occasionally, however, laws designed for a laudable purpose sometimes produce unintended results. Cases under the Hague Convention reveal an important gap in our knowledge about the impact of the Convention when there are allegations of domestic violence committed by left-behind parents against *taking* parents. Unfortunately, to date, most of the research on international child abduction has focused on studying the left-behind parents, presuming that in most cases this parent was the victim of the abducting or taking parent. This book chronicles the results of in-depth interviews of *taking* mothers and their attorneys and a published case analysis that paint a very different picture for one segment of taking parents—those who allege they are victims of domestic violence. For the first time, we have detailed accounts from battered mothers describing their experiences in other countries, their motivations for moving across borders, what they faced when responding to a Hague petition in US courts, and what happened to them and their children after the Hague decision was rendered. The deep and rich accounts of these mothers are compelling, and the experiences of their attorneys detail the steep hill that must be climbed to defend these mothers and their children.

The Convention was drafted long before policymakers understood the devastating impact that exposure to domestic violence has on children, or understood the dynamic of parents taking their children across borders to escape abuse. It is to the credit of those who drafted this treaty over three decades ago that they foresaw the need to provide exceptions to the return of children to the country from which they were taken. The US Supreme Court, in its 2010 *Abbott v. Abbott* decision, suggested that domestic violence could be considered as a potential risk to a child and therefore an exception to returning a child. The study reported in this book argues for a closer look at adult-to-adult domestic violence and not only the risk it represents for children, but also the role that violent coercion and deception play in establishing a child's habitual residence.

Ultimately, we need to know that the systems we design to ensure the well-being of children are focused on their best interests. The Hague Convention has this goal at heart, but in the actual application of the treaty, the safety of children and of battered women may be compromised. Judges must carefully analyze the circumstances that have led to the Hague petition and develop a nuanced understanding of the ways in which domestic violence occurs in families. When judges decide to return a child to the habitual residence where the father resides, more coordinated efforts are needed to safeguard children and their mothers. As this study suggests, the use of voluntary undertakings is often an insufficient mechanism for protecting children and mothers upon their return.

This book will help judges, attorneys, domestic violence advocates, and others better understand the plight of taking parents who have been victims of domestic violence. It has been my pleasure to work with, and learn from, the authors and their colleagues for almost a decade as we have studied this issue together. I hope the information in this book will provide you with a deeper and more nuanced understanding of the Hague Convention—both its power to help victims of family violence and its possible unintended consequences.

Chief Justice Barbara Madsen
Washington State Supreme Court
Olympia, Washington
June 2012

Preface

This book began because of one woman who reached out for help after fleeing her physically abusive husband. Although all of us who worked on this book have extensive backgrounds in research and practice with women survivors of domestic violence, none of us had heard of the Hague Convention on the Civil Aspects of International Child Abduction until this woman came forward. Her story mobilized us to explore further the intersection between international law, domestic violence, and the safety of women and children. We acknowledge this woman's bravery in her efforts to protect herself and her children, and we thank each of the women who shared deeply personal, difficult stories with the research interviewers with the wish that their experiences could help other families. We acknowledge their strength throughout the experiences they had, and their courage in sharing their stories with us.

Our intended audience for this book is fourfold. First, we know that many legal professionals who work with families in Hague Convention cases are unfamiliar with the dynamics of domestic violence. We wrote this book to inform people outside the domestic violence field about theory and available research on domestic violence and its effects, and to provide examples from women's experiences that can sensitize and enhance how legal professionals assess and respond to abuse claims. Second, domestic violence advocates are generally unfamiliar with the Hague Convention. Through an in-depth review of the policies and practices surrounding Hague Convention cases, we hope to provide advocates with information that can help them in their interactions with domestic violence survivors in the United States and abroad. Third, international treaties such as the Hague Convention are implemented and administered by a variety of national and international policymakers and government officials. The Hague Convention was written to protect children, but as this research will demonstrate, without fully understanding the reasons underlying the decision to leave one country for another, officials may return children to situations that are harmful to them physically and psychologically. Policymakers and administrators are in a position to advocate for a more thorough awareness of what is happening in these families. Fourth, the experiences of the women and children who participated in this study illuminate deeper theoretical concerns related to globalization, gender, and cross-cultural experiences of domestic violence. We hope, therefore, that this book will be useful to scholars in these areas.

This research would not have been possible without the efforts of Sudha Shetty, former director of the Access to Justice Institute at Seattle University Law School, and the students who worked with her to create the first project on Hague Convention cases where domestic violence was alleged. These early efforts were transformed through the volunteer efforts of attorneys at Thomson Reuters and law students from the Minnesota Justice Foundation into the ongoing website for the Hague Domestic Violence Project located at www.hague dv.org.

In a research undertaking such as this, the final product is the result of the collaborative support of many individuals and institutions, although we fully acknowledge that any errors are the responsibility of the authors. In particular, we would like to acknowledge the support given us to conduct this research by our home institutions, the University of Minnesota and the University of Washington Schools of Social Work, and the staff of the National Institute of Justice (NIJ) who shepherded this project: Leora Rosen, Karen Bachar, Bernie Auchter, and Christine Crossland. We were assisted by members of our National Advisory Board in the recruitment, analysis, and dissemination of the research: Hon. Barbara Madsen, Chief Justice, Washington State Supreme Court; Hon. Ann Schindler, Judge, Washington State Court of Appeals; Prof. Merle H. Weiner, Philip H. Knight Professor, University of Oregon School of Law; Chad Allred, JD, attorney-at-law, Ellis, Li & McKinstry, Seattle, Washington; Barbara Hart, JD, Battered Women's Justice Project and University of Southern Maine; Paula Lucas, founder and executive director, Americans Overseas Domestic Violence Crisis Center, Portland, Oregon; Sarah Ainsworth, JD, Counsel Emerita, Legal Voice, Seattle, Washington; and Roberta Valente, JD, then general counsel, National Network to End Domestic Violence, Washington, DC.

We especially want to thank the attorneys and advocates who helped recruit women to our study, and those who also participated in interviews themselves. We want to acknowledge the many volunteer lawyers and web designers from Thomson Reuters' West and FindLaw divisions, and the law students who worked with us on this project through the sponsorship of the Minnesota Justice Foundation. They all helped us tremendously in developing our project websites and in identifying published Hague Convention cases. Finally, we would like to thank our colleagues at the Hague Conference on Private International Law for their helpful reflections on the content of this book, and Sietske Dijkstra and Anita Schreurs-van Dijk of Avans University, the Netherlands, for hosting a presentation of these findings in Utrecht, the Netherlands.

Many colleagues have given of their time to read drafts of this work, including Merle Weiner, University of Oregon School of Law; Jane Gilgun, University of Minnesota School of Social Work; and Justice Shireen Avis Fisher, Justice of Appeals, Special Court for Sierra Leone and a retired trial judge for the state of Vermont; Helene Starks, Clarissa Hsu, Tatiana Masters, and Mark Wicks of the University of Washington Qualitative Research Writing Group; and the three anonymous reviewers obtained by NIJ. This book would not have been published without the encouragement of Claire Renzetti and the patience and faith of Phyllis Deutsch, our editor.

The opinions or points of view expressed in this book are those of the authors and do not necessarily reflect the official position or policies of the US Department of Justice.

Authors' Note

Although many international conventions are administered by the Hague Conference on Private International Law, for ease of reading in this book we refer to the Convention on the Civil Aspects of International Child Abduction as the "Hague Convention" or the "Convention."

For reasons we discuss in the introduction and in appendix B on the research method of the women's study, the confidentiality of people involved in Hague Convention petitions can be more easily breached because these cases are relatively rare. We have taken measures to ensure the anonymity of the participants in this study, including changing details about states, countries, and family members involved. In all cases, the original names of the women and children in our study have been changed (please see appendix B for more information on protection of the research participants).

Because such a high percentage of the couples were married at some point in their relationships, we usually refer to the men as "husbands" rather than the more generic "partner."

Throughout the book, when we describe aspects of the women's cases, we note those women whose children were returned to the other country with an asterisk (*) each time we tell one of their stories, so the reader can visualize the patterns (or lack thereof) in the experiences of women who had their children returned to the other country versus those whose children remained with them in the United States.

In transcribed quotations from our interviews, pauses in the respondent's speech are noted by ellipses . . . to denote longer-than-usual times of silence. Bracketed ellipses [. . .] are used to denote words in that have been dropped to limit unnecessary repetition, remarks from the interviewer, or information not directly relevant to the overall point of the quoted excerpt. Explanations of unclear referents in an excerpt are also included in brackets.

Battered Women, Their Children,
and International Law

Introduction
Globalization, Families, and Domestic Violence

The Hague Convention in Practice

Falling in love and starting a family is one of the joyful events of life. We are planning for the best when we begin a romantic relationship, full of ideals and hope. But what if the hope of the early days of love becomes a landscape of conflict and destruction? What happens when conflict erupts into physical violence, and into threats that may be worse than violence in the mind of the victim? And what if all of this occurs in another country, far from family and friends who could provide material and emotional support? If this happened to you, would you try to go to a place where your family could help? What if you left your harmful situation, but were now in legal trouble because you'd been accused of child abduction after taking your children across international borders? What if the courts decided to send your children back to the person from whom you had fled?

No one starts a relationship expecting to become a victim of domestic violence. For the women whose stories are the center of this book, these questions are not hypothetical. Each has been subject to a legal petition in US courts for the return of their children under the Hague Convention on the Civil Aspects of International Child Abduction. The Hague Convention was originally conceived to protect children who were retained unlawfully by a non-custodial parent in another country (Weiner, 2000). Its intent was to provide legal recourse to the primary caregiver of the children, usually the mother, to obtain the prompt return of her children if taken from the country without permission. In practice, the intended beneficiaries of the Convention have become its primary targets. In the case of a family harmed by a father's violent and abusive behavior, mothers have been repositioned as wrongdoers, as "child abductors" who are harming their children when they flee their husbands' violence (Shetty & Edleson, 2005). It is a situation that evokes the tragic—the policy solution to help the intended victims (custodial mothers) has become a tool in the hands of abusive fathers. Women attempting to protect their children and themselves from a husband's violence are recast as harmful child abductors by the very treaty that was intended to help them overcome a father's hostile behavior.

The flight of battered women and children across international borders raises two paradoxical issues. First, women are traditionally castigated for staying with violent husbands. Since the earliest writing on battered women in the 1970s, many have asked, "Why does she stay with an abusive partner?" (Martin, 1976). For mothers who finally flee the batterer, but end up crossing an international border to do so, the ironic focus becomes the exact opposite: "Why did she leave?" Second, under the current policies and procedures emanating from the Hague Convention, the treaty indicates that women should stay with their children in the country where they are living, even in the face of serious abuse, under the often incorrect assumption that services and resources are available to assist them in the other country (Bruch, 2004; Weiner, 2001). Ultimately, the implication of the Hague Convention is that women can either choose to save themselves and leave their children behind if they need to escape the violence, or stay in the other country and risk trauma, injury, and potentially death at the hands of their abuser in order to comply with the directive that decisions on their children's custody be made in the country of *habitual residence*.

The original goals of the Hague Convention were worthy ones that continue to be relevant today: to ensure the prompt return of children to their habitual residence; to protect children and left-behind parents from the harm caused by abduction; and to assist non-abusive parents with valid claims to their children. The way in which the Convention unfolds in the lives of battered mothers who have fled with their children from sometimes horrific violence is a different story of the Hague Convention's impact, and one that this research sought to illuminate.

This book is concerned with the intersection between what is usually considered *private* (that is, transnational family relationships and domestic violence) and the *public*, namely the legal processes that are evoked on behalf of children in a global context. Women and children are on the front line of changes caused by the macroeconomic and structural shifts associated with globalization, but their stories often are not central to debates on the effects of these transformations. We seek to center their concerns in this book, and to link them to broader issues and scholarship on globalization, citizenship, and gender justice.

To help orient readers to common circumstances in Hague cases that involve domestic violence,[1] we begin with a brief story. This case study, though based on information we gathered from women and attorneys, should be read as an exemplar, not as the story of a particular family. Every aspect of this story was told to us during our interviews, but the story itself does not represent a particular family, country, or set of actors. Instead, we describe certain dynamics that were shared by many of the women. We follow this composite case study with specific information about the Hague Convention before considering the larger theoretical landscape of globalization and how transnational processes frame the research we present in this book.

The Paradox of Leaving: A Case Study

Lena and Alberto met while both were at college in a small town in the United States. Theirs was a stormy romance, with Lena feeling enchanted by Alberto's charm and solicitousness, but dismayed by his jealous reaction to her friends. As the couple grew closer, Lena saw less of her friends to keep the peace with Alberto. They both enjoyed making plans for a life shared between Lena's small-town Indiana home and Alberto's family in Italy. After a year of marriage, their son Tomas was born. Alberto became increasingly angry after Tomas's birth, berating Lena repeatedly for what he saw as her deficiencies as a mother and a wife. When Tomas was two, Alberto announced that he wanted to move to Italy to give Tomas a chance to know his father's culture and family. Lena was uncertain about moving, but she hoped that by doing so, her conflict with Alberto would lessen.

When they arrived in Italy, Alberto became even more controlling of Lena. The first time he saw her trying to speak with a neighbor in her rudimentary Italian, he grabbed her by the arm, leaving bruises, and locked her in a bedroom. He insisted that Lena stay in the house and not speak to anyone outside his family. He would often leave the house for hours at a time, not coming back until late at night. The couple began to argue more. One night when Lena demanded to know where he was going, Alberto began punching her, yelling that

---

1. We use the term *domestic violence* instead of *intimate partner violence* or *gender-based violence* because it is the term most prevalent in US legal discourse. We understand that there are conceptual limitations to this term, particularly its focus on place (that is, the home, even though victimization occurs outside of cohabitation) and on violence (which is usually defined as physical harm, although emotional harm can be equally or more disturbing), and its gender neutrality in the face of evidence that women worldwide bear the brunt of victimization.

she had no right to question him. She could hear Tomas crying as Alberto beat her. The next morning, seeing the bruises on Lena's body, Alberto was contrite, telling her that he was upset by her questions and not to pester him about where he was going. Over the next few weeks, he was as charming as when they had first met, taking her out to dinner, and driving her and Tomas through the countryside. The good times faded as Alberto became angrier and angrier—about his business, about Tomas's crying, about Lena's failings. He would slap her when dinner wasn't ready, or if he was upset with her. When he became really angry, he would raise his fist to show that he would hit her again if she didn't stop what she was doing; sometimes he hit her anyway. He told her that he would take Tomas away if she defied him. He took their passports and hid them so she couldn't "run away."

Lena lived in chronic fear of angering Alberto. She had no friends and spoke very little Italian. She had no money and no way to talk with anyone in the United States without Alberto listening. Alberto insisted on sex, regardless of how she was feeling. She became pregnant again, but began having trouble with her health. Lena asked Alberto to let her return with Tomas to the United States for a visit and to see the doctor who had helped her through her first pregnancy. Alberto agreed to a one-month trip, and accompanied them to her parents' house in Indiana. However, once they were there, Lena had a miscarriage. Alberto returned to Italy a few days later because of a business emergency.

Lena's parents could see the tension in their daughter and in Tomas. Lena finally told them what had happened over the past years. Her parents encouraged her to stay with them, even though Lena was afraid of what Alberto would do if she didn't return. They convinced her to begin divorce proceedings. One month after Lena told Alberto that she had filed for divorce, federal marshals arrived at her parents' house. They served Lena with what they called a "Hague petition" and took Tomas, crying, from the house. The Hague petition stated that Lena had unlawfully prevented Tomas from returning to his home in Italy. Alberto, with the assistance of the US State Department, had found an attorney to file a case in federal court to have Tomas returned to him. Lena was told to be in court in three days for the hearing. She was not allowed to know where Tomas was being taken.

Lena's divorce lawyer had never heard of the Hague petition. He requested more time to prepare for the hearing, but the judge denied the request, saying that it was paramount to return the child to his habitual residence as quickly as possible, and that any issues regarding divorce and custody would have to be worked out in the other country. A few days after the hearing, the judge ruled that Lena had improperly kept Tomas in the United States, and that he was to be returned to Italy immediately. During the court proceedings, Lena learned that if she were to return to Italy, the Italian police had a warrant for her arrest on charges of child kidnapping. Lena's appeals were denied, and three weeks later, Tomas was with Alberto on a plane back to Italy. In Italy, Alberto was given sole custody of Tomas, after persuading the judge that Lena had kidnapped the boy. Although the criminal charges against her were eventually dropped, Lena has not been able to see or talk with Tomas for several months. She is not sure when—or even if—she will see her son again.

Women whose partners are abusive often turn to family members for assistance in coping and in repairing their lives. When returning to family means leaving one nation for another, a web of international treaties may be invoked that can result in a woman who has fled from abuse being held responsible for unlawfully removing her children, and potentially being subjected to legal proceedings related to child abduction. Mothers who flee with their children may have few other options to ensure their own safety, and their children's, in the face of their partner's violence; yet they remain vulnerable to being treated by the courts as an abducting parent.

Although it is unknown what proportion of Hague Convention cases involve domestic violence, it is clear from case law and legal advocacy work that some women come to the United States with their children every year because they are afraid for their safety (Weiner, 2003). Despite the fact that the Hague Convention has been in effect for more than 30 years, we know very little about the circumstances of women and children who have fled from abuse and then faced a Hague petition here in US courts. In fact, outside of a small cadre of international family law attorneys, US State Department administrators, and the handful of judges and individuals who have been involved in Hague Convention decisions, few people know of the Convention. As the world shrinks through processes of globalization and economic migration, situations in which the Hague Convention comes into effect are increasing, but our information about what happens before, during, and after these legal proceedings is limited. For people concerned about the safety and well-being of women and children exposed to violence, our lack of knowledge is worrisome.

Transnational relationships have become more common, and negotiating the dissolution of these relationships is increasingly complicated. Many of the women who participated in our research are American citizens, but some are not. Most are married to men who are citizens of another country, but this is not always the case. Children sometimes are allowed to remain in the United States, but often they are returned to the other country, and, as we will show in the cases we studied, to an abusive parent. To understand the legal position of transnational families, we turn now to a discussion of the Hague Convention.

What Is the Hague Convention on the Civil Aspects of International Child Abduction?

In 1980, the Convention on the Civil Aspects of International Child Abduction was finalized at The Hague in the Netherlands and has now been adopted by more than 80 countries around the world (Hague Conference on Private International Law [HCPIL], 2010). The treaty was designed to protect children from the harmful effects of having one parent unilaterally decide to leave a country in which the child had lived, without the permission of another parent, and in violation of the custody rights of that parent. Parents were thought to take this action when they were dissatisfied with their current access or custodial rights to the child, or when they thought they might receive a more favorable hearing in the court of another (usually their home) country, a tactic referred to as "jurisdiction shopping."

Certain definitions are commonly used within Hague Convention proceedings, and we use them in this book, so it would be helpful to spell out some of them here:

Left-Behind Parent: Parent in the country of habitual residence who asserts that a child has been wrongfully removed through a Hague application or petition.
Taking Parent: Parent who has removed the child from the habitual residence.
Petitioner: In a Hague Convention case, the left-behind parent; usually a father in this study. Sometimes also referred to as the applicant.[2]
Respondent: In a Hague Convention case, the taking parent; usually a mother in this study.[3]

2. This study does not address petitioners who are left-behind parents in the United States who experienced domestic violence and whose partners are perpetuating the violence by abducting the child.

3. In this book we will refer to respondents as mothers and petitioners as fathers, as this was the legal status of the individuals in the US cases we reviewed. However, if a father has abducted children to a country other than the United States (an outgoing case), the mother would be considered the petitioner and the father the respondent.

Outgoing Case: In reference to the United States, a child who has been taken from the United States to another country.

Incoming Case: In reference to the United States, a child who has come from another country to the United States.

Discussions held at the time of the treaty's crafting centered on the grave negative implications for a child's development and well-being caused by parental abduction, leading to the Convention drafters' conclusion that a prompt return of children to their country of habitual residence would facilitate a better outcome for the child (Perez-Vera, 1981). Children's habitual residence is understood to be the country in which they are usually resident, although this term has not been defined within the parameters of the Convention, and court rulings on what constitutes habitual residence vary. Parents who take their children out of the country without the permission of the other custodial parent can be taken to civil court to have the children removed and returned to the habitual residence and often to the left-behind parent. Criminal kidnapping charges may also be made against the taking parent through each country's criminal justice system. Although the Hague Convention, ostensibly, does not adjudicate child custody arrangements in families, a decision to return a child to the other country often becomes a de facto custody decision, as mothers' stories of the Hague process will demonstrate.

Nations party to the Convention are expected to help quickly return abducted children to their habitual residence, where other issues, such as custody, can be resolved by local jurisdictions (Beaumont & McEleavy, 1999; Garbolino, 2000; Hilton, 1997). The focus of the treaty is on the speedy resolution of questions related to the return of a child to his or her habitual residence, assuming that the legal system of that country would be best equipped to ensure the child's best interests. This assumption rests on principles of cooperation between nation-states and respect for diverse cultural and legal systems. The citizenship of the parents and children is not considered when reviewing a Hague petition. As a result, families can be citizens of one country and habitually reside in another, and it is the court of the habitual residence—not the court that represents the citizenship of the family—that is charged with making decisions about custody and visitation rights.[4]

---

4. For example, the 2010 *Abbott v. Abbott* case in the US Supreme Court involved two American citizens living in Chile. The mother returned with her child to the United States, and the father filed a Hague petition requesting the prompt return of the child to Chile.

The Hague Convention was framed with the understanding that the most frequent and typical parental abductor was a non-custodial father who took children from their primary caregiver mother. This belief was reinforced in the public's mind by the subsequent publication of the story of Betty Mahmoody in a book and movie *Not without My Daughter* (Mahmoody & Hoffer, 1987). Mahmoody went to Iran with her husband and young daughter for what she thought was a visit, but her husband intended them to remain in his country, and forcibly kept them in Iran. Mahmoody eventually smuggled herself and her daughter out of Iran and back to the United States. This story reinforced the beliefs that policymakers held about the likely targets (non-custodial fathers) and beneficiaries (mothers and children) of the Hague Convention (Weiner, 2000). As a result, the public perception exists that taking parents have committed wrongful acts that have both civil and potentially criminal consequences, and that left-behind parents and children have been unfairly harmed by abductions.

A recent global analysis of the characteristics of taking parents demonstrates the flawed nature of these assumptions. In 2008 Professor Nigel Lowe of Cardiff University Law School, in cooperation with the Permanent Bureau of the Hague Conference, undertook the third global survey of signatories to the Convention (Lowe, 2011). Hague petitions had increased by 45% across surveyed countries since the second survey in 2003. Internationally, 69% of the taking parents who were respondents to Hague petitions were mothers; 88% of these respondent mothers were the primary caregivers of their children, and 51% had gone home to a country in which they held citizenship. Unfortunately, the international community has been slow to recognize that some abducting parents may be battered mothers fleeing from their habitual residence and going home to seek safety for themselves and their children.

The Hague Convention was implemented in the United States through the International Child Abduction Remedies Act ([ICARA] 42 U.S.C. § 11603) passed by Congress in July 1988. ICARA established substantive and procedural mandates for handling cases in which children are removed from or retained in a country other than their habitual residence in violation of custody rights. These are civil and not criminal (that is, kidnapping) cases, so they are heard in civil, not criminal, courts. The US Department of State (2010b) reports that the US government has accepted more than 70 countries and territories as partners to the Hague Convention, although more have signed the treaty but have yet to become US partners. Most of the US treaty partners are located in Europe and the Americas. However, each year new countries are signing onto the Convention, thus expanding the populations covered by the treaty and the number of potential US partners. Currently, China, India, Russia, and most of Asia, Africa, and the Middle East are not signatories to the Convention, so alternative legal remedies must be pursued for return of children in those nations. Globally, the United States accounts for the highest number of incoming Hague applications, approximately 14.4% of all petitions filed in the most recent survey available (Lowe, 2011).

Under the Hague Convention, US law distinguishes between incoming and outgoing cases. Incoming cases are those in which the parent and child have come into the United States, leaving behind the other parent in a different country. In these cases, a Hague Convention petition is initiated by the left-behind parent's legal representative in a US court.[5]

In outgoing cases, a child has been taken by a parent to another country from the United States. In these cases, the US Department of State, acting as the US Central Authority, assists the left-behind parent in receiving help from the other country's Central Authority to file a Hague Convention petition in the courts of the country where the child is believed to now reside. The most recent highly publicized example of an outgoing case is that of David and Bruna Goldman (Semple, 2009). In 2004, Bruna took the couple's four-year-old son to Brazil, and then filed for a divorce in that country; she subsequently died giving birth to a daughter with her second husband. The US father initiated a Hague petition in Brazilian courts and was reunited with his son almost five years later, after numerous legal and diplomatic disputes.

The actual rate of international child abduction remains unknown. The most recent National Incidence Study of Missing, Abducted, Runaway, and Thrownaway Children (NISMART-2; Hammer, Finkelhor, & Sedlak, 2002) estimated that 203,900 American children were abducted by family members in 1999. Unfortunately, this survey did not separately identify international abductions from domestic ones. Of the estimated total US abductions in the NISMART study, only one-quarter (56,500) were reported to authorities. Similarly, the actual number of international abduction cases is likely higher than the number reported to the US Central Authority. Left-behind parents may

5. To date, no Hague petitions have been filed in the United States by same-sex partners who are legally married in countries outside the United States. Ten countries have legalized same-sex marriage as of 2010 (Argentina, Belgium, Canada, Iceland, Netherlands, Norway, Portugal, South Africa, Spain, and Sweden). All of these countries are Hague treaty partners with the United States, so it is conceivable that Hague petitions could be filed on behalf of same-sex partners in the future.

Table I.1 Countries with Largest Number of Outgoing and Incoming Cases of International Parental Abduction Reported to US Department of State, October 1, 2008–September 30, 2009

Origin	Outgoing (child taken from US to other country)		Incoming (child taken from other country to US)		Total	
	Cases	Children	Cases	Children	Cases	Children
Mexico	309	474	75	120	384	594
United Kingdom	48	71	31	44	79	115
Canada	74	104	29	39	103	143
Germany	50	71	18	20	68	91

US Department of State, 2010

choose not to engage in legal or governmental action, may attempt to negotiate directly with the other parent, or may pursue cases in state or federal courts and not report their activity to the Department of State, making it impossible to have a true count of these cases. Making such a count even more difficult is the fact that Hague petitions may be filed in either state or federal courts in the United States, resulting in more than 30,000 judges who may hear such a case.

Table I.1 lists the figures on international parental abduction cases reported to the us Department of State in a recent report to Congress (CY 2009). The us Department of State's Office of Children's Issues (2012a; 2012b) reported that 1,728 children were allegedly abducted by parents into or out of the United States during 2011, of which 1,015 were taken to Hague partner countries and 336 to non-partner countries. There were 345 children removed from other Hague partner countries and brought into the United States, while 16 were brought into the United States from non-partner countries, as reported to the us Central Authority. Fleeing mothers who are the focus of this study would be included among the incoming cases from Hague partner countries if the petitioner requested the involvement of the us Central Authority, that is, the Office of Children's Issues. Some mothers may face Hague petitions that were filed directly with a state or federal court that did not involve the us Central Authority. Currently, no system exists in the United States for tracking cases that are not voluntarily reported to the Office of Children's Issues.

The United States assigned coordination of incoming cases to the National Center for Missing and Exploited Children (NCMEC) until April 2008, when coordination was returned to the Office of Children's Issues. This same office has provided assistance to left-behind parents in outgoing cases since ratification of the Convention. Now the Office of Children's Issues facilitates the provision of *pro bono* or reduced-fee legal assistance for the left-behind parent in incoming cases (in this study, the fathers). The Office of Children's Issues may fund travel for left-behind parents to attend legal hearings or to be reunited with a child in the United States if the parent cannot afford this, and also provides information and tracking of cases (us Department of State, n.d.). Currently, the Department of State offers no formal assistance to taking parents, but will provide them with a list of attorneys experienced in Hague legal proceedings and other information on request.

The Hague Convention and Domestic Violence

Conceived of as a treaty that focuses exclusively on the child, the Hague Convention does not expressly recognize domestic violence against a spouse as a reason to deny the return of the child to the habitual residence.[6] Domestic violence is not mentioned in the Convention, and none of the exceptions explicitly mentions domestic violence as a reason to consider when making a decision about whether the child should be returned to the habitual residence. With little legal scaffolding, courts around the world have been left to wrestle with the role that adult-to-adult domestic violence should play in making decisions about child residence. The total number of battered mothers subject to legal proceedings under the Hague Convention is impossible to ascertain because there is no central repository of all Hague cases, or international divorce and custody disputes that include allegations of the presence of domestic violence. The absolute number of us Hague Convention cases is small compared to the total number of domestic child custody cases, and Hague cases involving domestic violence are also relatively small compared to estimated levels of domestic violence globally (see Johnson, Ollus, & Nevala, 2008 for a recent overview of international domestic violence rates).

The Hague Convention was not conceived as a remedy to issues of domestic violence. In fact, it was drafted three decades ago, at the beginning of the

6. Although domestic violence was not explicitly mentioned in the Convention, discussions during the drafting of the Convention did recognize that children may be taken out of a country for reasons related to domestic violence (Weiner, 2000). However, these discussions were not necessarily available to us judges, particularly those in state family court systems, so these framing concerns have not been central to implementation of the treaty.

modern movement to end violence against women and before numerous research studies were conducted that have revealed the potentially damaging effects of domestic violence exposure for children. The Convention is focused on the potential harm to children caused by parental abduction, without consideration for the reasons the "abduction" might be occurring. Although the treaty was not envisioned as a policy response to the issue of serious domestic violence and child abuse within families, those who drafted the Convention were aware that there would be circumstances under which children would face a grave risk of harm, an intolerable situation, or a violation of their human rights if they should be returned to the country of habitual residence. These concerns led the drafters to include exceptions to the child's return, such as Article 13(b) (grave risk) and Article 20 (human rights violations), to allow for judicial discretion when addressing unforeseen dangers that would result from the return of children. Despite these articles being an integral part of the Convention, they are often viewed as potentially undermining its intent (Silberman, 2000).

Only a few nongovernmental organizations have undertaken small studies or investigations of parents involved in Hague Convention cases, and only one of these studies has directly focused on the issue of domestic violence in the lives of taking parents. The most active organization has been Reunite International, located in the United Kingdom. Reunite has completed three separate studies that, in varying degrees, focus on international abduction cases. In the first study (Reunite International, 2003), international abductions involving 33 returned children in 22 families were examined. Of the 22 abducting parents, 14 were mothers, and 13 had returned to the child's country of habitual residence either with their child or at the same time as the child. Six abducting mothers raised concerns about domestic violence against them on return, and two others raised concerns about child abuse on return. In a subsequent Reunite study that focused on the impact of abductions (Freeman, 2006), there is mention of abducting mothers alleging domestic violence by left-behind fathers, and a belief by at least one mother that the Hague Convention was used as a method by the left-behind father to maintain contact not with his children but with her. Reunite's third study (Freeman, 2009) focused on relocation issues and makes little mention of the role of domestic violence in international relocations.

Two other investigations, one by International Social Service (ISS; 2007) in Australia and another by the Ombudsman Foundation (2002) in the Netherlands, provide additional information. ISS investigated the link between domestic violence and international child abduction, with a focus on recommendations for service delivery. Unfortunately, only 4 of 12 parent interviews conducted were with taking mothers; the majority were with women whose husbands had taken their children out of country. As a result, limited information was available on mothers who may have fled domestic violence. The ISS report concluded that "the overwhelming consensus from all the interviews where domestic violence or alleged domestic violence was present is that the primary motivator for mothers who abducted was the violence they experienced" (p. 9). The Dutch investigation (Ombudsman Foundation, 2002) was more of a journalistic review of seven cases that involved child abductions between the Netherlands and other countries. Although domestic violence was seldom mentioned in the case summaries, the authors concluded that the return of a child was not necessarily in the child's best interests, and that children were often victims and not beneficiaries of the Hague Convention's enforcement. At this time, little systematic evidence is available to guide our understanding of domestic violence issues in Hague Convention cases.

Exceptions to Return of a Child under the Hague Convention

Although domestic violence is not explicitly mentioned in the wording of the Hague Convention, the treaty does recognize that there may be times when returning a child to the habitual residence may not be warranted. Subsequent conversations among treaty members have made clear that domestic violence may be a circumstance in which the return of a child should not occur. For an exception to be granted (and the father's petition for return denied) in the United States, a judge must first decide that the habitual residence of the child was in a country other than the United States, and second, that the retention in or removal to the United States was indeed wrongful. That is, the removal or retention breached the custody rights of the left-behind parent under the laws of the habitual residence, and those rights were actually being exercised or would have been exercised but for the removal or retention of the child. In cases where the child is 16 years or older, the Hague Convention does not apply.

Once it is established that the child has been wrongfully removed from a habitual residence other than the United States, five exceptions or defenses may be available to a mother to prevent the return of the child to the country of habitual residence. Although these exceptions, once established, allow the court to refrain from returning the child, they do not obligate the judge to order that the child stay in the country of the taking parent. The exception that is most applicable for battered women is premised on Article 13(b) of the Convention. This provision states that a child should not be returned to the habitual residence if there is a "grave risk" that the child will suffer "physical or psychological harm." This argument also applies if return would place the child in an "intolerable situation."[7]

A second exception provided by the Convention involves the issue of consent. If the parent filing a Hague petition initially consented to a child's removal, then the taking parent can offer the other parent's consent as a defense against a Hague claim under Article 13(a). US courts have stated that consent for the child's removal needed to be a formal "act or statement," such as "testimony in a judicial proceeding; a convincing renunciation of rights; or a consistent attitude of acquiescence over a significant period of time" (*Friedrich v. Friedrich*, 1996, p. 1070). In other words, evidence based on more than just the opinion of the taking parent is needed to show that the left-behind parent consented to the removal of the child.

Third, the Convention allows a child to remain with the taking parent if the filing of the action in the US court has not occurred within one year of the removal or retention. This exception is provided for by Article 12. It is important to note that subsequent judicial opinions make clear that if a taking parent has hidden a child from the other parent, thus preventing the left-behind parent from contesting the removal, then the start of the one-year period may be delayed until the time when the left-behind parent knew the location of his or her child. The one-year time limit was designed to prevent a left-behind parent who was aware of a child's location from delaying initiation of court action for the child's return to the habitual residence, and to protect the child from further disruption to his or her home life once a substantial period of time had elapsed.

Fourth, Article 13 of the Convention states that if a child objects to returning, and has attained an age and degree of maturity at which it is appropriate to take his or her views into account, the child's objection may constitute an exception. The Convention allows each country to set its own standards regarding when and whether a child's testimony may be solicited as part of the proceed-

---

7. The Hague Convention was drafted well before the social science literature on domestic violence and its risks for children emerged, and nowhere in the language of Article 13(b) is exposure of a child to adult domestic violence cited as a rationale for finding grave risk. However, Switzerland recently expanded the definition of an intolerable situation in its implementing legislation to take into account a child's best interests, and has been a strong advocate for international change to recognize children's exposure to domestic violence as a form of psychological harm (Weiner, 2008).

ings in determining residence. A child's objection to return (if allowed to be offered in court) may not be sufficient to allow him or her to stay in the new country, but it is to be considered in the judge's ruling.

Finally, a court may refrain from ordering a child's return when return would contravene "the protection of human rights and fundamental freedoms" (Hague Conference on Private International Law, 2010, Article 20). Typically, this defense has been understood to refer to conditions such as war or extreme famine in a country, which could potentially result in harm to the child. Weiner (2004), however, has argued that separating a child from the primary caregiver (the mother) and returning him or her to a home where domestic violence exists could be construed as a human rights violation under Article 20. Similar judgments about separating children from their mothers in cases involving domestic violence have been found to be a violation of both the mother's and child's constitutional rights in US courts in the *Nicholson* decisions (see Lansner, 2008). As we will show in our analysis of US judicial opinions related to domestic violence and Hague Convention cases, the human rights defense is rarely used.

Theory and Context of Globalization in the Study of Hague Convention Cases

We began this study of battered women, who had Hague Convention petitions filed against them, using a theoretical lens that saw violence against women as an intersectional, structural issue (see, for instance, Crenshaw, 1991; Hunnicut, 2009; and Lockhart & Danis, 2010). Each person on our research team had worked directly with women who had experienced serious physical and emotional abuse from a partner (male and female). As we will discuss in chapter 1, we viewed domestic violence as a systemic issue related to gender inequality and patriarchy, but we saw that women were differentially at risk and had varying coping capacities as a result of their position within other social hierarchies (that is, of race or ethnicity, financial and class resources, mental and physical ability, sexuality, and religious or spiritual beliefs). What we came to understand through this research is that these commonly applied theoretical insights were insufficient to explain the complex issues of state-to-state relationships that are embedded in global legal frameworks and that clearly affected decisions about the battered women, children, and their safety in this study. We turned to the literature on globalization to further aid our conceptualization of domestic violence within this unique transnational context involving international institutions, human rights, and issues of citizenship.

Globalization is a contested concept. Some scholars suggest that globalization processes have been occurring for hundreds of years but have accelerated with recent technological innovations (Eriksen, 2007). Others believe that the concept of globalization as it is currently used reflects a new phenomenon that is the product of neoliberalism and the transnationalization of global capital in the latter half of the twentieth century (Scholte, 2000). As a focus of scholarship, the primary effort has been to understand globalization's economic ramifications, and secondarily, its cultural effects. On the economic front, globalization has fundamentally changed the flow of capital facilitating the growth of multinational corporations (Eriksen, 2007); migration from the global South to the global North has swelled in recent decades (Stasiulis & Bakan, 2003); technological changes in communications and transportation have accelerated (Eriksen, 2007); and products have been standardized, fostering the worldwide "McDonaldization" of items for consumption (Ritzer, 2007, 2008). Arjun Appadurai (1990), a leading scholar of the cultural changes wrought by globalization, has summarized these shifts along five dimensions, which he terms *scapes*: (1) the movement of people for economic, political, and recreational reasons (ethnoscapes); (2) globalized media and information systems (mediascapes); (3) the rapid spread of technologies based more on wealth than national residence (technoscapes); (4) the circulation of global capital (finanscapes); and (5) the spread of political ideas and ideologies (ideoscapes). These macrosocial theories have illuminated some of the processes associated with globalization, but they have been silent on or obscured the gendered costs and consequences of globalization in the lives of women, children, and families.

Recent works by a handful of feminist and globalization scholars have considered issues outside of a strictly economic realm, such as gender (Davids & van Driel, 2005), the family (Trask, 2010), or love (Padilla, Hirsch, Munoz-Laboy, Sember, & Parker, 2007). These works center the gendered nature of intimate relationships within a globalizing context. For example, Trask (2010) discusses the shifting definition of the family and the inclusion of previously excluded groups, such as lesbian and gay families, within the globalization discourse. Even within theoretical analyses of the recursive relationship between gender and globalization processes, long-standing issues of violence against women and children in families have not entered into the discussion. When issues of gender victimization arise in examinations of globalization, they are usually in the context of labor exploitation, the sexual trafficking of women by criminal enterprises, or the use of rape in wars between nation-states or during interethnic conflicts. As Padilla et al. (2007) note,

Because theoretical discussions of globalization are concerned with political, economic, technological, and cultural transformations on a broad scale—such as the increasing flexibility of global capital, neoliberal state policies, the rise of global media and communications technologies, and escalating population mobility— they have frequently failed to articulate how these large-scale processes are embodied and experienced, or how they come to influence the most intimate aspects of one's life. (p. xi)

Padilla et al. (2007), Trask (2010), and others recognize that globalization processes are inherently destabilizing to traditional gendered norms around autonomy and power within the family, yet the effects of these changes in terms of women's and children's safety have not been brought to the forefront.

This book seeks to remedy this omission by centering the voices of women as they discuss their experiences of domestic violence in a transnational context. We are concerned with the gendered nature of intimate aspects of family life, both in the ways that domestic violence is perpetrated and in the creative strategies that women develop to maximize their own and their children's safety. We are particularly interested in three theoretical aspects of globalization that are implicated in Hague Convention cases: (1) the role of transnational institutions in the brokering of intimate relationships, (2) the relationship between human rights and domestic violence, and (3) the ways in which citizenship is constructed within competing discourses about migration, and how each of these affects the experiences of women fleeing with their children across international borders.

The Role of Transnational Institutions in Brokering Intimate Relationships

Over the last century, a growing number of international bodies have been developed to address issues that have arisen from the increasingly complex networks of financial, military, environmental, and humanitarian relationships between countries. Institutions such as the United Nations (UN) and the International Criminal Court are examples of transnational efforts to find ways within the rule of law to address international concerns. The Hague Conference on Private International Law (HCPIL) was formed in 1893, 50 years before the United Nations, with a mission to develop civil conventions that responded to global issues related to the protection of children, family, and property relations; international commercial and financial law; and international legal cooperation and litigation.[8] Seventy-one nations and the European Union are members of HCPIL; membership includes most European and Latin American nations, China, India, Russia, and the United States. Not all members of HCPIL have signed on to all of the conventions that have been established. (We describe in detail the processes surrounding the Hague Convention on the Civil Aspects of International Child Abduction in the next section of this introductory chapter.)

In 1995 the United Nations held the Fourth World Conference on Women in Beijing, China. Governments across the world signed a Platform for Action that included "a commitment to achieve 'gender equality and the empowerment of women'" (Moser & Moser, 2005, p. 11) through a process called *gender mainstreaming*. Gender mainstreaming seeks to expand equality for women by analyzing institutional policies of international organizations for gender bias, and ensuring that organizations take action to address gender inequalities in the implementation of their policies (Eveline, Bacchi, & Binns, 2009). Most efforts that have been made to address gender issues in international institutions have happened in the field of economic development. Though significant critiques of this approach exist (for examples, see Eveline et al., 2009; Moser & Moser, 2005; Rao, 2006), the underlying premise of gender mainstreaming is relevant to the questions at hand in the implementation of the Hague Convention: namely, is there evidence of gender bias in women's experiences in Hague cases?

In this book we trace the ways that this particular international treaty is enacted transnationally, through the courts of various countries and the United States, and its resultant influence on "the most intimate aspects" of these families' lives (Padilla et al., 2007, p. x). By looking closely at the stories of the women and children at the center of these cases, we are able to follow the path from transnational institutional agreements to the lived experiences of individuals, and by doing so, to build an argument that a "gender-neutral" application of the Hague Convention disadvantages women who have been the victims of domestic violence.

Human Rights and Domestic Violence

The foundation for transnational legal efforts has been the human rights framework established with the passage of the Universal Declaration of Human Rights

8. See the website for the Hague Conference on Private International Law: www.hcch.net.

in 1948. A legal definition of *human rights* has traditionally been predicated on a strict differentiation between the acts of public (that is, state or governmental) entities or actors and the private world of the family. As Libal and Parekh (2009) note, issues of domestic violence fall in a gray zone in reference to traditional understandings of human rights: "Only a state or someone acting on behalf of a state could violate human rights . . . For example, part of the official definition of torture . . . is that it is done by a governmental official or someone acting on behalf of the government . . . The exact same brutal actions when done by private citizens may be considered immoral or illegal, but they are not . . . human rights violations" (pp. 1480–1481). Because human rights law has focused on violence perpetrated in the name of the state, its purview has been on harms that primarily affect men (Edwards, 2010).

As a result of these conventional theories of human rights, the kinds of violence that often affect women most directly may be excluded from consideration under a human rights framework, and thus from the purview of most international bodies. This distinction between the behavior of private citizens and that of state actors has been contested. The United Nations has encouraged attention to women's human rights through measures such as the Convention on the Elimination of All Forms of Discrimination against Women (CEDAW). Other international bodies, such as the World Health Organization (WHO), have also taken up issues of gender-based violence using a human rights framework (see, for instance, Garica-Moreno, Jansen, Ellsberg, Heise, & Watts, 2005) as have domestic violence theorists such as Stark (2007) in his theory of coercive control, which we discuss further in chapter 1. Through documentation of women's experiences of violence, we draw attention to ways in which a human rights framework could be used to protect women and children from further victimization.

Migration and Citizenship

Finally, the international migration of individuals and families raises significant issues related to citizenship and its role in providing support to people within a nation's boundaries. For example, contradictions abound in how nations determine citizenship, as well as in the rights and responsibilities it confers (and withholds). Some countries confer citizenship only through "blood right," while others (including the United States), confer citizenship based on "birth right" (Stasiulis & Bakan, 2003). As Stasiulis and Bakan note in their study of women who migrated to Canada, "While the designated 'rights' of capital to travel freely across borders have increased, the citizenship rights of people, particularly the most vulnerable people, have tended to decline" (p. 1).

As we will see in our discussion of women's experiences with the Hague Convention, citizenship is not relevant to the legal decisions that states are asked to make regarding child abduction. However, citizenship is clearly implicated in the stories women told of their experiences both in other countries and in the United States. In particular, access to many resources within a country may be restricted to those who are considered to be citizens of that country. Both the legal and human service infrastructures in many nations remain tied to notions of citizenship that prevent migrants from accessing avenues of recourse within the country to cope with the violence they experience. Reflections on these three areas—transnational institutions, human rights, and citizenship—are woven into subsequent chapters. In chapter 8, we conclude with a discussion of what studying Hague Convention cases that include domestic violence contributes to our understanding of these three areas.

Why Study the Hague Convention and Domestic Violence?

On January 12, 2010, the US Supreme Court heard, for the first time, an appeal of a lower court's Hague Convention decision. The transcripts of the Court's *Abbott v. Abbott* (2010) hearing reveal judges expressing concern for the safety of the mother in this case, and the ramifications of possibly separating her from her children.

JUSTICE BREYER: She has to choose between her life and her child. And— and is that what this—this convention is aimed at? (p. 5)

JUSTICE GINSBURG: What happens to the woman who, now she has abducted the child to Texas, and she says to the Texas court: If you send me back, I am going to be beaten by this man who has a history of being a batterer? . . . You are saying that the court . . . is helpless, that it's automatic that if there is a custody right the court in the State to which the child has been taken must order that the child be returned? (p. 9)

CHIEF JUSTICE ROBERTS: In other words, in the case that we have been discussing, if the woman would be subject to whatever persecution or domestic violence, but the child—you know, there is no suggestion of any harm targeted to the child, that would not be a case in which they could grant refuge? . . . So the woman would be subject to—if she wanted to remain with the child, there would be no protection. She would have to choose between subjecting herself to violence or being apart from the child? (p. 10)

In *Abbott v Abbott*, the court considered questions related to the Hague Convention and the custody rights of a non-custodial parent with a *ne exeat*[9] right under a country's laws. The court ruled that "a parent has a *ne exeat* right of custody under the Convention by reason of that parent's right" (p. 1). In short, the left-behind father had standing to file a Hague petition in US courts despite the minimal rights of custody he had been granted by his country of residence.

Many people may wonder how useful it would be to study the situations of women who have been the subject of Hague Convention petitions, when the number is so low compared to the number of women who experience domestic violence but are not involved in transnational legal processes. Even though the number of women who are the subject of a Hague petition is low, understanding the experiences of battered women facing these legal processes is critically important for three broad reasons.

First, these cases reveal several theoretical issues that are of concern to domestic violence, child maltreatment, globalization, and legal process scholars. Children are at the heart of these cases, and there is currently considerable legal dispute as to what constitutes "harm" to a child whose mother is a victim of domestic violence. Their experiences provide insights into how US courts regard domestic violence and consider it when making decisions that affect family relationships. These cases exist at the fulcrum point between individual and nation—they both reflect and determine critical issues such as citizenship rights, the rights of women and children, and the legal responsibility to *comity* between nations (comity means legal reciprocity; in Hague cases, it is the respect of one nation for the laws of another nation). Understanding the circumstances surrounding how US courts treat Hague Convention cases involving domestic violence reveals important dimensions of treaty interpretation, domestic law, consideration of children's best interests, and the legal rationales required to ensure safety for battered women and their children in the context of globalization.

9. A *ne exeat* order in a child custody case allows one parent to prevent the other parent from leaving the jurisdiction of the court, even if that parent does not have custody rights (sole or joint). In *Abbott v. Abbott*, the father who did not have custodial rights in Chile filed a Hague petition for the return of the child after his ex-wife relocated to the United States.

Second, a series of pragmatic issues drive attention to Hague cases. As the world becomes functionally smaller through transportation, migration, and communication changes, we can anticipate a growing number of transnational families. For example, the number of American children with at least one foreign-born parent increased from 15% in 1994 to 22% in 2008 (Federal Interagency Forum on Child and Family Statistics, 2009). Worldwide, approximately 214 million people live outside their country of birth, with 60% living in industrialized countries, usually Europe or the United States (United Nations Department of Economic and Social Affairs, 2011). With increased migration between countries, we can expect an associated rise in the number of battered mothers who flee across national borders seeking help from family and friends to ensure safety for themselves and their children. Each year additional countries become signatories of the Hague Convention or sign bilateral agreements with the United States with terms similar to the Hague Convention, thus expanding the possible number of cases entering our courts. India, with over 1 billion citizens, is expected to become a signatory to the Hague Convention in the near future. The recent *Abbott v. Abbott* (2010) decision by the US Supreme Court will also expand the number of people eligible to file petitions in the United States. In other words, for a variety of reasons, the number of families that become engaged in Hague Convention cases will continue to rise. This fact is borne out by the most recent world census of Hague Convention cases, in which Lowe (2011) found a 45% increase in petitions in the five-year period between 2003 and 2008.

Third, as we will show through analysis of the women's stories, abused women face a paradoxical injustice in Hague Convention cases that should be remedied. Frequently, the public asks, "Why does she stay?" when confronted with women who have been abused by intimate partners, rather than focusing their attention on the abusive partner's behavior (Anderson & Saunders, 2003). This question rests on a lack of understanding of domestic violence and its dynamics, particularly in relation to the potential for life-threatening violence after separation (Campbell, Webster, Koziol-McLain, Block, Campbell, Curry, et al., 2003). Asking this question also presupposes that battered women should (and have the resources to) take responsibility for the violence and remove themselves and their children from the situation. The paradox for women who are respondents to Hague petitions is that they *didn't* stay, that they *did* take action by fleeing to secure their safety and that of their children. But now they are forced through the legal system to answer the question, "Why did she leave?" because they crossed an international border with children and without a spouse's permission. Women who are respondents to Hague petitions in US courts are also simultaneously denied resources (in terms of limited Central Authority assistance, knowledgeable legal representations, time to acquire evidence, and so on) to make these complex legal arguments, while the fathers in these situations are given assistance and can have legal fees reimbursed by the mother if she loses the Hague petition. By actually taking action to protect herself and her children, a mother who crosses international borders may end up without her children and in legal limbo as a child abductor. For reasons of fairness and justice, it is important to understand these women's stories.

Finally, the consequences for failing to grapple with the complex issues surrounding domestic violence in transnational families can be fatal for the women and children involved. Recently, courts in Australia and Canada returned children to fathers who had long histories of abuse against their wives. In 2009, Cassandra Hasanovic was stabbed to death by her husband in front of her children and mother after she returned with her five- and three-year-old sons when they were ordered back to the United Kingdom pursuant to a Hague petition filed by their father in Australia (Husband guilty of murdering his wife, 2009). A Canadian court ordered the return of 10-year-old Deyan and 12-year-old Danyela to their father in Texas in 2010 after he filed a Hague petition against their mother. Six months later, Deyan was shot to death by his father, and Danyela was hospitalized with eight gunshot wounds (Ravensbergen, 2010). These two tragic incidents illustrate the gravity of the decisions being made in Hague Convention cases that include domestic violence, and demonstrate why research is urgently needed on the circumstances of these families.

Details of the Research

To date, no empirical research has examined the experiences of women who face domestic violence and are subject to Hague petitions in US courts. Our interest in this study was to describe what is occurring in these situations from multiple points of view to obtain a deeper understanding of how these mothers experience the intersection of domestic violence and our society's responses to them as child abductors. The research encompassed interviews with women, attorneys who represented both mothers and fathers in Hague Convention cases, and analysis of judicial opinions that had been written concerning domestic violence in Hague cases. Because so many Hague cases involve Latin American countries, we specifically sought a subsample of Latina mothers to participate in our study.

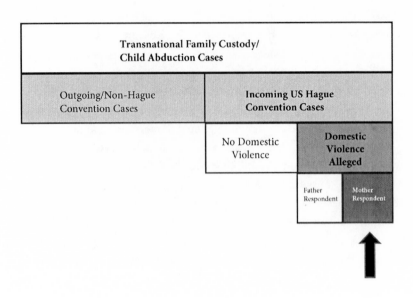

Figure I.1 Target Sample for Domestic Violence and Hague Convention Study

Figure I.1 illustrates the relationship of international parental abduction to the types of Hague Convention cases that are the focus of this study. The boxes in this figure are not sized proportionally to the number of cases; rather, they identify the segment of the population of all Hague Convention cases that we studied. As noted previously, international child abduction cases can be resolved outside of the legal system, or they may be heard as custody cases within state court systems without invoking the Hague Convention. In these cases, decisions are made at a local level. Left-behind parents in other countries have the right to initiate Hague proceedings if they feel their children have been wrongfully removed or retained in another country. These cases in the United States are split between incoming and outgoing Hague petitions. The focus of this study is on the *incoming* cases, those that are heard in US courts and, therefore, raise issues related to the treatment of battered women within the US legal system. An unknown proportion of incoming Hague cases include allegations of domestic violence in the family, so these cases in particular were sought as part of this study. Finally, either a father or a mother could be identified as the taking parent in an incoming Hague case, but as noted earlier, the clear majority of taking parents are mothers. The focus in this study is on those mothers who have left another country and relocated to the United States with their children, and who are identified as the respondents of a Hague petition filed in US courts.

Based on our experience in domestic violence services and research, we chose not to interview fathers about their views of the circumstances of these cases. We made this decision out of concern for the safety of the mothers who contacted the research team, and based on our knowledge that many women continue to experience harassment and physical violence from an abusive partner even after the woman ends an abusive relationship (Campbell, Rose, Kub, & Nedd, 1998; Fleury, Sullivan, & Bybee, 2000). However, we were interested in obtaining information on the perspectives of fathers, so we sought to interview attorneys who had represented fathers who were petitioners in Hague Convention cases.

To gain further information on how these cases are litigated and on the role domestic violence plays in the legal decision making in these situations, we interviewed lawyers who represented both mothers and fathers. When possible, we attempted to interview the mother, her attorney, and the left-behind father's attorney in the same case. We also interviewed additional informants, including expert witnesses, a guardian *ad litem*, a paralegal, and an advocate who had all worked on Hague Convention cases. Further information on the specific methods of the three studies (mothers' interviews, attorney interviews, and judicial opinion analysis) is available in appendices B, C, and D.

A final note on matters of epistemology—we are deeply aware of the socially constructed nature of the larger issues at play in this study: that is, the symbolic and structural nature of gender (Davids & van Driel, 2005); the contingent, emergent nature of globalization processes (Trask, 2010); and the evolving sense of what constitutes domestic violence. We also know that the interviews we conducted with each of the people who agreed to talk with us are characterized by a mutual co-construction of the interview narrative (Riessman, 2008). Telling the story of one's life or an event is not a straightforward, never-changing endeavor, but one in which each narrative recounting subtly (and sometimes dramatically) repositions the narrator herself in relation to changing understandings of an experience (Elliott, 2007). Although we fully accept the provisional nature of the information we gathered, we treat these data from a realist perspective—we analyze and report on the women's experiences as reflections of their current "truths" about their experiences. Our purpose here was not to prove who was "right" between mothers and fathers in a legalistic sense, but rather to illuminate the experiences of women who had previously been characterized one-dimensionally as perpetrators of child harm as parental abductors.

Overview of the Book

In the chapters 1 through 5, we describe and analyze aspects of the situations of women who had faced a Hague Convention petition in the United States. We begin in chapter 1 with an examination of current definitions of domestic violence and illustrate how women's experiences did and didn't reflect these ideas. The women's stories display a range of tactics used by their husbands, but most common across these stories were the ways in which men emotionally terrorized their family members in order to control their behavior. We end with a discussion of the ways in which torture has been defined, and use this as an example of how a human rights framework could be applied to these women's experiences. Chapter 2 focuses on why and how the women left the country in which they were living, and how these decisions relate to the central Hague Convention concept of habitual residence. The premise of the treaty is that families voluntarily make decisions on where they live (their habitual residence), but this assumption is challenged when women discuss how domestic violence affected their decisions on residence. In chapter 3, we discuss in more detail the special circumstances of Latin American women who came to the United States, and examine the different situations they faced as Hague respondents without citizenship resources in this country. The experiences of Hispanic women highlight the issues of citizenship and how these play out in Hague Convention cases. Chapter 4 shifts attention from the women's lives to the children's lives in these families. We review scholarship, which has evolved since the creation of the Hague Convention, on the detrimental effects of domestic violence on children even when they are not the direct victims of a parent's abuse. By examining children's experiences in the light of domestic violence research, we build the case for why exposure to domestic violence should be considered a "grave risk" to children, in the language of the Hague Convention. In chapter 5, we address the decisions regarding the return of the children in each woman's case, and link these decisions to aspects of the domestic violence occurring in these families. To date, little information has been systematically collected on what happens after a Hague case has been decided. This chapter provides one of the few systematic examinations of this issue in the literature.

The final three chapters turn to other players in the families' lives. In chapter 6, we discuss the views of the lawyers who both pursued and defended against Hague Convention petitions. The "lawyering" of Hague cases was an important contributor to the resolution of these petitions. Lawyers for respondents and petitioners often had differing views on the importance of domestic violence in the cases they litigated. This chapter describes some of the barriers to effective representation of women in Hague cases. Chapter 7 reports on an analysis of the currently available published judicial opinions involving the Hague Convention and domestic violence. Most judges who hear Hague cases have never presided over a treaty case before. As a result, the opinions that are written on these cases are of great importance because they represent the primary vehicle for conveying the legal understanding of what constitutes potential harm to a child. We end with a summary (chapter 8) of the major findings from this study, reflect on the theoretical issues raised by this research, and present thoughts on reforms that could lead to a more holistic response to these situations. The book concludes with an afterword by Sudha Shetty, the lawyer who brought to our attention the use of the Hague Convention in domestic violence situations. The appendices include information on where to find help if you are a battered woman or an attorney representing a survivor of domestic violence in a Hague Convention case, as well as more detailed information on how the studies of the women, lawyers, and judicial opinions were performed.

1 | Emotional Terror, Physical Harm, and Women's Experiences of Domestic Violence

When does bad behavior cross the line and become abuse? This question has different answers depending on whether it is asked by a legal professional, a violence researcher, or a concerned friend. In instances of rape or physical assault, the line may seem clear, but even in these circumstances, women's safety is not necessarily the paramount concern in the policy arena. For example, some jurisdictions do not protect women against rape in marriage; of the 192 member countries of the United Nations, only slightly more than one-half have statutes that make it possible to prosecute marital rape (Secretary General of the United Nations, 2006). Many people believe that certain behaviors (such as disobeying one's husband or being suspected of infidelity) are good reasons for a man to beat his wife (Garcia-Moreno et al., 2005). How a society defines domestic violence has implications for the legal protections available to victims, the availability of supportive services, and the likely responses that survivors will encounter from friends, family members, and others in their social networks.

In American courts, domestic violence is usually defined in reference to existing statutes that criminalize assault and battery. From this standpoint, the important issue is whether physical harm has occurred to a person. Domestic assaults (if they come into the court system at all) are usually charged as misdemeanors, and the majority result in dismissal of the charges (Ventura & Davis, 2005). Most states have enacted statutes that either specifically address domestic violence or provide for enhanced penalties under already existing assault and battery laws for domestic violence incidents (Miller, 2004). The federal Violence Against Women Act of 1994 (VAWA; Pub. L. No. 103-322, Section 3[a]) hews to a similar definition, stating, "The term 'domestic violence' includes felony or misdemeanor crimes of violence committed by a current or former spouse of the victim" or other person with whom the victim has cohabited or shared a child. In general, US legal definitions of domestic violence focus on physical acts that cause harm to the victim.

To understand dynamics related to domestic violence, it is important to reach beyond legal definitions to also consider the experience of victimization from a survivor's perspective. The Domestic Abuse Intervention Programs (Duluth Model, n.d.)[1] and other researchers (such as Smith, Smith, & Earp, 1999; and more recently, Dutton & Goodman, 2005; Stark, 2007) have interviewed battered women about their experiences, and have concluded that physical and sexual assaults are events that need to be understood within the context of one partner's ongoing effort to establish power and control over another. For example, Smith, Smith, and Earp (1999) note,

> Our research revealed battering to be an enduring, traumatic, and multidimensional experience conceptually distinct from episodic physical assault . . . We found that battering in women's lives continuously shapes their behavior, views of self, and beliefs in the controllability of their own lives. We also found that battered women are actively engaged in this experience; they want to improve their situation and . . . they are continuously engaged in both intrapsychic and active coping. . . . Based on this, we derived the following definition of battering: A process whereby one member of an intimate relationship experiences vulnerability, loss of power and control, and entrapment as a consequence of the other member's exercise of power through the patterned use of physical, sexual, psychological, and/or moral force. (p. 183)

More recently, domestic violence researchers have argued for a reconceptualization of domestic violence as *coercive control* (Dutton & Goodman, 2005; Stark, 2007). Coercive control is an enduring pattern of behavior by the dominant partner that uses intimidation, fear-inducing threats, and episodic physical and sexual assaults to control another's behavior, relationships with other people, and independent action in the world. In the context of coercive control, physical violence may be rare because reliance on the threat of harm is effective at producing the desired outcome. The dynamics of coercion differ from the kind of conflict found in other couples in which there is occasional or situational

---

1. The Domestic Abuse Intervention Programs in Duluth, Minn., developed the "Power and Control Wheel" that is commonly used to educate people about the experience of domestic violence.

violence, but whose violence is not clearly associated with an ongoing effort to control the other person's behavior. For example, Johnson (2008) differentiates between *intimate terrorism*, which he defines as physical or sexual assaults with behaviors focused on coercive control, and *situational couple violence* in which physical assaults occur (often under the influence of alcohol), but where an ongoing effort to control the partner is absent.

According to Stark (2007), definitions of domestic violence should center on coercive control rather than narrowly construing physical assaults as the signifying aspect of abuse. This shift in recognizing the importance of repeated attacks on one's personhood would concentrate attention on the ways in which a woman's agency and ability to control basic aspects of her own life have been compromised by the abuser. A revised definition of domestic violence would then include the following:

recognition of the cumulative effects of violence, particularly as it is used to target a victim's personhood;
a perpetrator's assumption of sexual privileges regardless of the victim's desires;
structural constraint (that is, isolation, prohibiting a victim's independent decision making, and control of resources) used by perpetrators to enforce women's compliance;
spatial and temporal extension of abuse to all facets of a victim's life;
entrapment based on a fear of physical harm to oneself or loved ones; and
women's social vulnerability to persistent discrimination which is the underlying social process that facilitates the enactment of coercive control.
(Stark, 2007)

This definition refocuses attention from episodes of physical harm (while not denying their seriousness), to the underlying, chronic dysfunctional pattern of controlling behavior by the perpetrator of abuse.

National and international organizations have drawn on this information to varying degrees in their efforts to define domestic violence, as can be seen from the definitions provided in table 1.1. These definitions expand attention from physical assaults and forced sex to the ways in which violence and threats of assault are used to control, intimidate, and coerce survivors to do as the abuser wants, in accord with our understanding from victims of domestic violence. However, as we will review in the next section, global (and us-based) studies of domestic violence continue to focus more on behaviors that are equated with criminality (that is, physical and sexual assaults).

Table 1.1 Selected Organizational Definitions of Domestic Violence

Organization	Definition
United Nations Declaration on the Elimination of Violence against Women[a]	"'[V]iolence against women' means any act of gender-based violence that results in, or is likely to result in, physical, sexual or psychological harm or suffering to women, including threats of such acts, coercion or arbitrary deprivation of liberty, whether occurring in public or in private life."
American Bar Association[b]	"The term 'domestic violence' means an act or pattern of acts involving the use or attempted use of physical, sexual, verbal, emotional, or other forms of abusive behavior by one person to harm, threaten, intimidate, harass, coerce, control, isolate, restrain, or monitor another person with whom they have or have had a physically, sexually, or emotionally intimate relationship, an intimate partner relationship, or any other relationship covered under the domestic or family violence laws of the jurisdiction."
American Medical Association[c]	"Intimate partner violence is characterized as a pattern of coercive behaviors that may include repeated battering and injury, psychological abuse, sexual assault, progressive social isolation, deprivation, and/or intimidation. Regardless of the specific behaviors, the intent of intimate partner violence is for one partner to exert power and control over the other."
American Psychological Association[d]	"Physical, visual, verbal, or sexual acts that are experienced by a woman or a girl as threat, invasion, or assault and have the effect of hurting her or degrading her and/or taking away her ability to control contact (intimate or otherwise) with another individual (p. xvi) and which is 'committed by one partner against the other in a relationship.'"
US Centers for Disease Control[e]	"Physical violence: the intentional use of physical force with the potential for causing death, disability, injury, or harm. Physical violence includes, but is not limited to, scratching; pushing; shoving; throwing; grabbing; biting; choking; shaking; slapping; punching; burning; use of a weapon; and use of restraints or one's body, size, or strength against another person. Physical violence also includes coercing other people to commit any of the above acts."

Table 1.1 *Continued*

Organization	Definition
	"Sexual violence: 1) use of physical force to compel a person to engage in a sexual act against his or her will, whether or not the act is completed; 2) attempted or completed sex act involving a person who is unable to understand the nature or condition of the act, to decline participation, or to communicate unwillingness to engage in the sexual act, e.g., because of illness, disability, or the influence of alcohol or other drugs, or because of intimidation or pressure; and 3) abusive sexual contact (intentional sexual contact against the person's will or when they are unable to understand the act as in #2)."
	"Threats of physical or sexual violence: Use of words, gestures, or weapons to communicate the intent to cause death, disability, injury, or physical harm. Also the use of words, gestures, or weapons to communicate the intent to compel a person to engage in sex acts or abusive sexual contact when the person is either unwilling or unable to consent."
	"Psychological/emotional violence involves trauma to the victim caused by acts, threats of acts, or coercive tactics. Psychological/emotional abuse can include, but is not limited to, humiliating the victim, controlling what the victim can and cannot do, withholding information from the victim, deliberately doing something to make the victim feel diminished or embarrassed, isolating the victim from friends and family, and denying the victim access to money or other basic resources. *It is considered psychological/emotional violence when there has been prior physical or sexual violence or prior threat of physical or sexual violence.* In addition, stalking is often included among the types of IPV."

[a] United Nations, 1993.

[b] American Bar Association Commission on Domestic Violence, 2004.

[c] Brown, 2002, p. 4.

[d] American Psychological Association Intimate Partner Abuse and Relationship Violence Working Group, 2002, p. 8, as quoted in Koss et al., 1994.

[e] US Centers for Disease Control, 2002; emphasis added to final definition (see www.cdc.gov).

Global Context of Domestic Violence

Violence against women is a serious global problem and encompasses more than domestic violence, although that is the focus of this study. Domestic violence exists within a web of interrelated forms of gender discrimination that result in violence and abuse against girls and women across the life span (Watts & Zimmerman, 2002). For example, female fetuses are more likely to be aborted, and girl babies are more likely to be victims of infanticide, or the intentional killing of infants (Singh, 2008). From adolescence to old age, women are more likely than men to experience sexual and physical violence from a partner (Black, Basile, Breiding, Smith, Walters, & Merrick, et al., 2011; Watts & Zimmerman, 2002). Extensive literature discussing perpetration of domestic violence reveals that men disproportionately perpetrate violence against women in intimate relationships (see Hamby, 2009, for a review).[2]

Over the past 20 years, efforts have been made to assess the prevalence of violence against women in several nations. Early attempts to measure the occurrence of adult domestic violence largely focused on behavioral definitions that prioritized the experience of physical assault (Straus, Gelles, & Steinmetz, 1980). In 2005, the World Health Organization conducted the Multi-Country Study on Domestic Violence and Women's Health, followed by the more recent International Violence against Women surveys (IVAWs) (Johnson, Ollus, & Nevala, 2008). These surveys were the first in the world to use comparable measures, data collection processes, and analyses that allow cross-country comparisons. Rates of physical and/or sexual violence ranged from 9% to 40% in the IVAWs (Johnson et al., 2008) and from 15% to 71% in the Multi-Country Study (Garcia-Moreno et al., 2005), with most countries reporting substantially more physical than sexual violence. As understanding of domestic violence has grown, efforts have been made to modify research measures, to expand the behaviors assessed to include sexual violence and psychological and emotional abuse that reflect victims' experiences of coercion and intimidation. For example, in the wHO Multi-Country Study (Garcia-Moreno et al., 2005), four aspects of emotionally abusive behavior were assessed: "being insulted or made to feel bad about oneself; being humiliated or belittled in front of others; being intimidated or scared on purpose, . . . and being threatened with harm (either directly

2. We recognize that domestic violence is an experience in which men can be the victims of female perpetrators, or men and women may be abused by same-sex partners. However, we focus on men's violence against women both because of its frequency and because of its relevance to Hague Convention cases.

or in the form of a threat to hurt someone the respondent cared about)" (p. 35). Across the 10 countries, between 30.9% of women (in Bangladesh) and 75.1% of women (in Ethiopia) had experienced at least one of these behaviors from an intimate partner. Between 4.6% (in a Japanese city) and 26.4% (in a Peruvian province) of women reported three or more of these experiences from an intimate partner.

In 2011, the United Nations Entity for Gender Equality and the Empowerment of Women (UN Women, 2011) issued the first-ever listing of national prevalence data on physical and sexual abuse from 81 countries.[3] Unlike the WHO study, these data are not necessarily comparable across countries because of variations in how physical and sexual violence were defined, how samples were created and recruited, and how data collection techniques were handled (that is, asked in person, over the phone, anonymously, and so on). Although these data may not be comparable between countries, they are the best estimates currently available for each country and were usually derived from population-based studies. Table 1.2 lists the lifetime prevalence estimates for countries that are also listed as signatories to the Hague Convention. Rates of lifetime physical violence range from 6.4% in Morocco to 39.3% in Turkey; lifetime sexual abuse from 2.9% in Albania to 15.6% in Chile; and combined rates from 7.0% in Canada to 46.7% in Mexico. Of the 21 countries with combined physical and/or sexual violence estimates, the majority, including the United States (Black et al., 2011), report that at least one-quarter of the female population has had these experiences. Most Hague signatory countries have significant levels of reported physical and sexual violence. However, from the standpoint of a definition of domestic violence that centers coercive control, these levels would be considered as indicators of a potentially much larger problem.

A common set of risk and protective factors for physical and sexual violence has begun to emerge from these cross-national studies. For example, Abramsky et al. (2011), in their analysis of the WHO multi-country data, found that "alcohol abuse, cohabitation, young age, attitudes supporting wife beating, outside sexual relationships, experiencing childhood abuse, growing up with domestic violence, and perpetrating or experiencing other forms of violence in adulthood" (p. 10) all increased the risk of domestic violence in most countries. Access to education, higher socioeconomic status, and marriage (versus cohabitation)

3. Measures of coercive control have not yet been included in most national studies, so these are not listed. The listing does provide additional information on non-partner physical and sexual violence, the percentage of women whose first sexual encounter was forced, and the percentage of women abused during pregnancy.

Table 1.2 Prevalence of Intimate Partner Violence in Selected Countries That Are Signatories to the Hague Convention[a]

Country	Lifetime Physical Abuse (%)	Lifetime Sexual Abuse (%)	Lifetime Physical and/or Sexual Abuse (%)
Albania	8.2	2.9	—
Australia	25.0	8.0	27.0
Brazil (city/province)	27.2/33.8	10.1/14.3	28.9/36.9
Canada	—	—	7.0
Chile	15.0	15.6	35.7
Denmark	20.0	6.0	22.0
Finland	17.6	4.3	—
France[b]	2.5	.9	10.0
Germany	23.0	7.0	25.0
Ireland	13.0	8.0	14.5
Italy	12.2	6.1	14.3
Mexico	—	—	46.7
Morocco	6.4	6.6	—
Netherlands	21.0	—	—
New Zealand	30.2	14.1	33.1
Norway	13.9	9.4	26.8
Paraguay	19.3	7.6	—
Peru	31.2	8.0	38.8
Poland	14.0	12.6	—
Romania	15.1	3.1	28.5
Serbia	22.8	6.3	23.7
Slovakia	15.0	9.0	27.9
South Africa	12.5	4.4	—
Sweden	18.0	—	—
Switzerland	9.0	3.0	10.0
Turkey	39.3	15.3	41.9
Ukraine	12.7	3.3	13.2
United Kingdom	18.9	3.8	28.4
United States	22.1	7.7	24.8

Note: Abuse data taken from United Nations Women (2011). A dash indicates that data are unavailable for this estimate.

[a] Countries that are signatories taken from the convention status table of the Hague Conference on Private International Law (www.hcch.net). Not all countries that are signatories to the Hague Convention have developed estimates of physical and sexual abuse.

[b] France did not assess the experience of violence throughout a woman's life, but asked about its occurrence only during the previous 12 months.

were all protective factors associated with lower likelihood of domestic violence. Other cross-national comparisons have found similar risk factors, particularly in terms of young age, poverty, early experiences of violence, and alcohol abuse (Kury, Obergfell-Fuchs, & Woessner, 2004).

The research reviewed here indicates that domestic violence is a significant worldwide problem. Efforts to determine the central aspects of domestic violence suggest that partners who are sexually or physically violent often use physical force to ensure their dominant status in the relationship. The underlying dynamic is not based solely on aggressive or angry feelings, but rather is an attempt to control another (and ensure one's own dominance) through coercion, intimidation, and threats.

For the purposes of the research presented in this book, we defined *domestic violence* as an ongoing pattern of intimidating behavior in which the threat or use of serious physical and/or sexual violence is employed to accomplish the overall goal of controlling the partner. This definition recognizes that domestic violence is more than an isolated experience of physical violence, and that any act of violence has to be evaluated within the overall context of reported relationship dynamics. For example, a single episode in which a partner is hit in the midst of an intense disagreement, though violent, would not constitute domestic violence in this study unless it were coupled with behaviors intended to control the other person.

Participants in the Hague Domestic Violence Study

Basic demographic information about the parents and children were gathered during each mother's interview. As noted in table 1.3, the parents in this study were generally in their late 30s, most of the mothers were white, one was African American, and six were Hispanic. Although over one-half of the women in this study had a college degree, almost all of the men were highly educated. Fewer than one-half of the women were working while they lived in the other country, while three-quarters of the men were employed. Women who were employed in the other country generally worked in professional, managerial, or business occupations. The inequality of education, and particularly employment, became a problematic issue for the women when they attempted to obtain resources to cope with the abuse, as we will describe later.

The relationships between the parents tended to be long in duration, averaging 10.25 years (1.03 SD). All but one (95.5%) of the women were legally married to the father of their children prior to the Hague petition. However, six

Table 1.3 Description of Mothers and Fathers in the Study

Demographic	Mother	Father
Age	37.6 yrs.	38.9 yrs.
	(1.17 SD)	(1.01 SD)
% White	68.2%	n/a
% Completed at least BA	54.5%	86.4%
% Employed in Other Country	41.0%	77.3%

(27.3%) of the women were legally divorced at the time their ex-husbands filed a Hague petition. Forty-five children were involved in the Hague petitions, of which almost two-thirds (63.2%) were boys. On average, 1.81 (.15 SD) children were involved in the Hague petition and the mode was two children; family size ranged from one to five children. The children tended to be young, with an average age of 6.42 years (3.53 SD); children's ages ranged from 1 to 15 years. The women came to the United States with all of their children, except in two cases: one in which the father had taken the youngest child to another location, and another in which the mother had sent her oldest daughter (not biologically related to the Hague petitioner) to live with her parents prior to taking her younger children to the United States. For 13 (60%) of the women, the Hague petition was filed within the previous 5 years; and for 8 of the women, this period was from 5 to 10 years before the interview (information was missing on one woman).

Mothers in our study came to the United States primarily from three areas of the world. One-half of the women (n=11; 49.9%) came from countries on the northern and eastern coasts of the Mediterranean, six (27.24%) came from non-Mediterranean European countries, and five (22.7%) came from Latin America. Five women (22.7%) were immigrants to the United States, while 17 (77.3%) were US citizens. Of the men, all but one (95%) were citizens of the countries to which they moved their families. One father was a US citizen, but was working in the country from which he petitioned for the return of the children, also American citizens.

Women's Domestic Violence Experiences

In our interviews, we started by asking each woman to describe the events that led up to the Hague petition being filed. This question usually prompted a

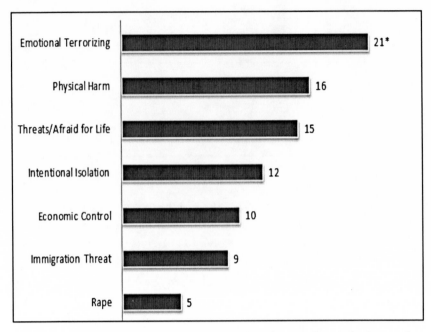

Figure 1.1 Summary of Types of Abuse and Number of Respondents Who Reported the Type (n=22)†
† Information on non-physical events unavailable in one case.
* Number for each type reported at the end of each bar.

description of experiences in the relationship that the woman eventually came to label as abuse. If a woman did not specifically report that she or her children were physically harmed, we asked directly about this possibility. Otherwise, we did not survey women on the types of abuse they experienced, but rather compiled the incidents they described. We categorized these experiences into seven broad areas: (1) emotional terrorizing, (2) physical harm, (3) threats to life, (4) intentional isolation, (5) economic control, (6) passport control and immigration threats, and (7) rape. The overall frequency of each type of abuse across the cases is reported in figure 1.1. These areas are well documented in literature related to domestic violence as typifying the kinds of behaviors used by abusive spouses to maintain control of their partners.

Emotional Terrorizing

By far the most common story told by the women we interviewed was one in which their husbands behaved in a manner designed to induce fear and terror, and to make the woman more controllable, that is, willing to submit to his demands. We label this behavior of the husbands *emotional terrorizing* because of the way the women focused on the fear they felt in their relationships. Although domestic violence literature has typically called this behavior emotional or psychological abuse, these terms did not adequately represent the depth of fear that the men's behavior created in the mothers interviewed for this study.

This form of abuse revolved around verbal threats or behaviors designed to intimidate and control without the use of physical force. For example, Tamara* described what it was like the last year that she was living with her husband. He had been diagnosed with a serious mental disorder by a psychiatrist in his country, and was prescribed medications for this condition. When he took the medicines, he was easier to live with, but he decided to stop taking them in the months leading up to Tamara's* decision to leave. Although his behavior had been difficult during most of their marriage, his threats and intimidation increased in the last year before she left, although he never hit her during this time. Here she describes the kind of behavior he exhibited:

> I lived in my son's room for the last year. I slept in my son's room because [my husband] was being so horrible. The first couple of months I lived in my son's room, [my husband] would come in at three or four o'clock in the morning, turn on all the lights, screaming and yelling "I'm going to kill you." [. . .] scaring the crap out of all of us. And so, that's when the kids and I started locking our doors at night. . . . The girls shared a room next door to my son's room, so I would tell the girls to lock their room at night and I locked ours, just because you never knew what he would do at night. And then, there were days I would come out of that room in the morning and he would be sleeping on the floor in front of the door. [. . .] It's the "eggshell thing" where you just never know what mood he'll be in and you never know what you do or what you say, how it's going to make him react; if he's going to lay in bed for two days, not eat, and cry and say he wants to die . . . or if he's going to kill you.

This story is an example of the feelings of emotional intimidation and fear experienced not just by Tamara* and her children, but by almost all of the women interviewed. Tamara's* husband was using sleep deprivation, threats, and "screaming" at unpredictable times to express his rage. Tamara* reported that her husband had multiple firearms in the house. At times during their final

---

* Asterisks indicate women whose children were returned to another country. See Author's Note, page xv.

year, he threatened to shoot her when he was angry, providing substantial reason for her to feel afraid that his behavior might culminate in a serious attack.

In Sandra's case, her husband used intense emotional intimidation to express his anger against her to try to force her to take the actions he desired. They fought frequently about child care; he expressed resentment about having to watch their children, and wanted to hire a helper so that Sandra could devote more of her attention to him. She describes a typical incident that occurred multiple times in their household:

> So he just got more and more angry over time and then probably the year before I ended up leaving [the other country], he just got more threatening and started to really scare me that he might hurt the kids or . . . So I just was always sort of trying to get him into rooms that would be far away from the kids [. . .] He just yelled a lot . . . said I shouldn't be afraid of him because he hadn't hit me but he'd have me backed into a corner with his fists over my head.

Although we do not have a physical description of either of these people, it appears from Sandra's story that her husband was larger than she, and he was capable of using his size to threaten violence with his fists. His yelling was designed to force her to accede to his demands, but the result was Sandra's escalating concern that her husband would physically harm their children.

Sometimes the husband's behavior was less focused on threatening physical harm, and more designed to discredit the woman in her own eyes or in the eyes of others in her support network or community. For example, Ellen* had a rocky marriage for several years, but no overt physical violence occurred. Instead, she found that her husband was trying to convince her and others that she was mentally ill. While living in his country, he took her to psychiatrists and told them she was mentally ill before she had an opportunity to talk with them, under the guise of explaining her situation because she was not fluent in the country's language. Ellen* discovered that, in her husband's country,

> if you're married, a spouse can sign a paper with the psychiatrist, and they could put you away. [. . .] I had people in the town where I lived later tell me that he was going around telling people that I need to go into a psychiatric hospital. So, I was in great danger. And I knew once the psychiatrist had contacted me and said that I was ten times sicker than my husband, that my husband obviously had convinced him that I was the unstable one. [My husband] had transferred his illness onto me; I was in serious danger because I was warned by people that all it takes is a signature and a doctor's signature and you're gone.

In this example, Ellen* interpreted her husband's behavior as an attempt to "poison the well" with any person or helping professional she might consult, in order to maintain his control over her. By assigning all of the problems in the relationship to her, he was able to avoid any scrutiny of his own behavior.

These examples describe specific efforts used by some of the husbands who pursued Hague petitions to intimidate, terrorize, and discredit their wives. All but one of the women had similar stories of emotional threats and psychological intimidation in their marriages.

Physical Harm

Most of the women in this sample (72.7%) reported some form of physical violence from their partners. These harms were serious. For example, women reported being choked, suffocated, punched hard enough to leave bruises, hit or attacked with dangerous objects, kicked while on the ground, and beaten up on multiple occasions. To illustrate the kinds of violence women were coping with, Marina reports on one of the incidents she endured at the hands of her husband:

> He pulled me out of the bathroom by the hair and started hitting me. I don't know for how long he was hitting me, five, ten, fifteen minutes, hitting me hard. I tried to escape and protect my face . . . he continued to hit me and my nose was bleeding. All of a sudden, he left. I heard some noises outside and when he came back, he had an ice pick in his hand. When I saw that, I . . . I was sitting on the edge of the bed. He put the ice pick to my stomach and held my jaw very tightly with his other hand, and said, "I can hit you all I want and I will never leave a bruise on you." He used to be a police officer before I met him . . . He left my jaw out of place. To this moment, I still have problems when I open my jaw.

In this example, Marina's husband beat her until she was bleeding, and dislocated her jaw. His physical violence was coupled with verbally threatening her life; his attack left her with permanent physical injuries to her jaw. This attack combined emotional terrorizing, direct physical harm, and the threat of more injury if she did not comply with his dictates. Each woman who reported physical harm described variations of this kind of serious physical event.

For instance, Austin* met her husband and relocated with him to his country in Europe to marry him. Her daughter was born two years later. She reports the following series of events at that time that culminated in her emergency departure from her home with her daughter:

Shortly after my daughter was born, we started having more severe problems. There
was a lot of verbal abuse, shortly after she was born—not so much physical abuse,
but verbal abuse. [...] About a year [after our daughter was born], things just came
to a head. We had a very huge problem. Basically, he kicked me, and threatened my
life. I went with my daughter to a [domestic violence] ... shelter.

Austin's* experience was severe enough that she fled the couple's home that
night and sought refuge in a shelter in the other country. Her action indicates
that she perceived the threat of continued physical violence from her husband.
For the majority of women in this study, physical harm was not a one-time
event, but rather it happened repeatedly within the context of emotionally terrorizing behavior.

In six cases, the husband either did not physically harm the woman during
the course of the relationship or used violence once, or else the woman reported that the physical abuse was something she felt was minor. Four of these
cases had no report of any physical violence, but did contain multiple reports of
emotional terrorizing, such as the verbal abuse and intimidation described earlier in Sandra's story. In one case, Tamara* reported that she and her husband
had a physical altercation after he was served with divorce papers, and she attempted to leave with her young son. She was explicit, however, that no physical
violence had occurred previously in their relationship. In Ellen's* case, she reported occasional and what she deemed minor pushing and shoving when she
would resist a directive from her husband, or when she would ask to go to the
United States. We categorized these six stories as having no or minimal physical
harm, because they differed from the stories of women who reported either
multiple experiences of violence or a single experience that was of such magnitude that it could have been life-threatening.

Threats to Life

Although threats were certainly a component of emotional terrorizing, 15
(68.2%) of the women specifically discussed either direct threats their husbands made to kill them or their children, or reported that the husband's abusive behavior was escalating so dramatically that the woman feared for her own
life and the lives of her loved ones. For eight of these women, their husbands
directly threatened to kill them, their children, a family member, or other people trying to help the women. In the seven other cases, the husband did not
explicitly tell the woman that he would kill her, but his behavior was erratic,

violent, or rageful enough that she feared for her life and the lives of her children.

Pamela married a European citizen who was a police officer in his country; she later discovered that he had a serious drinking problem. His behavior was bizarre when he was intoxicated. Once he tried to make a bomb that set fire to her parents' home during a visit. He wanted to return to his country after his son was born, but because he had already become abusive, she did not want to return with him. Pamela reports that he told her,

"I'm going to put you in a car with [our son] and I'm going to tell your parents that I'm driving us to the airport, and I'll leave the car at the airport and they can come and pick it up." And he said, "I will kill you on the side of the road, throw you in a ditch somewhere where you can't be found for weeks and by the time I get on the plane, and I'm in [my country], even if they do find you, [my country] does not extradite their own citizens to other countries for crimes." So, he said, "I can kill you in the United States and as long as I make it on a plane with my son, I won't serve a day in prison for killing you, because [my country] won't send me back to the United States to serve a sentence." Which is the truth; [his country] does not extradite their citizens. And so I was scared to death.

Pamela's husband told her at another time that he had killed people during his time as a police officer, and that it was like "stepping on a mouse." Coupled with the physical violence she was experiencing from him (including an incident in which he stabbed the bed multiple times while she was sleeping in it because he was angry at her for buying it), she felt that his threat to kill her was credible. She ended up returning to the other country in accordance with his wishes as a result of her concern about his dangerousness.

In other instances, the threat made by the husband was not only to kill the woman, but to kill the entire family. Fiona* and her American husband relocated to Europe for him to accept a temporary six-month job. After he was laid off from the job, he tried to secure other employment but was unsuccessful. Fiona* reported that during this period, he became increasingly violent and intimidating toward her. She describes a specific event that transpired after her husband was awakened by her infant son crying in the middle of the night:

And the scariest thing to me . . . this is really what . . . this whole thing . . . I really think how this whole thing started . . . is he . . . um, one night the kids woke up and one kid woke the other kid up and they were both crying and [he and I] were both tired. [. . .] And he said, "I can't take this anymore," and he left the house. [. . .] I thought, is he going to get a gun and kill himself? [. . .] He came back and I was sitting on the couch feeding our son and my daughter was sitting next to me, and [. . .] he said, "I feel so weird. I could just take a knife and kill this whole family." [. . .] And this—this is really scary for me [voice breaking]. [. . .] I had nowhere to turn to. I had absolutely no one. So—I didn't know what to do. I thought, you know, do I—do I just grab the kids and run out of the house or what?

In the context of her husband's other abusive behaviors, this threat felt credible enough to Fiona* that she immediately contacted her parents in the United States for help. They counseled her not to "set him off" or "rock the boat," and to try to get him to agree to return to the United States. They set up a safety plan in which she contacted her parents every day by email or phone until she was able to return to the United States.

While these two examples illustrate instances in which the men used direct threats to kill the woman and/or her children to enforce compliance, in other circumstances women had to interpret the level of danger they faced from their husbands. In seven cases, based on the totality of their experiences, women came to the conclusion that their husbands were capable of and heading toward an event that could end their own or their children's lives. In Rebecca's* case, after a period of intensifying conflict with her husband, she agreed to his wish to return to his country in an effort to try to save the marriage. Once there, his behavior escalated to life-threatening violence. He once beat her head against a wall to the point that she was bleeding and needed medical treatment; in another instance, he used an object to beat her that could have caused life-threatening injuries. As a result of these circumstances, Rebecca* came to this conclusion:

One day, I thought, okay, I'm either going to die, or I'm going to leave. [. . .]
    And I really believed that. I thought I was going to die one way or the other.
INTERVIEWER: *In the sense that he was either going to kill you, or you were going to die trying to leave?*
Yeah.

Kayla described a similar "felt sense" that something terrible was about to happen. She moved with her husband to his country in Europe after her youngest son was born. Soon after their move, her husband's physical violence began to escalate, and he became more emotionally volatile and out of control. During the time leading up to her decision to leave him, she reports the following experiences:

He would give me these strange looks, like "I'm gonna get you" type of look. Or the type of look where the hair on the back of your neck stands up, and you think that he's going to kill you, or get rid of the other kids, somehow. That's just . . . you know . . . it wasn't paranoia. It was . . . something's not right. He really is going to do something.

Women were coping with a combination of abusive behaviors from their husbands. In this context, they had to evaluate subtle behaviors or changes to determine the level of danger they faced. Fifteen of the women we interviewed came to the conclusion that they and their children were in serious danger. This realization became a motivating factor in their decision to flee from their husbands.

Intentional Isolation

Another common pattern occurring in over one-half of the cases was the effort the husband made to intentionally isolate the woman, both from people in the other country and from her family and friends in the United States. This enforced separation differed from the experience of cultural isolation that many of the women experienced as immigrant women to another country. In their new homes, most of the women couldn't speak the language or were unfamiliar with the customs of the people. In contrast, husbands' intentional isolation stemmed directly from their efforts to control the woman's contacts and activities.

Stephanie* relocated to her husband's country in Europe soon after the birth of their son. When their son was two months old, Stephanie's* husband began to hit her; she required medical attention for some of these attacks. She tried on multiple occasions to seek help from the police, but she was unable to speak the language and could not get them to intervene in her situation. She knew that she needed help, but her husband made efforts to prevent her from contacting others and telling them what was happening. As she describes the situation,

I couldn't go on the Internet. My husband was just keeping track of everybody I spoke to on the telephone, everybody. He would check my websites, whatever websites I visited. He would find a way to just track everything.

Tamara*, as we reported earlier, would protect her children from her husband by sleeping in one child's room and having the other children lock their doors at night. When she went to work in his country to help financially support the family, her husband became jealous and demanded that she not have social relationships at work. Tamara* also reported multiple instances during the marriage when her husband would physically isolate her from the rest of the family or from others. For example,

> He would lock me up. He was a big power. You know, taking away the keys to the car or locking me up in a room for hours at a time, even going so far as to shut off the electricity for that room in the fuse box.

Marta* reported similar efforts by her husband to control her behavior and her access to friends and family. She and her husband were citizens of a Latin American country and lived there until Marta* became so afraid of his repeated assaults that she fled with her children to her parents in the United States. She had few freedoms in the relationship, as she explains:

> He always had to decide on everything, what clothes I was to wear, whether or not I could have friends. He wouldn't let me fraternize with absolutely anyone; not with my friends, nor with my family. I lived isolated, and that depressed me and would cause me many problems.

Through threats and physical violence, Marta's* husband prevented her from having contact with her friends and family. For each of the 12 women who reported intentional isolation, the husband took specific actions to prevent his wife from physically or emotionally accessing help and support from others. For the majority of the respondents who were also immigrants to the country where they were residing, their isolation was intensified because most were unable to speak the language and were unfamiliar with the cultural traditions of their husbands' countries. The consequences of both his intentional isolation and her limited capacity to seek support within his country meant that many women turned to their families in the United States for help as much as they were able to do so.

Economic Control

As we noted earlier, most of the women in this sample were not working in the other country prior to their return to the United States. The reasons for their lack of employment were multifaceted, including the woman's desire to be the primary caregiver for her children, her husband's jealousy and efforts to limit her contact with others, and her citizenship status in the other country and the rights to employment (or lack thereof) that this status conferred on her. A substantial number of these women were dependent on their husbands for access to any finances because they did not work; several of those who were employed also had to give their earnings to their husbands, who would decide how to spend the money. As a result, almost one-half of the women had no independent access to money, which became an issue as they attempted to gain safety in the other country, and at the point when they decided to leave for the United States.

Stephanie*, like several of the other women in our study, described how her husband had "complete control" of the money in the household. Under these circumstances, regardless of whether the woman was the one earning the money (as was the case for Stephanie*), she had no ability to make choices regarding how the money was spent. Stephanie* describes the ways her husband controlled her independent functioning:

> He kept complete control of our finances, our money. I did not have any say whatsoever on how to spend it, where to spend it, when to spend it. I didn't possess any checks, any credit card, any debit card. If I withdrew money, it was with his permission, with his knowledge. If I wrote a check, it was with his permission, and with his knowledge.

Megan* reported similar economic control after she relocated with her husband to Europe when their children were two and four years old. Once they arrived in his country, her husband's behavior changed, and he became more threatening and angry. He moved out of their small apartment because he was upset with the children and the care they required. She found employment because of her English language skills, but this caused him to become even more jealous and angry and to exert more control. On one occasion, he choked her in front of the children and threatened to kill her. After this incident, Megan* tried to figure out how she could escape his abuse. She notes,

> I didn't have any money. Of course, he had control of *all* the finances in the marriage. So, what I started doing was, I was paid in cash and I started hiding money inside record sleeves, so he couldn't find it.

In this example, Megan* described her strategy for attempting to gather funds in order to escape from his country and return to her family in the United States. Because her husband was in control of the money that she made from her job, she had to covertly hide money in order to buy plane tickets to return to the States. Many of the women discussed the way they clandestinely attempted to gather funds to escape their situation.

Rebecca* reported on a different way in which her husband used their financial situation to control her. Without her knowledge, while they lived in America, he accumulated a large amount of debt. As she says,

> This made me feel like the most stupid, stupid woman . . . he had not paid our bills for close to two years, in the United States, and we owed about a hundred thousand dollars, which I had no idea about. My father called [after she moved to her husband's country] because he was receiving some of our mail, and he said "I'm opening these letters and you owe this, and you owe that" [. . .] and [my husband] said, "Well this is fine because we're never going back to the United States."

In this situation, Rebecca's* husband had amassed huge debt without telling her, debt that she feared she would continue to be responsible for as an American citizen and his wife. He told her that she would be responsible for this debt if she returned to the United States, effectively creating another barrier to her ability to her return.

Men in several of these families controlled all access to money and financial decisions. Women who had no independent access to funds had fewer options for coping with their husbands' violence. For example, they could not choose to move somewhere else in the country because they had no resources to enact this decision. As a result, many of the women turned to family members in the United States for financial help to flee their situation.

Passport Control and Immigration Threats

In the case of nine (41%) of the women we interviewed, their husbands took some action to control their movements by either destroying or limiting access to their passports. In the case of women who were immigrants to the United States, husbands often threatened to report the woman or other members of her family to American immigration officials. The special concerns of women who are immigrants to the United States are discussed in chapter 3.

Women who were US citizens but living in the other country needed access to their own passports, and their children's, to be able to leave the country. As a result, several of the men controlled the passports in order to control the women. For example, Ellen* relocated to her husband's European country soon after they were married, and gave birth to her children in that country. She petitioned for American passports for each of her children, but as she notes, her husband destroyed these:

He actually got into a big argument and he actually mutilated the passport, right in front of me; two of the passports, and the other two, I think, were damaged and then lost or something like that. So, right in front of me, ripped up my passport and my son's passport and said that I would never be returning to my country.

In this situation, Ellen's* husband was able to enforce his control over her and to prevent her from leaving his country by destroying the passports. In other cases, husbands hid the passports so their wives would not have access to them.

Men also used women's immigration status in the other country as a means of exerting control. For example, Katie* immigrated to a small, rural village in Europe with her husband. There she had two children. Seven years after relocating, she returned to the United States with her oldest daughter because her grandmother was terminally ill. Katie's* family talked with her about the fact that her husband was calling more often than seemed necessary to check on her whereabouts. They brought her materials on domestic violence, and she came to believe that she was a victim based on his controlling behavior. She decided not to return to his country, and was then subject to a Hague petition he filed for the return of their daughter. As a result of the Hague petition, Katie* discovered that her husband had created immigration problems that made it difficult for her to return to his country when she agreed to return with their daughter. As she describes this discovery,

He fiddled with my immigration. Apparently, what happened was, I had submitted all the necessary forms, at the appropriate times. However, from what I understand, they actually returned a form with a question, but it had to do with him, and he never replied. So basically, my immigration was defunct. [. . .] So, all I can say, it was very well . . . orchestrated. I mean, the fact that my immigration was messed up, and he tries to claim this Hague, although he knew the entire time where his daughter was. I think it's too coincidental. So, I think what he was hoping to achieve, was to just have her returned to him, then, and my not be allowed into the country.

In Katie's* view, her husband consciously chose not to provide information to immigration officials in his country with the intent of preventing her return if she should leave. In this case, his actions regarding her immigration paperwork led her to believe that he was intentionally using this tactic to separate her from her children.

Rape

Five of the women we interviewed volunteered information that their husbands had raped them. In one situation, Kelsey* moved with her husband to his country and a few years later gave birth to her first son. During a visit to introduce her son to his family in America, she explains, the following event occurred:

> And it was three months after [our son] was born, that we were in [the United States], and we were invited to his father's house to be there. [My husband] came into the bedroom, I had just finished breastfeeding [my son], and he just raped me. He just . . . that moment and that's how I got pregnant with [my younger son], and because his father was in the next room, he knew I couldn't say anything. It was just he left, came in, did what he did, and I was completely stunned. [. . .] And I kept saying, "Stop, stop!" But he knew that his father and his stepfather were in the next room. And we were in the States, and it was something that, what am I going to do? You know, he's my husband and you feel like I just got violated.

Other women also reported that their children were conceived after their husbands had raped them. In this way, sexual assault was a part of the pattern of abuse that some women reported in their descriptions of their relationships.

Each woman had some combination of the experiences described in the preceding pages. In table 1.4 we document each woman's unique pattern of abuse, ordering the cases from those with the most types of abuse present to the least. The narrative information and its summary in this chart lead to the conclusion that all but a handful of women in this study experienced serious, intense, and potentially life-threatening abuse. By the time they left the other country, most of the women were afraid for their own lives and their children's lives.

This table facilitates within-case and across-case comparison, and allows us to place the women into a mutually exclusive typology of domestic violence experiences based on the type of harms they experienced. This typology is found in table 1.5. We ordered this typology to differentiate between those women who routinely experienced serious levels of physical violence and those who did not report physical harm, but did report emotional terrorism inflicted by their husbands. This ordering reflects the emphasis in US courts on physical harm when determining that domestic violence exists. Sixteen (72.7%) of the women in the sample were frequently physically harmed by their husbands and lived in a state of intimidation and control. Four women reported chronic emotional terrorizing, but that their husbands never physically hurt them (Katie*, Sandra), that any physical events were minor in the woman's reckoning (Ellen*),

Table 1.4 Types of Domestic Violence Reported by Each Woman

Woman	Emotional Terrorizing	Physical Harm	Threats to Life	Intentional Isolation	Economic Control	Immigration Threats	Rape
Belinda	◆	◆	◆	◆	◆	◆	
Amanda	◆	◆	◆	◆	◆	◆	
Ilana	◆	◆	◆	◆		◆	◆
Fiona*	◆	◆	◆		◆	◆	
Lara	◆	◆	◆			◆	◆
Ruth*	◆	◆	◆	◆	◆		
Megan*	◆	◆	◆	◆	◆		
Pamela	◆	◆	◆	◆	◆		
Marina	◆	◆	◆	◆			◆
Ellen*	◆		◆	◆	◆	◆	
Caitlin*	◆	◆	◆	◆			
Kendra	◆	◆	◆	◆			
Jennifer	◆	◆	◆				◆
Kayla	◆	◆	◆		◆		
Rebecca*	◆	◆	◆		◆		
Stephanie*	◆	◆		◆	◆		
Austin*	◆	◆	◆				
Marta*	◆	◆				◆	
Tamara*	◆		◆	◆			
Katie*			◆	◆		◆	
Kelsey*	◆						◆
Sandra	◆						

Note: Women were not surveyed on each of these areas of abuse (with the exception of physical harm), so they may have had experiences that they did not report during the interview process.

or that physical violence happened only once, rather than as a pattern of harmful attacks (Tamara*).

In two cases, the actual categorization of the women's experience was ambiguous. Both these women self-identified as victims of domestic violence, but compared to the other 20 women, their stories had two different elements, one related to the timing of abuse and the other to the content of the woman's story. In Amanda's case, a marriage of over 15 years deteriorated over the course of several months after her husband had an affair and brought his mistress to the country where they were living. Prior to the affair, Amanda said that there were no examples of emotional terrorizing or other abuse. After the mistress appeared, Amanda and her husband had a fight that resulted in her requiring hospital care for a knife wound to her hand. Amanda reported that she believed

Table 1.5 Typology of Women's Domestic Violence Experiences

	Mother Physically Harmed	Emotional Terrorizing with No Physical Abuse	Ambiguous Cases
Total	16	4	2

this injury was accidental, but after this incident, she began to feel afraid of her husband and what he might do next. She did not report that he had harmed their children, although the children were upset by the frequent fighting. Amanda's case differed from those of other women, who reported chronic abuse that occurred over many years, throughout the course of the relationship.

In the second case, Kelsey*, unlike the other women interviewed, did not spontaneously relate information about a pattern of coercion, intimidation, or physical violence in her marriage. She did not describe incidents of emotional terrorizing or other abuse prior to the separation, with one exception: she reported that her second child was the product of her husband's raping her, a very serious allegation of violence that may have haunted her throughout their relationship and the separation. She felt intimidated by her husband after they separated, especially in his efforts to limit her access to their financial resources, and in disagreements over custody of the children. Her narrative was characterized by a degree of incoherency and contradiction not seen in the other interviews—this kind of incoherency can be characteristic of people who have unresolved traumas that manifest as disorganized thoughts and emotions (Jelinek, Randjbar, Seifert, Kellner, & Mortiz, 2009; Porter & Peace, 2007; Uehara, 2007). As a result, it was unclear whether this respondent did not understand what she was being asked to describe, or if she had not experienced an ongoing pattern of intimidation and coercion. Unlike the other women in the study, who easily described multiple instances of various forms of abuse, Kelsey* did not, although she clearly saw herself as abused and was living in a domestic violence shelter. Her main concern was that she believed her children had been exposed to sexually inappropriate situations by her husband.

These two cases illustrate the difficulty in creating a conclusive definition of domestic violence that is inclusive of typical abuse experiences and also differentiates abuse from other forms of couple conflict. In both cases, these women self-referred to the research study based on their evaluation that they were victims of domestic violence and fit the eligibility criteria for the study. It may be that these women did not recognize patterns of emotional terrorizing that had gone on earlier in their marriages (that is, the abuse was more chronic than they recognized), or perhaps coercive control did not occur earlier in the marriages. Aspects of the two women's stories were consistent with the reports provided by the other women, including isolation, a feeling of threat to life, economic control, and immigration threats in Amanda's case; and rape early in the marriage and emotional intimidation after separation in Kelsey's* case. For each woman, however, the time frame or content of her reports were not similar to those of the other 20 mothers in the study. We have discussed these two cases at this level of detail to illustrate the difficulties people external to the families may face in determining whether the women's accounts would be evaluated as domestic violence.

Domestic Violence as a Human Rights Concern

One of the questions confronting legal professionals is whether women's domestic violence experiences are serious enough to constitute a "grave risk" to the psychological or physical health of their children. We will discuss this issue in depth in chapter 4, but here we want to emphasize a central point: the majority of women we interviewed were physically harmed by their husbands and lived in situations of intense fear for themselves and their children. These circumstances were not trivial—instead, they were potentially life-threatening. On a daily basis, women had to strategize around their husbands' violent tendencies and efforts to restrict their agency and autonomy. The context of this level of violence is the backdrop for assessing their subsequent decisions to leave their husbands and come to the United States.

The women in this study described situations that exemplify the concept of coercive control and demonstrate how domestic violence is not just a matter of how frequently or seriously a woman is physically assaulted. Husbands often made sustained efforts to degrade, humiliate, and intimidate the women in order to ensure their acquiescence to the men's control. The women's experiences are frightening, troubling, and upsetting. Yet, it is important to recognize that even with as much specificity as the examples we have given, women's actual experience of entrapment is elusive. As Stark (2007) notes, the domestic violence research literature

documents violent acts and harms they cause in agonizing detail. But this work suffers from the fallacy of misplaced concreteness: no matter how many punches or injuries or instances of depression are cataloged, the cage remains invisible . . . We see the effects of dominance, anger, depression, dependence, fear, substance use, multiple medical problems or suicide attempts, calls to the police or visits to the ER or shelter, but not *domination itself*. (p. 198; emphasis added)

These stories are, by and large, tales of domination, of the efforts of one partner to exert complete control over the other. In contexts outside of the family, the behaviors reported here—physical assault, threats of harm to the victim or family, isolation, and degradation—are consistent with human rights definitions of acts of torture (Dutton, 1992; Edwards, 2010; Jones, 1994). Traditionally in international law, domestic violence has not been viewed as a human rights violation because these acts are perpetrated by "private" individuals rather than "public," that is, state-sponsored, actors. Despite the fact that domestic violence has been conceived of as a private matter, scholars have noted the parallels between abuse and other forms of "terrorism." For example, in 1994, Marcus notes "that people or groups wishing to terrorize others use three basic tactics: (a) surprise and seemingly random (but actually well-planned) acts of violence, (b) psychological and physical warfare to silence protest and minimize opposition, and (c) the creation of an atmosphere of intimidation in which there is no way to escape" (as cited in Perilla, 1999, p. 112).

The United Nations and other international bodies generally find that torture includes four elements: (1) severe physical and/or mental pain and suffering; (2) intentionally inflicted; (3) for specified purposes; (4) with some form of official involvement (Copelon, 1994). As Copelon (1994) notes in her comparison of domestic violence and torture, the first three of these components are easily identified in domestic violence victimization. The question of whether domestic violence denotes a human rights violation is inextricably bound to the issues surrounding the dichotomization of public versus private space. When only those forms of violence that are perpetrated in the public sphere by state actors are acknowledged as torture, then the experiences of women can be relegated to a level of lesser priority. Yet Copelon argues that this dichotomy trivializes the world of the private and deprives women

of one of the key mechanisms of defense, healing and survival—the identification and condemnation of clearly wrongful authority. Indeed, once the gravity and comparability of intimate violence is acknowledged, the problem is not that the meaning of torture is diluted but that the practice of torture is pervasive. Recognition of gender-based violence as torture . . . is problematic because it reveals the banality of evil and the enormity of suffering that society has accepted and must confront. (p. 139)

The Hague Convention on the Civil Aspects of International Child Abduction exists within a web of interrelated beliefs and decisions about what constitutes human rights, and how these rights are understood in a legal context. The Convention itself recognizes the abrogation of human rights as a reason to prevent the return of a child to the habitual residence, yet exposure to domestic violence has not been considered a human rights violation. Because the treaty primarily focuses on the child, it is possible to ignore the violations happening to the mother, even though some US domestic courts have made clear that separating a child from his or her non-abusive parent violates, for both, their constitutional rights of access to each other (Lansner, 2008; Weiner, 2004). If domestic violence were understood as a violation of human rights, rather than as the impulsive behavior of private individuals, it is likely that these issues would be more at the forefront in decisions affecting transnational families. As we will show, the question of domestic violence is not a central feature in decisions regarding the return of children to their habitual residence under the Hague Convention.

2 | The Misinterpretation of Domestic Violence

Recasting Survival as Child Abduction

The purpose of the Hague Convention is to return children to their habitual residence as quickly as possible, because the assumption is that the taking parent has abducted the child, and that abduction is harmful to the child. The treaty priority is to have courts in the country where the child has usually resided make decisions about issues of custody and visitation when a marriage or partnership is dissolved, rather than allow a parent to "jurisdiction shop" for a legal venue that would be most favorable to his or her concerns.

The Hague Convention does not define *habitual residence*, so courts have been left to determine their approach to this concept. As a result, US courts differ on what standards should be used to determine the habitual residence of the child. Vivatvaraphol (2009) has reviewed jurisprudence in this area and found that courts evaluate the shared intent between parents to reside in a certain place, and that this intent is not dependent on a certain amount of time elapsing, but rather on the "settled purpose" (p. 9) to make the new location the habitual residence in the "ordinary and natural" sense of these words (*C v S [minor: abduction: illegitimate child (1990)]*). Courts can look to certain facts as evidence of settled purpose, including "child's enrollment in school, the primary language spoken by the child, the quality and duration of the child's stay in a particular country, and the relationships formed by the child with friends and relatives" (Vivatvaraphol, 2009, p. 17). Citizenship is not considered in the question of habitual residence—it may be that none of the people in a Hague Convention case is a citizen of the country that is found to be the habitual residence. If a judge determines that the other country is the habitual residence of the child, then the mother would have to prove one of the defenses against return described in this book's introduction.

An underlying assumption about habitual residence not explicitly stated in the Convention is that both parents have voluntarily agreed to reside in another country with their children. Without this presumption of voluntariness, one parent could force another to live in his or her country, and then claim abduction if the coerced parent leaves with the children. For this reason, legal scholars have stated that fundamentally, habitual residence must "entail some element of voluntariness and purposeful design" (Clive, 1997). When habitual residence is narrowly framed by looking at school attendance or length of time in the other country, what is often overlooked are the ways in which men may entrap women in other countries, even if the women initially agree to relocation.

Moving to the Other Country

In this section, we examine how the women in our sample came to be in these other countries, and we demonstrate the role that domestic violence played in some cases in determining the habitual residence of the children. We focus on the 17 cases in our sample of American women who moved to other countries to be with their husbands.[1] This excludes the cases of five women who were citizens of other countries and who relocated to the United States to escape their husbands' abuse.[2] We focus on the cases of American citizens because they include a decision to move to the other country *prior* to the decision to flee back to the States, whereas the Latina mothers were not in "foreign" countries prior to their leave-taking.

In 15 of the cases, women discussed how they came to be in the other country.[3] We categorized the reasons women gave for moving to the other country

1. In most cases, the father was a citizen of the country to which the family moved. In two cases, an American husband, wife, and children relocated to Europe for economic reasons, but all were US citizens.

2. In the cases of the immigrant women we interviewed, the habitual residence of the child was understood by all parties to be the other country, because both parents (and the children) were generally citizens of that country and had lived there most, if not all of their lives, prior to leaving. In contrast, women who were American citizens made a decision at some point to immigrate to the other country, and as we will show, issues of coercion were sometimes involved in these decisions. We will take up the special issues of women who are immigrants to the United States in chapter 3.

3. In two of the cases, no determination could be made as to the reason and circumstances of the move to the other country, either because of the degree of incoherency in the story, or because the focus in the interview was on the woman's current difficulties, and not enough time was available to cover this aspect of her situation.

into four mutually exclusive areas, based on the degree of voluntariness involved in the move.

Voluntary Move

For the majority of the women (60.0%), the move to the other country was for voluntary reasons that were not influenced by domestic violence. In the language of previous court rulings, the coupled voluntarily shared a "settled purpose" to reside in the other country. In Sandra's and Jennifer's cases, they had jobs in the other country that facilitated their moves. Sandra's American husband accompanied her to another country; Jennifer sought professional employment in her husband's country, and when she secured this, they moved there. For Fiona*, Caitlin*, Austin*, Kayla, and Ruth*, the family moved so that the husband could take a job in the other country. Tamara* was a student in her husband's country when she met him, married him, and decided to settle there with him.

In these eight cases, there was no indication that the women felt the marriage was in trouble prior to the move to the other country. For Megan*, however, the move to her husband's country came after a year in which her husband had separated from her and the children to travel around the United States because he was dissatisfied with the relationship. He returned to the family and suggested that they move back to his parents' home country, as he believed they would have better opportunities there. Megan* agreed to do so, feeling that this would be an opportunity for her to live abroad, and that their relationship would improve. In each of these nine women's circumstances, domestic violence was not a factor in the decision to move to the other country.

Move Accomplished through Threats or Trickery

In six cases (40.0%), the women were tricked into relocating, immediately prevented from returning when they arrived in the other country, or forced by potentially life-endangering threats to accompany their husbands to the other country. In each of these women's situations, there is a clear absence of a voluntary decision to travel to, and remain in, the other country. A pattern of coercion and physical threat associated with domestic violence were factors in each of these six cases.

Within this group of women, Pamela's situation is the clearest example of coercion. She reports on the way her husband threatened her to make her move with him to Europe.

We lay in my parents' house while my son slept, and he said to me, "You're going back to [my country]. I don't want to stay in the United States. Me and my son and you are going back." And I told him I didn't want to go. I wanted to stay here, and that is when he said to me: "You will go back or I'll kill you." And he proceeded to tell me that he knew [how to kill] . . . which he did. That was his job. And he told me that in his career as a [. . .] policeman [. . .] he did secret vigilante work and that his last time, he had killed seven people. [. . .] And so I was scared to death. From that day on, I just cried [. . .] because I knew what I was headed for. That I was going to live my life being tied to this abusive man who was an alcoholic, and he never showed not one ounce of attention to my son even from the moment this child took his first breath. He never fed him. He never touched him. He never held him. He didn't change his clothes. He didn't tell him he loved him. Nothing. Nothing. [. . .] Yet, he was willing to kill me because he saw his son as a possession . . . And he saw me as a possession, and that's all that I was. So, out of fear of death, [. . .] I went back to [his country]. Not because I wanted to, but because I was told that I would die if I didn't. And coming from a man who looks you straight in the face and says, "I've killed seven people before, and it won't mean anything to me to kill one more."

Pamela's story shows how her husband used his ability to threaten her with death (a threat that she found credible based on his past employment, his behavior while they lived in the United States, and the stories he told her) to force her to return with him to his country. Pamela's husband filed a Hague petition against her after she escaped with her son and returned to the United States, but the case was never heard in court, and no decision was ever made because her husband, for reasons unknown to Pamela, did not pursue the case after filing it in a US court.

In the five other cases, some level of subterfuge and coercion was used by the men in these families to either trick their wives into moving to the other country, or to keep them there once they had arrived.[4] Once each woman had

4. In terms of subterfuge, Katie* felt that her husband lied to her to facilitate the move to the other country, but it is unclear what role domestic violence might have played in this decision. She voluntarily agreed to move to his country, but came to believe later that he had manipulated her into the move in order to put himself in a better position should they divorce. She believed that he encouraged her to go to the United States to be with a dying relative, planning all along to use the Hague process to obtain custody of his daughter, while simultaneously preventing Katie's* return because he had not filed necessary paperwork for her immigration status. Katie's* attorney counseled her to agree to a voluntary return to his country, as the court had ruled that this was the habitual residence of her daughter.

accompanied her husband to the other country, within days to weeks she realized that he would not allow her to return to the United States, and that he would force her to stay in his country. Ellen's* husband told her that they would be visiting his country, but once there, he destroyed her passport and her child's, to prevent her from returning to the United States. Several months later she managed to get new passports issued from the US Embassy, and fled with three of her four children (the fourth child had been taken by her husband to another location). Once she and the children were in the United States, he successfully used the Hague process to force the children's return to his country. Ellen* was unsure if evidence about the coercion involved in their continued presence in the other country was presented to the US court.

In Kendra's case, after the birth of her son, she agreed to temporarily visit her husband's country, only to discover after being there for a few weeks that he intended all of them to stay.

> The baby was eight months, [. . .] and we were going to go back for the summer and do the usual, you know [. . . We] had to show the baby off. You know, take the baby and show it around [. . .] and everybody's happy and life is a party. We went back and it was . . . really nice for a while, and then I sort of discovered quite by accident that his mother had arranged a permanent job for him that—well . . . and things sort of escalated from there.

Kendra discovered after learning of her husband's new job that he had no intention of leaving his country and returning the family to the United States, where they had lived for the previous two years since marrying. It is unclear whether this was her husband's plan before they began their visit, or this decision evolved during the weeks they were initially there. After deciding to stay, he moved them into a family compound, where Kendra was isolated from contact with others because it was against the beliefs of his culture to allow women to be in public unescorted. Soon after Kendra's husband revealed that they would be staying in his country, he began to physically and emotionally abuse her. This abuse continued for several years, during which time Kendra made two attempts to escape. Her husband found her after ten months in hiding; the second time she fled to the United States and went into hiding with her son. Her husband hired a private investigator, found her location, and had her son removed from her custody as a result of the Hague petition. Kendra argued in court that she had never agreed that his country would be their habitual residence. She eventually settled her Hague case, the court returned their son to her custody, and they were allowed to stay in the United States.

For Rebecca* and Amanda, their husbands clearly planned their efforts to force the women to remain in the other country once they had arrived. Rebecca* and her husband were having serious conflicts while in the United States. The couple had previously lived together in his country, so they decided to return; Rebecca* hoped this would help mend their relationship. Rebecca* recounts the situation she experienced immediately on moving to her husband's country:

> I moved with my husband and my two children to [his country] [. . .] and the day after we arrived there, I realized that I had made a mistake. Our marriage had been falling apart, and literally the day after we arrived, I told him that I had made a mistake and I wanted to go home, and I wanted a divorce. What I didn't know was that before we had moved, he had set it up so that I couldn't go home. He had . . . in [his country], there's such a thing as a restraining order so that somebody can't leave the country. [. . .] He had set up, with his family, a meeting with an attorney, which he did immediately, got a restraining order against me, and I could not leave the country. I was trapped.

Rebecca's* husband hid his intent to force the family to stay in his country. Once Rebecca's* legal entrapment occurred, the physical violence from her husband escalated to the point that he was inflicting potentially life-threatening violence, including attacking her with dangerous objects. After several months, Rebecca* managed to obtain his agreement that she and the children could visit her parents in the United States for a few weeks. Once she arrived in America, she immediately filed for a divorce. Her husband submitted a Hague petition and was successful in enlisting the US courts to force the return of the children to his country. Even though she had been attempting to leave his country from almost the moment she arrived, the US court did not acknowledge the role that his coercive and violent behavior played in determining their residence in the months preceding her move with the children back to the United States.

Amanda also was unaware of her husband's ulterior plan to enforce their move to his country. She moved to his country in the hope of repairing a marriage that had been fractured by his adultery. She describes the following history:

> I was born and raised, you know, here in the United States, and my husband was here [when] I met [him]. We were married for ten years and he's from [Europe], and we were here, married nine years, and he decided to go back to [Europe]. [. . .] He told me we were going to go there for a while, just to see if it worked out. [. . .]

So, we pretty much went on a trial basis. But as soon as I got there, things started changing. [. . .] He didn't say too much at first, and we were there for like about a month, and then, he told me to come back because we had one of our businesses running here [. . .] So I came back and I paid the rent, and then, I went back to [his country], and then I found out that we weren't going back. He took my passports away, and the kids' passports away. [. . .]. So, he took our passports away and he said that we weren't going anywhere. [. . .]. I wasn't even in [his country] more than six weeks when all this chaos started going on.

Amanda's story demonstrates the coercive nature of the decision her husband made, once they were in his country, to stay there. Soon after his announcement that they would be staying, the encounter happened in which she was cut with a knife he was holding during an altercation. Amanda managed an elaborate escape and returned to the United States with her children; he served her with a Hague petition soon after. Interestingly, Amanda's was the only case in which the judge decided that the father's country was not the habitual residence of the children. However, from Amanda's understanding, the judge's rationale for this decision was based on the length of time they were in the other country and the fact that the couple had maintained a business in the United States. When he ruled on the children's habitual residence, the judge did not cite as a reason the coercive actions on the father's part that had kept Amanda and her children in the other country until they escaped.

In summary, most of the women in this study went willingly to the other country with their husbands, or met and married their husbands while resident in the other country. In these nine cases, domestic violence did not play a significant role in determining the habitual residence of the children. The decision to live in the other country was mutual, or one already made by the woman without coercion.

For a significant minority of the women, the decision to be in the other country was either a result of a direct threat from the husband, or was a product of the husband's intimidation and efforts to control the woman and children. In these cases, some level of deception or coercion in the relocation to the other country was involved. In the context of abuse, some children were residing in the other country because their mothers were not free to negotiate their residence as a result of the father's abuse and intimidation. A mother's decision to remain in another country may reflect a strategy to ensure her own and her children's survival, more than a voluntary decision to reside in this location.

The dynamics of the decision of where to live, coupled with the previous description of the abuse that the women reported, indicate that the question of the child's habitual residence is far more complex than a simple calculus of time or a child's attachment to social institutions. Children may have spent several years in another country, so they may have been enrolled in schools or been a part of a social community. However, these actions may be rooted in the initial efforts of the father to entrap the mother and children in the other country through his abusive behavior. As a result, the issue of habitual residence in these families has to be carefully explored to uncover whether the decision to reside in the other country is a mutual and voluntary one. To determine the child's habitual residence solely on the basis of length of time in the other country, without acknowledging the underlying reasons for this residence, is to further perpetuate abuse of the women and potentially further harm the children.

Taking Mothers and Their Reasons for Crossing International Borders

As we have suggested previously, women facing Hague Convention cases are placed in the paradoxical position of having to justify their decisions to take action to end the abuse. The traditional question—why does she stay?—is turned on its head, with the legal system forcing her to defend why she left when leaving means crossing international borders. Work with domestic violence victims in the United States shows that women turn most frequently to informal support networks (family and friends) for help in coping with relationship troubles (Postmus, Severson, Berry, & Yoo, 2009). When these efforts are unsuccessful, women often turn to formal resources, such as the police or legal professionals, medical providers, or domestic violence–specific resources to try to handle their circumstances.

The women in our study were surprisingly resourceful and persistent in seeking help from outside sources to cope with the violence and to attain safety within the other country. But as we will show, women were unable to secure resources in the other country that ensured their safety and allowed them to survive economically outside marriage to their husbands.[5]

5. As we note in appendix B, none of the women reported successful efforts to obtain help from criminal justice or legal resources in the other country. This may be an accident of sampling (we may not have been able to reach the women who successfully obtained help but came to the States anyway), or it may reflect an underlying reality that women who cannot access these resources are the ones most likely to return to the United States.

Ending the Relationship in the Other Country
Did Not End the Abuse

The women made multiple attempts to change the actions of an abusive partner, either by directly challenging his behavior or by engaging others on their behalf to confront him about his violence. In general, as we will show, these efforts were unsuccessful, leaving the women with few options other than continued exposure to violence or figuring a way to escape. Six of the women had already taken steps to remove themselves from the violent behavior of their spouses before fleeing to the United States, but leaving the relationship did not end the violence and, in some cases, only escalated it further. Of these six women, three had initiated divorce proceedings, and three had already divorced their abusive spouses prior to their decision to flee to the United States. In these instances, the legal end of their relationship did not stop these six men from continuing to stalk and physically attack the women. For example, Lara had been married to her husband for more than five years before deciding to obtain a divorce because of his abusive behavior. However, her ex-husband's violence did not end after the divorce, but escalated, as she notes:

> I filed for divorce and separated from him. I lived in another house, but then it was worse because he would go to the house and if I wasn't there, he would break everything. On two or three occasions, he went and broke the door, and started throwing things around [. . .] And like I told you, the tone of things was escalating. When I couldn't take it anymore, I went to the authorities, when things got too ugly in front of my son. [. . .] So, he came in breaking the door down, as it was his custom, and he started to hit me in front of my son. [. . .] I ran for the phone to call the police and he left immediately. But, since that time, he hit me harder.

Even though Lara had taken every step available to her in the other country to physically, legally, and emotionally separate from her abusive husband and to begin the process of rebuilding her life, her husband continued to stalk and attack her in her new home. The effects that the violence and disruption were having on her son became a primary concern, compelling Lara to reach out to the authorities in her city. Unfortunately, in her efforts to get her husband to stop attacking her, Lara was stymied by the unwillingness of the institutions she contacted to address the domestic violence.

For Lara, and for five other women, taking steps to end the relationship did not end the husband's abuse. In fact, these women's decisions to separate escalated the men's attempts to try to regain control of them. These women were

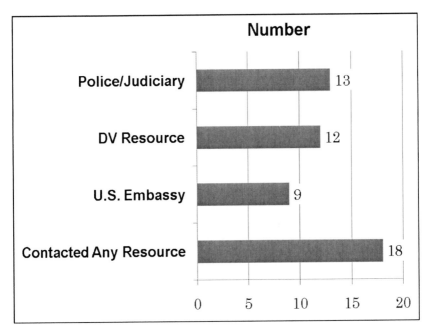

Number

Police/Judiciary	13
DV Resource	12
U.S. Embassy	9
Contacted Any Resource	18

0   5   10   15   20

Figure 2.1 Resources Accessed by Women in Coping with Domestic Violence

doing what they could to increase their safety and remove themselves and their children from the husband's abusive behavior while still living in the other country. Unfortunately, they were not successful in stopping the violence.

Obtaining Help in the Other Country Didn't Stop the Abuse

Like Lara, women in the study sought a variety of resources to cope with the violence. Most women (85.7%) contacted at least one of three resources—police or judicial system, other domestic violence resource, or the us Embassy—in the other country. In figure 2.1 we note the number of women from the 22 in our sample who contacted these three resources and summarize how many contacted any formal system in the other country. Next, we provide more detail about the responses women encountered from the formal institutions in the other country.

Contacted the Police or Judicial System

When women did reach out for formal help, they were most likely to turn to the police and judicial system for assistance. More than one-half of the women in the study (59.1%) sought help from the criminal justice system in the other country to cope with the abuse. In addition, three of the women contemplated contacting the police but chose not to, either feeling the system would not be responsive because she was a foreigner, or feeling unsafe contacting police because her husband was a police officer or knew people on the force. Overall, only six women did not consider approaching the police in the other country.

Strikingly, however, of the 13 women who contacted the police or court system, none received assistance with domestic violence. The reasons for this lack of help varied, but the most common response of police and court officers was to support the husband overtly or covertly in continuing his abusive behavior. In six cases, the police or court openly sided with the husband in his efforts to control the woman. For example, Kendra was violently attacked by her husband, and she did what she thought any woman would do in this circumstance—she contacted the police. When they arrived, this is what happened:

> The police did come; they actually came up in record time. They were there in about less than 30 minutes, if I remember correctly. And they looked at me—by then, you know, things are beginning to show. I had hand marks around my neck so that for days I wore a turtleneck to hide. And they informed him that since I was still up talking and able to complain he hadn't done his job properly (begins to cry).

Kendra interpreted the police comment that her husband had not "done his job properly" to mean that he had not exerted his control over her sufficiently to prevent her from calling the police. The police were overtly supporting the abusive husband's right to use physical force to control his wife, even to the extent of endorsing the possibility that he could do something to prevent her from being "up talking." Marta* encountered a similar dismissive attitude among the court officials she approached for help as the violence escalated:

> At first, I didn't do anything because he always found a way to make me feel like it was my fault [that] he was aggressive with me. "It's your fault I beat you. It's your fault." So I didn't do anything. But the last time he beat me, I went to court and I told them I wanted to file a violence complaint, and they laughed at me and told me to go make my husband happy, because most of the women who went there to file a complaint would bail their partners out a short time later. So I didn't pursue the complaint. The only thing I had was a medical report, which stated the lesions I had. This was the report I was supposed to use to file the complaint. But, they didn't [. . .] want to take my complaint [. . .] they said that all the women who filed a complaint against their partners for domestic violence, would later turn around and bail them out of jail, and that was a lot of work for them to do and that it didn't

make sense for me to file a complaint if I was going to bail him out myself, later. They told me to go make my husband happy so that he wouldn't beat me.

Marta*, after many beatings, felt desperate enough about what was happening to seek help from the court, but the officials she encountered didn't want to take complaints that caused extra work for them when the women wouldn't pursue legal action. Marta* does not indicate that they assessed her situation, offered her alternatives to the violence complaint, or helped her to plan for her safety in another way. Instead, the officials implied that they saw her as responsible for the violence because she was not making her husband happy. Their advice was to do something to modify her behavior so he would stop beating her.

In both Kendra and Marta's* encounters with officers of the criminal justice systems in the other countries, the men who heard their complaints not only didn't treat the situation seriously, they actually aided the violent husbands in evading responsibility for any aggressive actions. In Kendra's case, officials directly communicated to her husband, in front of her, that there would be no consequence for him. In Marta's* case, court officials placed the responsibility for his actions on her, so he was not held accountable. These two examples should be interpreted as instances of institutional sexism in which women's safety needs are systematically discounted in favor of bolstering the role of the man in the relationship.

In accessing law enforcement help, other women encountered difficulties that were less overtly discriminatory, but that still inclined toward supporting the men engaged in aggressive behaviors. Stephanie* called the police on multiple occasions to report that her husband had hit her, but she was unable to convince them to come and investigate her story. She had to enlist other legal help to pressure the police to respond:

> I told [my] attorney [in the other country] what had happened, that my husband had been physically violent, and I told her that I had been trying to call the police; that I had called them, and they always respond with "We want to speak with your husband. We want to speak to your husband." My husband would talk to them, calm them down, tell them, "She's crazy. Nothing's happening. I'm not abusing her. She's crazy." So, they wouldn't come . . . until finally, this attorney called the police and said, "I'm demanding that you check on her." They finally did.

Stephanie* was not fluent in the language of her husband's country and was unable on her own to activate the police to intervene with her husband. She had to find another legal authority who pressured the police to make a visit to the home and assess the situation. Unfortunately, when the police came to investigate, they pulled her husband aside and told him to safeguard the children's passports from her, as described earlier in the section on passport control and immigration threats. The police did not investigate the husband's violence or help Stephanie* to identify what could be done to increase her safety. This lack of intervention by the authorities led her husband to feel even more empowered to beat her, because he believed there would be no consequences to his actions.

Several women encountered bureaucratic barriers to obtaining help from the criminal justice system in the other country. Rebecca* told of a common barrier the women reported, namely that the police could intervene only if they were present when she was being physically attacked.

> They said they couldn't do anything after the fact. They needed to be called when it was happening.
> INTERVIEWER: *Can you tell me a little bit about the incident that led you to go to the police?*
> He had picked me up . . . the houses and apartments are built out of stone. Everything is built out of stone there. And he had picked me up and was slamming me against the wall and had bashed the back of my head open. All of my hair was bloody and matted, and I went to the police and . . . you know . . . they said they needed to be at my house when it was happening. They needed to see, you know, what was happening at the time: who was doing it, how it was done.

The likelihood that a woman would be able to phone the police during a physical assault, and then have them arrive in time to witness the attack, seems remote. This emphasis on firsthand witnessing of violence severely limited Rebecca's* ability to obtain safety for herself through help from the police. This example illustrates a bureaucratic barrier relative to how systems define a legitimate domestic violence report. In Rebecca's* case, only an eyewitness account by a police officer would satisfy the need to determine if domestic violence was occurring. The evidence of the aftereffects of the assault (her bloody head) was insufficient to galvanize a response.

Other women also found that they didn't "fit" the bureaucratic protocol used by authorities to determine if domestic violence was happening. In Jennifer's case, she was a professional woman, and she and her husband lived in an affluent part of town. The police were disinclined to become involved in her case. She believed that they saw abuse as more of a problem for those in poverty, so her professional, affluent status was a barrier to receiving help. For Marina, her husband's abuse was so serious as to knock her unconscious, but because he didn't leave bruises in typical places, the police said there was nothing they could do. Tamara* also sought help from the police, both on the night when she served her husband with divorce papers and he became violent, and in the weeks that followed once he discovered her whereabouts and began stalking her. The police tried to help her find shelter the first night, but there was no shelter space available; subsequently, they told her there was nothing they could do about his stalking, as he had the right to be on the street outside of where she was staying because it was public space.

The police and court systems were the most frequent resources the women approached to try to stop the abuse. However, these systems often functioned either overtly or covertly to support the battering husband in his efforts to control the woman, or the bureaucratic response to the abuse was such that these systems did not effectively intervene on behalf of the women. Across 11 countries, the experiences of the women who chose to leave were remarkably similar—the police system was not able to protect them and their children from abuse.

Sought Help for Domestic Violence in the Other Country

In the context of the social safety system of the police and courts providing no effective intervention, over one-half of the women turned to another formal resource for assistance with the abuse. In Austin's* case, a physical attack by her husband was so severe that she had to flee the house with her young daughter, and they ended up living in a domestic violence shelter in the other country for a few days. In the other eleven cases, women did not seek out typical domestic violence services, but rather sought help from attorneys, religious authorities, social service providers, and medical workers who treated their injuries. These services, particularly the attorneys that practiced in the other countries, tended to be more supportive of the woman than were the police and courts. Eight of the women reported that the other formal helpers they encountered were empathetic and attempted to help them cope with the violence.

However, some of the services the women approached perpetuated the same problems as found with the police, namely, they did not hold the batterer accountable for his actions. As a result, these resources were ineffective in helping the women to create a safer situation for themselves and their children.

Stephanie* notes her experience with a mediation service that the police suggested could help the couple more effectively negotiate the problems they were having:

> We went to see the mediator once. We had appointments to go see this mediator. Again and again my husband blocked these mediations claiming he was ill, claiming that he had to work late. And I have all of those papers. I've always had all of those documents. It's his own handwriting, with his own signature making excuses of why he couldn't attend, or why we couldn't attend these mediation appointments. The mediator when we saw her once, told us that there were a lot of problems, that my husband should go to a psychologist and that we should also try family therapy. He never once set foot anywhere. He said he didn't have time. He said he didn't believe in it, and that he wasn't going to do it and nobody was going to make him. And it's true, nobody did. So, after he blocked the mediation three times, the mediator stopped. They didn't call. They didn't write. They never wrote to me or called me saying, "Madam, we have to talk to you. Are you in agreement with this, that we stop this? Is it true what your husband is saying that he's this, that he's that . . ." They just dropped the ball. They just didn't do anything.

This example documents a struggle similar to that encountered when the women tried to obtain a police response to the violence. Although the mediator was able to see that the couple was having problems and needed further assistance (particularly for the husband), this assessment did not lead to further action. In fact, when the husband refused to continue participating, there was no consequence for his decision, and the mediation service stopped contacting the couple. Stephanie* sought help from the police and from this mediation service, but neither helped address the violence. After these efforts, she notes that she was in a "desperate and delicate position," because her husband now believed he could enforce his will on her physically and emotionally without suffering any consequences.

For five of the women, their own understanding of the situation didn't facilitate self-identification as victims of abuse, and thus, they didn't access domestic violence–specific services. Two of the women expressly noted that they didn't think of themselves as having been abused until they chanced upon a brochure on domestic violence when they came to the United States. Because these women didn't self-identify as victims, they didn't seek help from battered women's programs.

Contacted US Embassy in the Other Country

Nine of the women directly contacted the US Embassy in the country where they lived, to ask for help. The embassies responded in a variety of ways to the women. Kendra was told that the domestic violence was a personal issue that the embassy couldn't address; similarly, Sandra called the embassy during a frightening altercation with her husband, and was told that they couldn't help. Two embassies gave advice to the women that contradicted the underlying premises of the Hague Convention. For example, Tamara's* mother contacted the US ambassador in the other country, who said, "If it was my daughter, she'd be out of here." And as Tamara* recounts,

> So, for my mother and I, after hearing from our lawyer and from the ambassador, we left. But, it wasn't the true story. It isn't . . . you have to know 100% what the law is. And I thought that as long as I had custody of my kids, which I was given custody of [by the other country's court after separating from my abusive husband], that I would be able to leave. And it wasn't true.

Tamara's* children were returned to her husband in the other country, and Tamara* has been engaged in legal action in the other country for several years to regain custody. Ellen* also received similar advice to flee her abusive husband from the US Embassy in the country where she lived. In both women's cases, the US judges ordered the return of their children to their husbands in the other countries, saying that the women needed their husbands' permission to leave the country of the children's habitual residence. Both have faced accusations in custody hearings that they were parental kidnappers. In retrospect, both women wished that the US Embassy officials had known more about the Hague Convention and had advised them differently, although they were unsure if different advice would have changed their decision to flee.

In Amanda's case, the US Embassy was a critical resource in helping her escape with her children back to the United States. Her husband hid their passports after informing her that they would remain in his country. Through Amanda's tenacity, she was able to contact the US Embassy when her husband was out of the house and start the process of creating replacement passports for herself and her children. After her husband injured her, and her subsequent hospitalization, US Embassy officials requested documentation and questioned the doctor about whether the injury was self-inflicted. Once they were assured that Amanda's story was credible, the embassy staff initiated several efforts to help her return to the United States. As Amanda notes, one of the embassy officials planned every detail of their trip away from her husband's country:

> [The person] from the embassy was there [at the airport]. And [. . .] he had told me, "When you get there, just walk straight to the counter." We already had planned that two nights before. He had tickets for me, and he had [our] passports, [. . .] as soon as he gave us the tickets, he goes to me, "Go through the gate right away. Don't wait out here. And when you get inside the plane, call me." [. . .] As soon as I got in, they put us on board right away. [. . .] When the plane landed, they said [Amanda], "Come to the front." . . . [I was so scared] we would be arrested. But, no, what it was, was that the embassy, the US Embassy had already arranged for an attendant, an employee to pick us up with a cart, you know those carts that they drive the people around . . . [. . .] Then, they [. . .] rushed us through a back elevator that came down, and they took us straight to the podium. They gave us our passports, and they put us immediately on that plane. I mean, we were the only ones allowed on that plane before . . . the plane wasn't even ready. You know? But, they stuck us in there immediately, and as soon as I got on the plane, [the US Embassy official] called me [to reassure me].

This story highlights the strategic role that US Embassy personnel played in assisting some of the women trapped in other countries. In Amanda's case, the embassy official not only assisted her with obtaining passports, he also arranged transportation to the United States for her and the children on short notice, and smoothed the way for the family at each of the transit airports. The US Embassy's actions helped Amanda to successfully escape from her husband.

Across these three sets of resources—criminal justice, domestic violence programs, and the US Embassy—a consistent pattern emerges: 18 of 22 women actively sought help to address the domestic violence from at least one formal source in the other country. Thirteen of the women sought help from more than one formal source. It is clear from these stories that women made multiple efforts to find a solution to their situation while in the other country. In the case of the criminal justice system, these efforts to improve the women's safety were routinely stymied by overt and covert actions of the police and courts that supported the batterer and not the woman. Outside the criminal justice system, women were more successful in obtaining support, but the assistance was not sufficient to ensure that they could safely stay in the other country. Part of the reason these women were unsuccessful in securing safety in the other country had to do with additional barriers they faced.

Additional Barriers to Safety in the Other Country

Besides the barriers noted so far (such as the ineffective action of police), women also consistently noted three other areas of difficulty in creating safety for themselves and their children in the other country: (1) language barriers, (2) barriers created by the other country's laws, and (3) immigration status.

Language Barriers

Excluding the women who were immigrants to the United States and, therefore, fluent in the language of the other country, only five women (29.4%) were conversant in the language of the country where they resided. This lack of fluency contributed to the women's social isolation and, as seen in previous stories (particularly with Ellen* and Stephanie*), their inability to converse gave their husbands the opportunity to control the information provided to formal services to which the women turned for help.

Some additional pragmatic language issues also come to light for the women. For example, some of the women lived in countries whose alphabets are not Latin-based; in one woman's case, she was able to speak the language, but she couldn't read it, so she was unable to do simple things like look up resources in a telephone book. Two women reported that they were unable to receive translation of courtroom proceedings concerning divorce, custody, visitation, or criminal charges of kidnapping filed against them by their husbands after they fled the country. A woman's lawyer would sometimes have a person try to whisper in her ear what was happening in the court, but formal interpretation was not provided to these two women. Most of the women in this study were unable to communicate effectively with either formal service providers or informal networks, such as neighbors, in the other country.

Barriers Created by the Other Country's Laws

Several of the countries in which the women lived had laws deeply rooted in traditional patriarchal customs. For example, two of the women reported that they were not allowed to testify in court because women were not permitted to talk, although their husbands could speak freely during court sessions. In some of the countries, legal remedies available in America were not accessible, even though these countries were Hague Convention partners with the United States. For example, two of the women reported that there was no mechanism to obtain a restraining order against a spouse in the country where they lived, or, as in Sandra's case, the requirements to get the restraining order were too high. Sandra reported that she would have to be physically injured by her husband (for example, being "cut") in order to get a restraining order in the country where she resided. Her husband was emotionally threatening her and her family members, but he had never hit her or anyone else. Functionally, as she notes, it was impossible for her to get a restraining order against her husband:

> I was trying to find a way to live in [the other country] and do my work . . . But they don't have restraining orders there, so . . . I mean I was looking for any legal way to be protected so I could stay and do my job . . . I didn't want to leave . . . But that goal wasn't . . . you know . . . I had to pick my job or . . . you know, being safe [. . .] so when I found out there would be no way to get a restraining order, there would be no way to keep him from having a right to be in the marital home, I knew I couldn't live there anymore.

Other women commented on the difficulties they encountered in pursuing a divorce in the other country. Some countries did not have a provision for a no-fault divorce, so one member of the couple had to be identified as having wronged the other, a position that the men in these countries vigorously resisted taking. For example, Tamara* filed for divorce on the basis of her husband's abuse; he counter-sued her, claiming she was a bad mother because she had "abducted" the children and been forced to return as a result of the Hague petition.

Belinda endured many years of abuse by her husband. She was in a difficult situation, in that she lived with him in Latin America in a different country from where her marriage had taken place, and this made obtaining divorce legally unavailable to her where she resided. She reports,

> I had consulted with an attorney in [the country of residence] on one occasion when he beat me. I told the attorney I wanted a divorce and asked what I could do. He told me I couldn't get a divorce in [the country of residence], because we got married in [another country], and that's where I had to go to get a divorce. But he told me that, according to the law in [the other country], in order to get a divorce there, I had to be separated from my husband for two years. So I was caught between the wall and the sword because I couldn't get divorced in [the country of residence] because I was married in [the other country], and how was I going to get a divorce in [the other country] while living with him? [. . . Previously] I let him know I was not going back [to him] and I would ask him to divorce me. He would tell me he refused to divorce me.

Belinda was unable to get a divorce in her current country of residence, and her husband would not allow her to live separately from him for the two years required by the original country. Eventually, Belinda came to the United States with her six-year-old daughter to visit her family. When they heard how difficult things were for her, they offered to let her stay with them so she could pursue getting a divorce in the United States. In the state where her family resided, she had to be separated from her husband for only six months to obtain the divorce.

Immigration Status

A further difficulty confronting several of the women involved the restrictions they faced as a person with limited rights in the other country because of their immigration status. For many of the women, their status depended on their marriage. As long as they were married and residing with their husbands, they were able to live (but often not work) in the other country. Once they separated from their husbands, however, the women's status in the other country became even more tenuous. For example, Tamara* had married in the other country and resided there with her husband for ten years, but once she separated from him, her ability to live in the country was cast into doubt. As she explains,

I'm allowed to live here because I'm married to [my husband]. Then, when we separated, they said they had to decide whether I would be allowed to live here, or not. They did decide I was allowed to live here, partly based on the fact that I had kids here. But, first I had to get a job. [. . .] I found a job, which I still do now. [. . .] So, as soon as I could get a job, then, I was given, kind of, I guess what you would call a green card; a work permit [. . .] Then, it was no problem. As long as I have a work permit, and I have a job in this country, I'll be allowed to stay here now, even if we get divorced.

Tamara* was able to maintain her legal right to be in the other country after her separation and subsequent divorce proceedings because she was able to find a job. Because Tamara* was fluent in the language of the other country, she found work, but if she had not had this linguistic skill, she may not have been able to continue living in that country near her children after the separation. For other women, the combination of caring for young children, not being fluent in the other country's language, and holding a visa status that prevented employment were all barriers to obtaining jobs and, therefore, having independent access to finances that could be used to change their situations.

Finally, immigration status also created barriers for some women in their ability to use resources in the other country. Three women reported that they were told by domestic violence agencies in the other country that the organization did not have the resources to help non-citizens. Program staff explained that funding constraints prevented them from having enough services to meet the needs of women who were citizens of the country, so they were unable to serve non-citizens. In these cases, even when women reached out to domestic violence services, their immigration status in the other country precluded their ability to access these resources.

Women living in other countries faced many significant barriers to creating safety for themselves and their children. Most women made multiple efforts to enlist formal resources to stop their husband's battering, but they did so in a context in which they faced linguistic and legal barriers to remaining in the other country and ensuring their children's and their own safety. Because of the intensity and severity of their husbands' abusive behavior, the lack of accessible resources within the other country that could be mobilized in the service of safety, and the barriers that confronted these mothers, the women in this study eventually decided that relocating to the United States was most likely to provide them with the safety and support they needed to stop the abuse. In the next section, we describe ways in which women left the other country.

How Women Left the Other Country

Given the life-threatening nature of much of the abuse the women experienced, many reported that they knew it was a matter of life or death to find a way to escape their husbands. Considering their husbands' behavior, their resources, and the negligible amount of institutional support they were able to secure, each woman made a decision to leave with her children to try to find a safer place to live. In almost every case (18 of 22, 81.8%) women moved to the United States to stay with a family member, mostly their parents (14 women). If a woman's abuse happened domestically, it would be natural to expect that she would seek help from her family members, and this behavior would be encouraged. But in a transnational context, this decision to join with supportive family members can provoke a Hague petition and the label "child abductor."

Women left the other country in a variety of ways.[6] Four basic patterns of leave-taking occurred; these were (1) spontaneously fleeing after a physically

6. One woman's leave-taking story was not available (Caitlin*), and one woman's circumstance was not similar to other women's in the study. In Austin's* case, she divorced her hus-

violent altercation, (2) making a planned escape, (3) arranging for a visit to the United States with the intention of staying, and (4) after coming to the United States for other reasons, deciding to stay.

Spontaneous Flight

Five of the women reported a critical incident of abuse that forced them to leave suddenly with no or minimal forethought. In these cases, women left the homes they were sharing with their abusive husbands within minutes to hours; and within days to a few weeks, they left the country. For example, Jennifer recounts the sudden decision she made after a particularly serious episode of abuse that involved her newborn baby:

> So, coming home from the hospital the last hurrah was—it was kind of a blessing— he threw me down the stairs and threw me out of the house when I had my little three-day-old in my arms. And I grabbed my three-year-old and got in the car and we drove away. [. . .] I got [to a city in an adjacent country]. I had the clothes on my back. I had no more Kotex, just the one I had. I had no more diapers. [. . . The hotel clerk said there were no rooms] and I literally stood there with my diaper bag and my purse and my two kids and just cried [. . .] Well, the gift shop lady . . . the gift shop was right up by the front desk, came out and took pity on me . . . talks to the guy [. . .] and sure enough, I had a hotel room in about five minutes. [. . .] It was magic. It turns out that woman, she came up about a day later, delivering a pram full of diapers and Kotex and all this stuff. She [. . .] knew exactly what I needed.

As Jennifer's story illustrates, some of the women had to make sudden decisions after a particularly severe episode of abuse. Jennifer had financial resources available, and she was able to make arrangements to flee the country within few days. She drove to a nearby country to figure out what to do next, and was then able to arrange to return to her parents in the United States. Tamara* faced a similar dilemma when her husband assaulted her the day she served him with divorce papers. Unlike Jennifer, Tamara* had few financial

---

band after his abuse. After the divorce, Austin* remained in the other country to comply with a visitation order, but she needed medical care, so she eventually moved with her young daughter to the United States for treatment. Although she did have full custody of her daughter, she did not have permission from her abusive spouse to leave the other country. Austin's* husband had a *ne exeat* right, that is, the right to permit or deny the movement of his children from the country. Once Austin* and her daughter were in the States, he filed a Hague petition, and the us courts returned her daughter to the other country, stating that it was her habitual residence.

resources to draw on to cushion the hardships associated with her sudden need for escape. As she relates,

> The [bank] accounts, anyway, were closed because I filed for divorce. Everything was frozen and there I was, with [my children, my mother and myself], and I had the car because I had driven away with the car, but I had nothing else. I had none of our clothes. I had left with the passports, and the kids, and that's it.

Practically, Tamara* had nothing but "the clothes on her back" when she ran away from her husband after his violent outburst. In these circumstances, women had to make rapid decisions to ensure their safety, and possibly even their survival, in moments of intense physical violence. Jennifer's and Tamara's* stories illustrate the situations experienced by five of the women in the sample who were forced to flee under these volatile circumstances.

Planned Escape

In contrast to women who were forced to escape as a result of a particularly violent event, seven other women strategically planned, over the course of months to years, how to get themselves and their children safely back to the United States. Amanda's story illustrates typical aspects of these experiences and is recounted at length to demonstrate the nature and depth of the planning she undertook in order to get away with her children. The events we will detail follow three earlier incidents: her husband's announcement that the family would be staying in his country after they arrived, and his destruction of their passports; her physical knife injury and hospitalization after an altercation with him; and his decision a few days after she was released from the hospital to move the entire family to a rural village isolated from the rest of the country. In addition to already finding a way to be in touch with the US Embassy in the other country (as recounted previously), Amanda also crafted a careful plan to leave that she augmented once they were under way:

> [I told the US Embassy official that I overheard my husband say that he would be traveling in two days.] And [the official] goes, "Are you sure he's going to go?" He goes, "You better make sure," he said, "because we only have one chance. We can't mess up." [. . . So I had to find a way to get us to the airport, which was four hours away.] I saw a taxi coming by, and I jumped in front of it and I said, "Do you go to [the airport]?" And the guy said, "Yeah. Yeah." 'Cause I could speak pretty fluent [language]. [. . .] I asked him how much it was, and he said it was 120 euros, which

I had saved little by little 'cause I didn't have too much [because my husband restricted my access to money]. But it was whatever I saved, and then, I got into the kids' money. [. . .] I got two little backpacks. I got everything ready. I went to the store, and I got one backpack and I put snacks in it. The other one, a couple of their little things. I came back [to the United States] with nothing for the kids . . . 'cause I couldn't. I had to make it look like they were going to school. [. . .] And so when I got to the corner [where the taxi was supposed to pick us up], I said oh, my God, I pray to God that this guy shows up, and about two minutes later, the taxi showed up. So, it's like everything was starting to work. Everything the way I planned it. I was afraid that somebody would see us, 'cause everybody knows everybody in that village. So the taxi came, he picked us up, and I told the kids, "Lay down." I said, "'cause you guys were asleep," but really what I was doing was hiding them, right? [. . . The taxi driver] took me all the way to the airport, and inside my mind I was thinking I don't know if I want him to know where I'm going. So, what I did was we went almost all the way to the airport, but, across the street from the airport, there's a hotel. So I told him, "Oh, I'm going to be spending the night at that hotel." I said, "Then, I'll be leaving in a couple of days to [an] island." I said, "Drop me off across the street." So, he did. [. . . My daughter] got really scared. I mean, her eyes got huge and she goes, "Where's Papa? If he finds out, he's going to be mad at us." I said "No, [honey], Papa said that we can go for two days. Your [relative] is sick. So we have to go for two days. He said we can go. That's why we got our tickets. You see?" [The US Embassy official] had tickets for me, and he had passports, and the reason he had the pictures, a month before we were supposed to leave, or six weeks before, I had told my husband that I was going shopping and I saw a passport place and I ran in there real quick and I bought the pictures, and I had them all that time.

Amanda's story illustrates the ongoing efforts she made to arrange everything necessary to allow her to successfully return with her children to the United States. She planned for several months before her husband's absence presented a moment of opportunity that she seized. Each of the other six women took similar steps to receive new passports, amass money, find a way to get to the airport, and manage their children through the stress of making their escape.

Arranged Visit to the United States with the Intent of Staying

Four women arranged with their husbands to return to the United States for a short visit, usually to see family members. However, the women knew that they intended to stay in the States as soon as they were able to get there. To escape their husbands' violent behavior, the women did not reveal their underlying intent. Rebecca* explained this process in her description of how she managed to get her husband to agree to her temporary return to America with the children. This trip took place several months after the couple had relocated to his country and he had immediately obtained a restraining order to force her to stay. During these months, his abusive behavior escalated in severity with several serious physical attacks against her. She explains,

> I said I wanted to go home with the kids for the summer, and he agreed under the condition that I return in [a month], and if I didn't return, he would file the Hague, and kidnapping charges. And I said fine, I would return [to the other country], and the minute I got back to America, I filed for legal separation and temporary custody, and he filed the Hague Petition.

Rebecca* strategically agreed to cooperate with her husband's conditions for her return to the United States with her children. Once in America, they fought the Hague petition for several years before an appeals court ordered the return of the children to the father's country. The other women in this category reported similar experiences of strategically planning a visit to the States to see family, indicating compliance with their husbands' directives, and encouraging their husbands to believe that they would return after a short time, while secretly planning to stay.

Decision to Stay When Already in the United States

Four other women were already in the United States when they decided not to return to the other country, but they had not planned to stay when they originally came to America. For example, Katie* had come to the States with her daughter to care for her relative who was terminally ill. Once here, she decided to stay after gaining insight into the unhealthy and coercive ways her husband treated her. Fiona*, similarly, was in the United States because her husband had lost his most recent job, and then she decided to stay. She recounts the series of events that led up to her decision to remain in America:

> [My husband was fired and] you know, we just put everything into this move. Here we are in a foreign country. We're all US citizens and I'm pregnant and now you're without a job—that's just great. And he had had almost—I think it was 28 jobs in the last 20 years. [. . .] We had a discussion at that time that things are not looking good. We're four Americans in Europe without possibility of employment after the six-month contract expired, and what are we going to do? Maybe it would be better

just to go back to the States, establish our residency—[. . .] live with my parents. [. . .] We had started to shop around for tickets to come to the States. [. . .] We flew back to the States [. . .] we had return tickets, but our intention was to establish residency and he would send out resumes and look for a job, and if nothing pans out, I would stay behind and then he would go back and see what kind of jobs there were, and we would just take it from there. [. . .] He went back to [the other country]. And I told him, I am not coming back until you get settled. And he said, well, we'll see about that. [. . .] We'd been in contact and you know, I said how are things going? Are you finding any kind of jobs? Or you know, how are things going with resume searching? And he said there was one job—another temp job that he thought he might get but he wasn't sure yet. And then he asked me what my plans are. And I said, I told you, I'm not coming back until you—first of all, at this time I—because he was far away from me I felt more comfortable, I said—you ensure my safety. We have to go to some kind of counseling. And until you get your job situation straightened out. [. . . After that phone call, he] discontinued all communication. Nothing. There was no more contact at all with him. And he um, the next thing I knew [. . .] the US Marshals went in my parents' house, getting our passports. And that's the first time I heard of the Hague.

After years of moving around the United States and Europe following her husband's many jobs, and after years of physical and emotional abuse that included threats to kill her, Fiona* decided to remain in America. A large part of the reason for this decision was her husband's refusal to guarantee her safety and to seek counseling to change the dynamics between them. Fiona's* story shares some characteristics with reports by three other women in the study who were in the United States and decided not to return to the other country. For women in this category, returning to America was not done in an effort to escape a husband's abuse. Instead, they returned to the States to cope with other life stressors, and often to assist family members. Once separated from their abusive partners, the women became emboldened to demand changes in the relationship, changes that the men opposed. When they were not able to negotiate their safety if they returned to the other country, they decided to remain in the United States.

Child Abduction or Fleeing Domestic Violence?

We argue that in cases where women face serious and sustained abuse as documented in chapter 1, where they are forced to stay in the other country because of their husband's coercion, or where they are unable to find resources to help ensure their own and their children's safety, these cases should *not* be defined as child abduction. The threat of physical harm posed by domestic violence should negate the presumption of wrongdoing on the part of a taking mother who has experienced serious abuse. Until all women have equal access to resources to help them cope with a partner's physical abuse, fleeing from the situation will and should remain a reasonable and responsible option.

A rich literature exists on strategies that battered women employ to cope with abuse prior to their decision to leave the relationship (Brabeck & Guzman, 2008; Brown, J., 1997; Goodman, Dutton, Weinfurt, & Cook, 2003; Liang, Goodman, Tummala-Narra, & Weintraub, 2005; Wuest & Merritt-Gray, 1999). This research indicates that leaving a violent relationship is a process that unfolds as survivors find that their initial coping efforts are ineffective in ending the violence (see, for example, Goodkind, Sullivan, & Bybee, 2004). Most women begin by enacting private behaviors such as placating or resisting the abuser (Goodman et al., 2003) before seeking external resources. The women in this study turned to many formal institutions in the other country in their efforts to cope with the violence. They sought help from the police, courts, domestic violence shelters, hospitals, and social service programs. In addition, they sought help from US Embassy officials, and enlisted the aid of friends in the other country (if available). The women's efforts were multifaceted and ongoing; these women demonstrated courage in the face of their husbands' physical violence and threats.

Despite their efforts, the women were generally unsuccessful in mobilizing resources in the other country that could effectively help them secure a safer situation. They faced overt and covert efforts by the police to protect and reinforce the abusive husbands' position. Some US Embassy staff were remarkable in the assistance they provided, but others refused to aid these mothers and their children. In addition, the women faced barriers to accessing other help: these included language difficulties, immigration issues, and divorce policies that did not address their safety needs. Access to no-fault divorce might have allowed the women to separate from the abusive partner in a less legally stressful fashion than that faced by many of the women. Recent research on the effects of divorce policy indicate that access to unilateral divorce has been associated with large declines in domestic violence and intimate homicide (Stevenson & Wolfers, 2006).

The fact that none of the women could secure assistance from the legal systems in the countries where they resided may indicate an unanticipated bias in the sample. It may be that those women who were successful at garnering assistance from the police or courts in the other country were not as likely to leave the country (so would not be subject to a Hague petition nor, therefore, be in our sample) because they may have found resources to secure their safety in the other country. Assessing the role of legal services to assist women who are being battered in other countries would be a fruitful avenue for future research aimed at identifying resources to help ensure mothers' and children's safety overseas.

Five women in the study (22.7%) separated from their husbands in the other country and pursued divorce. But leaving their husbands did not end the physical violence, and in some cases, it escalated the men's abusive behavior. The occurrence of post-separation violence and stalking have been identified as serious aspects of domestic violence (Tjaden & Thoennes, 1998, 2000). In a study of battered women who had resided in a shelter, 43 percent were re-victimized by their former partners, even as long as 24 months after leaving the relationship (Fleury et al., 2000). The five separated women in our study did everything in the other country that is typically expected of domestic violence survivors— they sought help for the abuse, they left their abusive husbands, and they worked to establish themselves independently from their husbands. Despite these efforts, they could not secure safety for themselves and their children, and they faced continued abuse in the other country. They decided to move to a location where they could secure assistance from family; for these women, it was the United States.

Analyses of lethality risk factors suggest that the period after leaving an abusive relationship is a hazardous one in which women face heightened danger (Campbell et al., 2003; Campbell, Glass, Sharps, Laughon, & Bloom, 2007). These 22 women may not have been aware of the research literature linking departure from an abusive partner with a potential increase in their husbands' lethality, but they had an awareness of the danger they faced. Each came to the conclusion that she was in a situation with her abusive husband that could have serious consequences for herself and her children. In this context, all the women made a decision to flee, and in all but four cases, the women moved to be with family members, usually parents, in the United States.

For most of the women, the process of leaving was difficult. One-half of the women had to plan for a period of time (sometimes reaching into years) to create a way to leave safely without further endangering themselves or their children. Some women spontaneously fled the other country after a particularly violent episode of abuse. Unfortunately, because they crossed international boundaries in order to escape their abusers, the women were vulnerable to being legally defined as child abductors under the Hague Convention, such that their husbands were able to force the return of their children to the other country.

with Luz Lopez and Gita Mehrotra

3 | The Unique Situation of Latinas Responding to Hague Petitions

Currently, Latinos and Latinas comprise 16% of the total US population; their numbers grew by over 15 million between 2000 and 2010 to 50.5 million (Ennis, Rios-Vargas, & Albert, 2011). Demographic projections indicate that by 2030, one in four US residents will be of Hispanic descent (National Research Council, 2006). Because of "both employer demand for cheap, hardworking laborers and failed immigration policy" (National Research Council, 2006, p. 27), the number of migrants from Mexico and Latin America who are in the United States without documentation now surpasses 11 million. The stories of the Latina women interviewed for this study are framed by their experiences both as immigrants to this country and as undocumented residents in the United States.

The most recent national estimate of violence against women in the United States is the National Intimate Partner and Sexual Violence Survey (NISVS) conducted by the Centers for Disease Control and Prevention. According to NISVS, over one-third (37.1%) of Hispanic women have been assaulted in their lifetime by a current or former intimate partner, a higher rate than reported by white non-Hispanic and Asian or Pacific Islander women, but lower than other racial and ethnic groups (Black et al., 2011). Other studies with state- or city-based samples in the United States suggest that Hispanic women have an increased risk for domestic violence when compared to non-Hispanic white women (Vest, Catlin, Chen, & Brownson, 2002), and that among low-income women from Mexico, Puerto Rico, and the Dominican Republic, Mexican women report the highest rates of violence (Frias & Angel, 2005). Unfortunately, although Frias and Angel (2005) asked where respondents were born, none of these reports ascertains how many women were undocumented, as were the women who participated in our study.

Few quantitative studies regarding domestic violence in immigrant communities have been conducted in the United States (Raj & Silverman, 2002;

Sokoloff, 2008). Many authors have noted that it is even more difficult to assess the prevalence of domestic violence within the undocumented population because asking immigrants about their legal status can be a barrier to survey participation. In addition, immigrants are underrepresented in national surveys due to language barriers (Bhuyan, Shim, & Velagapudi, 2010); their decreased likelihood to report domestic violence to law enforcement (Wood, 2004; Sokoloff, 2008); and the high level of poverty experienced by immigrant Latinas, which can result in their being missed by prevalence surveys that rely on having a telephone (Haas, Dutton, & Orloff, 2000). Menjivar and Salcido (2002) assert that the incidence of domestic violence is not higher in immigrant communities, but rather that immigrant battered women's experiences are exacerbated by the distinctive constellation of issues (that is, communication barriers, discrimination in employment, and deportation concerns) they experience as immigrant survivors. Understanding the legal immigration status of Latina women is important, because several studies suggest that being undocumented is a barrier to seeking help for domestic violence (see Rizo & Macy, 2011, for a review).

Practitioners and researchers alike have identified several challenges facing Latina battered women, in particular, as they seek safety. These include language barriers; cultural or religious values regarding the importance of family and traditional gender roles; educational and income disparities that may affect actual or perceived access to resources; and lack of access to legal remedies (Pendleton, 2003; Klevens, 2007; Raj & Silverman, 2002). Immigrant battered women in the United States also often fear that they, their children, and/or their abusive partner could be deported, particularly if the abuse is reported (Klevens, 2007). As a result of these barriers, battered Latina women have been found to be less likely than other survivors of abuse to seek help for domestic violence (West, Kantor, & Jasinski, 1998; Bauer, Rodriguez, Quiroga, & Flores-Ortiz, 2000). However, like other victims of domestic violence, Latina survivors indicate that one of the main reasons they seek help is the severity of the violence and the threats they perceive to the well-being of their children (Acevedo, 2000; Rizo & Macy, 2011). Some researchers have also found that immigrant Latinas feel safer in the United States than in their home countries because of the presence of domestic violence laws in the States (Menjivar & Salcido, 2002). For example, a recent international review of laws to prevent violence against women noted that "the protection of the family and not of the woman is the priority in most of the laws of Latin America" (Vives-Cases, Ortiz-Barreda & Gil-Gonzalez, 2010), whereas US laws when implemented offer some safeguards to individual women.

Current research and practice regarding immigrant battered women has focused on women's experiences of violence once they are already living in the United States with their abusive partners (Raj & Silverman, 2002). For a woman who has legally immigrated to America with her husband, her immigration status may be tied to his. If she reports her husband to the police for domestic violence and he is arrested, he may be deported; as a result, she will lose her legal right to remain in the United States, potentially causing deportation procedures to be initiated against her. (Espenoza, 1999). In addition, researchers and advocates note that a woman's immigration status can be used as a tactic of control by a violent partner—he can threaten to report her to US Immigration and Customs Enforcement (ICE), or delay providing her with the paperwork necessary to secure her own citizenship status (Espenoza, 1999). These threats and others are part of the abuser's effort to maintain control over the woman and create barriers to safety and services, keeping immigrant battered women trapped in abusive relationships.

Advocacy efforts have centered on creating more options for immigrant and refugee battered women by helping them to obtain legal status in the United States independent of their abusive husbands (see, for example, Orloff & Kaguyutan, 2001; Pendleton, 2003; Wood, 2004). Three avenues are available to battered women who are not citizens to obtain legal standing in the United States as a result of having been the victim of domestic violence: the VAWA self-petition, the U-Visa program, and obtaining asylum.

The Violence Against Women Act (VAWA), passed in 1994 (and renewed in 2000 and 2005), created a provision for battered immigrant women that allows them to self-petition for legal permanent status without relying on an abusive husband for sponsorship. To be eligible to self-petition, the woman has to meet certain requirements, including being the legal spouse of the batterer, residing in the United States with her spouse, being in good moral standing, and arguing that she or her children will suffer "extreme hardship" if she is deported (Espenoza, 1999; Ganatra, 2001). Being separated from a child who was born in the States and is, thus, an American citizen, is not considered an extreme hardship under the law (Ganatra, 2001). If an immigrant woman takes action to end her relationship with the abuser before attending to her immigration status, she can be at risk for being deported to her country of origin. These requirements create many barriers for immigrant women who are in the country legally; for a woman who is undocumented or whose abuse occurred outside the United States, this avenue is not available.

Through the revisions to VAWA in 2000, a new visa program, the U-Visa, was created to grant legal immigration status to victims of crime (including domestic violence). To be eligible, the crime must have occurred in the United States, and the victim must be willing to participate in the prosecution of the crime (Northwest Immigrant Rights Project, 2000). For women who were subject to domestic violence outside of the United States and who fled to America seeking safety (like the women in the Hague study), this legal provision is also unavailable.

Legal advocates for immigrant domestic violence survivors have been fighting for years to have the United States acknowledge that battering is a form of persecution that could, and should, result in the victim receiving asylum in America. In 1996, the first woman ("R. A.") was granted asylum because of the domestic violence she experienced in Guatemala (Heyman, 2005). However, this ruling was overturned three years later, and since then, other battered women who have petitioned for asylum have been in legal limbo. Recently, the Obama Administration proposed new rules that would allow battered women to receive asylum under certain circumstances:

> In addition to meeting other strict conditions for asylum, abused women will need to show that they are treated by their abuser as subordinates and little better than property, . . . and that domestic abuse is widely tolerated in their country. They must show that they could not find protection from institutions at home or by moving to another place within their own country. (Preston, 2009, p. A1)

As a result of the shift in the government's views on domestic violence in asylum cases, R.A. was granted asylum in 2009, paving the way for others to argue that domestic violence exposed them to an extreme risk of persecution in their home country (Bullard, 2011).

Although all of these remedies have been critically important in creating a greater range of legal remedies for battered immigrant women, they have substantial limitations for immigrant women who are responding to a Hague petition (Pendleton, 2003; Wood, 2004). For instance, VAWA self-petitioning requires the applicant to be married to a US citizen or legal resident, which, as we will show, is not the case for Latina Hague respondents. Regarding the U-Visa, the domestic violence must have occurred in the United States; Latina Hague respondents have fled domestic violence in other countries, so they are not eligible for this legal remedy. And as for obtaining asylum as a victim of domestic violence, it is yet to be determined whether this will actually become an avenue available for undocumented immigrant women who have fled domestic violence in their countries of origin.

In the rest of this chapter, we document the ways in which the Latina mothers' stories both differed from and were similar to the stories of mothers who were US citizens. The situations of the Latina mothers subject to Hague petitions in the United States differed substantially from those of immigrant women battered in the States and also American-citizen mothers who fled back to their home countries.

Experiences of Latin American Mothers

To explore the unique concerns of immigrant women who relocate to the United States to escape the abuse they experienced in their home countries, we've analyzed in more depth the stories of the four Latina immigrant mothers in this study: Lara, Marina, Marta*, and Belinda. Each of these women's cases follows the general chronology of Hague Convention experiences that we found for the entire sample. Here we focus primarily on aspects of these women's stories that are a result of their status as Latina immigrant women, not US citizens like the other women. We've organized these mothers' unique experiences across five major domains, with illustrative quotes from their stories where appropriate.

Reason to Leave for the United States

Latina mothers' reasons varied regarding the decision to leave their native countries for the United States. For example, despite the fact that Lara had legally separated from her husband and was living in her own house with the children, the abuse did not stop. The continuation of the abuse led her to consider moving to the States to live with relatives. As she relates,

> He would come into the house with the excuse to bring the kids medicine because they were sick. He would start throwing things around in front of the kids, and inspecting my house. He would ask who was there and would push and shove me. I have a sister, who lives in the United States. I was alone in [Latin American country] with my kids and didn't have anyone to stick up for me and I was afraid. So I decided to leave and relocate to the United States.

Lara's neighbors heard the violence, and observed her husband pushing and shoving her and throwing things in the house. These neighbors did not offer assistance, and Lara did not know who to approach for help, other than her family members in the States. After a particularly serious incident of physical violence, she turned to the police in her home country. Here she describes what happened next:

First, I went to the police to accuse him. I went to file a report and they told me if I wanted to file a report, I had to go to the Red Cross so they can make a report on the bruises, in order to file a complaint with them. [. . .] I went to the Red Cross and they said, "You know what? You're not bleeding. You have bruises, and you've been hit, but you're not bleeding. We need for the bruises to be visible, in order to give you a paper that states this. Why don't you wait two days, until they're more noticeable so that we can make the report better?" Okay. I waited two days. Two days later, I went to the Red Cross. I tell them what happened. They said, "You know what? That was two days ago. Why do you come now?" I said, "Well, because that's what you instructed me to do." Then they said, "No, we can't give you that paper." It was very frustrating. I couldn't make a report. So, I went to the attorney who was helping me with the divorce proceedings, and he told me there was nothing we could do. He said we needed to wait until my husband hit me again and left me bleeding. I really felt desperate.

Lara's experience illustrates the problems faced by women as they tried to seek institutional accountability to stop the batterer from continuing his behavior. Despite evidence (her bruises) that she had been harmed by her ex-husband, neither the police nor the Red Cross intervened on her behalf to stop the violence. In fact, the process that Lara encountered in trying to document this physical assault could be characterized as an effort by the authorities to avoid accountability for any kind of intervention. Neither institution took responsibility for aiding her, and instead reinforced the idea that she would have to be hurt even more severely before they might intervene. In this encounter, bleeding was equated with severity, with the implication that other physical harm was not as serious. Lara's visible bruises were not a sufficient indicator that her ex-husband's behavior was a criminal problem. Her neighbors, police, and the Red Cross did not help her to safely remain in the other country, so she left with her children to seek help from family in the United States.

Marina's experience paralleled Lara's. The escalating violence of Marina's husband, and his threats to her life and the safety of her children, were the reasons for her decision to leave and relocate to the United States to obtain help from her family. Marina reports,

These events took place which made me fear for my life, and obviously for the security of my three kids. I told him something was bound to happen because he was blocking all of my ways out, and he was putting surveillance in the house. That house turned into a cage and I decided to flee.

Belinda was in the United States with her husband and children visiting her relatives. Her husband had to return from this family vacation earlier than anticipated, so Belinda stayed in the States with her son and her younger daughter. She reported considering contacting the police in her country, but she had heard that they would help a domestic violence victim only if she paid them. Only her husband had access to their money, so Belinda felt she had no access to help in that country. Her husband's absence, however, gave her the opportunity to consider what to do next. As she notes,

> When he left, I knew I had to make a decision, but deep down, I was scared because he was such a possessive, arrogant, and dominating man that I was very scared of him. I had to return to [Latin American country] the next day but I decided to stay in the United States.

Finally, Marta* speaks of her decision to leave her husband and go to the United States:

> So, after he beat me again that last time, I knew I had to leave. We were not safe and I realized he was not going to change. My parents were in the United States. I told them what was happening, but they told me they couldn't help me while they were in the United States and I was in [Latin American country]. So I consulted some attorneys in [Latin America], and I asked how I can take my kids out of this country without having to ask for my partner's consent. The attorneys told me that if I took the kids out of the country, he could accuse me of kidnapping, but that that was a very long process and hardly anyone did it. So I made the decision to leave.

In each of these women's situations, they experienced serious abuse, and they were unable to find help in their own countries to address the violence. Taking steps to end the violence and remain in the other country did not ensure the women's safety. In some ways, these women's stories are similar to those of the US-citizen women in our study—they, too, could not find help in the countries where they lived. As a result of the unavailability of resources in their home countries, the isolation, and the danger they faced, non-citizen women chose to bring their children to the United States, despite the legal barriers they knew would immediately confront them as undocumented residents.

Family and Other Support

Almost all of the US and immigrant women moved to the States to seek the support of parents or other relatives who were already residing here. Access to these informal support systems was critical to these women when making their decisions to leave. For example, Lara's sister lived in the United States, and Lara decided to join her. Similarly, Belinda's married sibling and spouse knew how difficult the situation was at her home, and they offered her a place to stay and financial help to leave her husband. Marina had family in the States, but her parents were in the Latin American country where she resided. For a long time, she did not tell her family about her situation because she feared their reactions would escalate the trouble at home. Finally, after an incident in which her husband hit her older daughter, Marina decided to tell her mother, who lived near them, about the abuse. She recounts,

> I spoke with my mom. I told her about everything that had happened. My mother was a bit surprised, and told me she never really liked him nor the way he would speak to me and the way he treated the kids. But she never expected things to be the way they were. She told me she didn't know why I had allowed it, and that I should've spoken up from the first time he hit me.

Once Marina disclosed to her family the reality of her situation, she began to rely on them more, and would take refuge at her mother's house. She finally fled to the United States, where she stayed with her sister. Marina's family support and validation of her experience were vital to her ability to seek safety.

Marta's* parents had already relocated to the States, and they encouraged her to leave her husband and join them. She had a visa, but her children (all age ten or younger) did not, so she had them taken across the border by friends who had them pose as their children. As she explains,

> I have my visa and passport. Some close friends of my father, who work in the United States and live in [Latin America], brought my kids across the border as their own. Once on the other side [US side] all I did was take a plane to [meet them]. My parents helped me, and once there, I also sought help at a legal aid center.

Immigration Threats

One of the particular challenges faced by Latina mothers in this study was the immigration threats made repeatedly by their husbands once they were in the

United States. In some ways, the Latina mothers' experiences were a mirror image of what happened to the mothers who were American citizens—for US-born mothers, the abuser threatened them with immigration troubles while they were in the other country; for Latina women, those threats were enacted using the criminal justice system of the United States. For example, Lara describes the following:

> My husband contacted me. and threatened me from [Latin American country] saying that he was going to come get me with the FBI, and he was going to use every means necessary to get the kids back. That is why I was so scared.

In Marina's case, her husband threatened to kill her or to kidnap the children. He also threatened to report her to the immigration authorities as a way to force her return to him:

> My husband always said to me, "If you leave, I'm going to find you wherever you go. I'm going to take your kids away from you and I'm going to kill you." Nothing compared to this. You know why? I lived day after day and night after night frightened thinking about what would happen next. I was sure if I left he would do something, report me [to US immigration authorities], and my kids were going to go back to [Latin American country]. It could be his way to get me to return.

When Belinda's husband learned that she was not returning from the United States and that she wanted a divorce, he said he would not grant it. On the contrary, reports Belinda, "He said he would send immigration and the FBI" so she would be arrested and sent to prison for taking the children. He also said that she would never be able to find a job. She would be dependent on her sibling, and their son would "turn into a drug addict."

The Hague Petition and Other Legal Processes

The Latina mothers differed from the US-born mothers in that their legal battles were on two fronts, as they dealt with both the Hague petition and other legal proceedings related to their immigration status. For example, after Lara's husband found her five months after her arrival in the United States, he located the children in their new schools and arranged for the police to take them away because he had filed a Hague petition. Lara relates these events:

> I was working. My son was with a provider in Head Start and my daughter was in school. So, I get a phone call and they tell me, "Lara, you know what? Your husband

is here. He just took your kids. And we need you to come to court right now." I was very scared, and I asked, "What happened?" I had advised the school not to give my kids to anyone, as I had done with the Head Start teacher. The teacher told me that many police cars had arrived and they took my son from her, and she didn't know what to do because many people came and took my son; they took both of them. The school could not stop them from taking my daughter either. So, we went to court, then. The judge wasn't very helpful because she said it was a problem for my country, and told us to go fix our problems in [Latin American country]. She was rude. What helped me was my immigration petition for asylum [on the basis of domestic violence] and my attorneys. I had letters. I . . . when he would go and hit me and/or destroyed the house, he would leave me written messages insulting me and saying things about me. I saved those messages and presented them in court, and they even showed him. They asked him if he had indeed written them.

Lara found a domestic violence agency in the United States that helped her petition for asylum on the basis of the family's domestic violence experience; the agency also helped her obtain a restraining order against her husband. At first, the judge ruled in favor of Lara's ex-husband's petition to return the children to the other country, saying that this problem should be addressed in the Latin American country's courts. However, Lara explains, "I already had the immigration asylum case petition pending, so they allowed the children to stay with me until the other courts made their decision." The immigration court couldn't make a decision because the Hague petition was still pending. Lara continues,

During the appeals process, my ex-husband filed again, asking for custody of the kids. So, it was like if you already filed through Hague, why are you filing for custody of the kids? So, I had all three courts at the same time, and none of the judges could decide. It wasn't until the Hague Convention decided that I could be here and have my kids that immigration made a decision and custody of the kids was decided on.

The first judge ruled against Lara. However, Lara explains that her lawyers helped her a great deal:

The Hague case was appealed, and the judge found in my favor a month later. She [the appellate judge] had documentation of the threatening messages he had written, letters about witnessing violent incidents from friends and neighbors in [Latin American country], documents from attorneys explaining the divorce, and the restraining order. After my ex-husband lost the Hague case, he filed for another custody determination. He now has visitation rights, including weekend visits when he wants to exercise them and a yearly vacation with the children in [Latin American country].

Marina also speaks of the police serving the Hague petition, and of her thoughts during this event:

A few months after I left to the United Sates, the police came to my house and took my kids away. I was told that their father was here and that I had kidnapped my kids. I explained to them . . . I speak English because I used to teach it in [Latin American country]. I explained to them, sometimes in Spanish, sometimes in English, because my mind was racing to figure out what I could do at a moment like this . . . I was told about having a hearing the next day, and an attorney from [the domestic violence agency] represented me because I couldn't find anyone else. So that attorney represented me at that hearing; I wasn't allowed to speak at all. I heard they were saying that custody would be granted to the father. I asked my lawyer to please let me speak because I had something to say. She told me I couldn't speak unless the judge allowed me to. I pleaded with her to ask the judge to grant me the opportunity to say a few words because I wanted to tell them my kids were being abused. I asked that the kids be put in a foster home, but they didn't listen. They simply granted the father custody, and I was given visitations of two hours on Sundays and a ten-minute phone call per day. They gave us a court date in three weeks. I can tell you that what I went through those three weeks was like hell. What he did to us in [Latin American country] was very hard and that was the last straw.

Marina searched for an attorney who would help her keep the children in the United States, and she found one experienced in Hague cases, who told her that this would be costly.

They gave us a court date for three weeks later. I found an attorney, which was very expensive. You know something? When you talk to attorneys and you explain the situation; that you are fleeing for a specific reason, they don't want to take the case. They all said the kids would have to go back, and that was not the answer I wanted to hear. Finally, I found an attorney who told me he had some experience with Hague. He told me he handled a Hague case about three years ago, and that he could help me, but that his services are very expensive. I decided to work and borrow money, do anything I could do to pay him.

Marina's oldest daughter testified in the second court hearing about the abuse she had endured and also what she had witnessed being inflicted on her mother and siblings. The two other children were too young to testify, but a psychologist performed an evaluation, and the report was also presented during the court hearing. The judge returned the children to Marina's custody after this testimony and denied the father's Hague petition request. Marina also had an immigration asylum case based on domestic violence pending.

Belinda's husband accused her of keeping the children in the United States without permission, and he demanded that their youngest child, who then was seven years old, be returned to live with him. Belinda received the Hague petition papers and had a hearing scheduled in eight days. She found assistance through a local legal aid office in the community where she was residing. The lawyer assigned to her had never been involved in a Hague Convention case, but did research and represented her (*pro bono*) in the three-day Hague hearing. The judge ordered the couple to negotiate a solution to the situation. Both parents asked for the same: to have the child during the school year, and for the child to go on vacation with the other parent during the summer. Belinda told the judge, "Please understand that my daughter is very young, and young kids need their mother. My husband could also be violent." She explained the history of domestic violence, but the judge said that was not part of his jurisdiction in this case. However, due to the age of the daughter, the judge did grant custody during the year to Belinda and visitation with her husband in his country during the summer.

Marta* was the only one of these four mothers to have her children returned to the other country. Once Marta* and her children were relocated in the United States, her husband, the father of the two younger children, petitioned for the children's return and was also granted custody of the children in his country. Marta* describes what happened:

Just as the attorneys in [Latin American country] had advised me, he did all the paperwork to bring me to court for taking the kids out of [the country] in order for him to file for custody of . . . in order for the Hague law to be effective, he had filed for custody of the kids in [Latin American country]. He asked the INTERPOL and the FBI for their support. He even went to television stations here, in [Latin America]. The case was televised and in the newspapers. He got support from a missing kids' agency there, in [Latin American country], and through all these agencies, he was able to get in contact with some attorneys in the United States who offered their services at no cost, *pro bono*.

After ten months in the United States, Marta* was served with a Hague petition, and her two younger children were taken from her home by six police officers. The officers gave her a legal document, about 200 pages long, with information on the Hague petition that had been filed against her. The Hague petition required that Marta* appear in court that day. She was given two hearing continuances, but the judge ordered the children returned to their father on the basis of the child custody document from the other country. The judge noted that domestic violence was not relevant to the determination. The children returned with their father to the Latin American country, but Marta* could not return immediately because he had filed criminal kidnapping charges against her in that country.

> When he returned to [Latin American country] with the kids, it was televised. He came off the plane hugging the kids, in a triumphant attitude. As if he were the good father, and he was the father who regained his kids. Television portrayed him as the good one and me as the bad one. As if I wanted to separate my kids from their father. When he told the kids he was going to put me in jail, the kids told him they didn't want their mother to be in jail. So he told me that he didn't pursue putting me in jail, only because the kids asked him not to.

Finally, through a lawyer, Marta* negotiated with her husband, and the kidnapping charges were dropped. As she recounts,

> So I asked him to tell me what he wanted. He told me all he wanted was his kids to remain with him. I said, "Perfect. I'll give you custody of them *even though* you took the custody without my giving it to you, but I'll give it to you. In exchange, I want you to drop the [kidnapping] charges from the federal court." He agreed, and the charges were dropped since that's a charge that is pursued per petition of the plaintiff. He dropped the charges and kept the kids.

Unfortunately, for the first one-and-one-half years that Marta* was back in their country, her husband did not allow her to see the children. The neighbors told her that the children were alone in the afternoons, so she began to sneak to see them, but the kids eventually told their father. At that time, Marta* and her husband made an agreement that she could see the children on Saturdays. This was the current state of affairs at the time of our interview.

Resiliency and Resourcefulness

One characteristic of all the Latina mothers in our study was their resilience and resourcefulness in the face of both the Hague proceedings and their status as immigrants. Whereas many of the US-born women had family who were able to temporarily support them financially, the Latina mothers' families had fewer financial resources. As a result, the Latina women had to find work (while not having citizenship documentation), and often had to begin learning English in order to maintain employment. For example, Lara was able to obtain a work permit, and at the time of our interviews, she was working and taking English classes. She stayed with her sister for two days before she found an apartment with a roommate. She was able to find a domestic violence shelter to help her with a restraining order, as she describes:

> When I arrived in the United States I was inquiring about a [domestic violence] shelter at the family court, and I told them I was in danger because someone was coming to get me, and they advised me to get a restriction [protection] order and that is what I did.

Lara received assistance from the lawyers in the domestic violence shelter and a private religious charity. The children were able to fit in well in their new school, and they were being seen by a child psychologist to help them with their traumatic experiences. Lara was relieved and determined to make their lives better and safer.

Despite her resourcefulness, Marina tried but was unable to secure the assistance in her home country to stop the potentially deadly violence she experienced at the hands of her husband. Marina was adapting to her new life in the United States at the time of our interview. Though language and limited resources were barriers for the other Latina mothers in this study, this was not so much the case for her. Marina was able to hire an attorney to help her with the Hague case. She also found employment. As she notes, "I'm not afraid of working. I want to improve my children's lives." She is happy her children are safely away from the violence and are receiving therapy. She is also paying the lawyer fees with her work.

Belinda's sibling petitioned for her to remain in the United States, and the immigration service then extended her visa. At first, Belinda found a job with a cleaning company and worked about 14 hours per day. Her children stayed with her sibling for the first month, after which Belinda was able to save enough money to buy a used car and rent an apartment. Now Belinda has a better job and her children are doing well. "And thank God," she says, "my kids' father can't say that my son turned into a drug addict, because . . . you know mothers are the kids' foundation."

Marta's* story is probably the most difficult. Her oldest daughter, now a teenager, resides in the United States with Marta's* parents. Marta* has returned to where her younger children live with their father, and does not have enough money to visit her daughter. She is also uncertain if she would be able to obtain a visa to travel. Mother and daughter communicate via the Internet. Marta's* younger children are showing psychological impacts of their situation, including aggressiveness at school. Marta* has tried different ways to stay more in touch with her children after her husband gained custody, but she continues to worry about the effects of her husband's behavior on them.

The Special Needs of Immigrant Respondents to US Hague Petitions

Most of the literature on domestic violence against immigrant women focuses on their abuse experience *after* they migrated to a new country. In contrast, the Latina women involved with these Hague cases experienced significant domestic abuse while living in their home country, and then fled with their children to the United States while their abusive partners remained in the home country. The experiences of the Latina mothers in this study are also in contrast to the majority of the women in the study sample, who were US citizens living abroad with husbands (who were usually citizens of the other country) when they experienced domestic violence and then returned home to the States.

As with most of the other women in our sample, the Latina women came to the United States to seek the support and safety of family members already living here. All four women had a high level of concern for their own safety and their children's well-being due to the domestic violence they were experiencing. However, unlike the US-citizen women in the sample who sought help mainly from parents, the Latina immigrant women turned to a variety of family members, including siblings or extended family in the States, to help them transition into the country and give them initial (and sometimes ongoing) support. Research on help-seeking among Latina survivors of domestic violence suggests that when women reach out, they are most likely to turn to their mothers and sisters for help (Rizo & Macy, 2011), although these sources may be only moderately helpful (Brabeck & Guzman, 2008).

The Latina mothers encountered language barriers in the US court system because Spanish was their first language, and the legal terminology of the Hague petition documents was often unknown to them. They had little money, and through their own resourcefulness they found shelters, legal aid offices, and lawyers who could help them navigate the legal and immigration systems and also could advocate on their behalf. Three of the four Latina women were represented by legal services or legal aid attorneys, whereas the US-citizen women were more likely to have private family law attorneys. Also similar to the other mothers we interviewed, the Latina women faced a quick timeline for Hague legal proceedings, and were often expected to appear in court within hours to days of being served with the Hague petition. The rapid progression of US Hague proceedings was even more challenging in the context of the language and cultural barriers these women faced. The issue of the mothers' immigration status in the United States was a unique aspect of the Latina women's cases. US-citizen mothers were not simultaneously engaged in both Hague and immigration hearings, as were the immigrant mothers. Because of the specific circumstances of these domestic violence cases involving the Hague Convention, legal remedies that are available for other immigrant battered women were not options for the population of Latina women reflected in our sample. For instance, the VAWA self-petition requires that the husband be a legal resident or citizen of the United States, but all of the Latina women in our sample had husbands who were still in the home country and did not have legal status in the States. Similarly, they were not eligible for U-Visas because the crime of domestic violence occurred outside of the US.

Interestingly, the Latina mothers had access to one significant resource that was not available to the US-citizen mothers: the law permits petitions for asylum in the United States in instances where domestic violence has occurred. Two of the women in this study found lawyers who helped them initiate an asylum process in US courts. When they had the Hague petition hearing, these asylum petitions were still open. It may be that these two women's lawyers were knowledgeable about preparing an asylum claim based on domestic violence, and had already assembled the supporting documentation and evidence for the asylum claim when the Hague petition was filed. It appeared in these cases that judges ruled in favor of allotting time for the resolution of the asylum question and, in the end, rejected the Hague petition. The fact that the judges took this asylum immigration process into consideration was a crucial factor that led to the denial of the fathers' Hague petitions.

The current shift in government policy regarding asylum for domestic violence survivors means that this legal recourse may become more available to immigrant women who are subject to a Hague petition in the future. US asylum policy will move from proving that women are members of a "particular social group" at risk of persecution (Gomez, 2003, p. 961), to a focus on an asylum applicant's ability to prove that the government of her home country is unable or unwilling to protect her from domestic violence. As legal scholars note, proving a government's inability or unwillingness to intervene in domestic violence will be challenging because of the difficulties women face in taking action against an abusive partner. In addition, an asylum application will have to overcome

> the commonsense notion that the government, with overwhelming power compared to an individual persecutor, should be able to control that persecutor. A domestic violence applicant's argument that the government is unable to control her persecutor is much more challenging than that of an asylum applicant arguing a militant faction or influential cultural or social group is uncontrolled by the government . . . Significant crime or strife would need to exist within a country to imagine a situation where law enforcement resources were entirely consumed such that a single individual could not be controlled. Country condition reports alone will usually be insufficient to demonstrate that a functioning government is incapable of controlling an individual. An applicant will need to supplement general country condition information with her own personal experience where it will be difficult to demonstrate law enforcement inability if she has not reported her abuse. (Bullard, 2011, pp. 1886–1887)

Thus, although legal asylum for a victim of domestic violence may be more possible in the future than it has been so far, it is likely to remain challenging to ensure the safety of battered immigrant women through the asylum process.

In conclusion, this subset of Hague cases from Latin America reflects similarities and differences when compared to other Hague cases in our sample. In both types of cases, women were unable to find resources in the other country that would allow them to safely remain there; they came to the United States to be with family members. Once here, however, the immigrant battered mothers had experiences that differed markedly from those of the US-citizen mothers, because of the barriers they faced regarding language difficulties and their status as undocumented residents of the United States. The experiences of these four women were similar to those of other Latina immigrant women who were subjected to domestic violence while in the United States. However, the fact that Lara, Marina, Belinda, and Marta* were abused outside of the United States meant that legal strategies such as VAWA self-petitions and U-Visas, available to other immigrant women, were not accessible to them. Yet, three of the four women were able to remain in the United States with their children, suggesting that the asylum process may be a viable option for assisting battered immigrant mothers who are subject to Hague petitions.

4 | Child Exposure to Abduction and Domestic Violence

Up to this point, we have focused primarily on the experiences of mothers in Hague petition cases. In this chapter we explore the situations of the children who fled with their mothers. We review research on parental abduction and the effects of exposure to domestic violence for children to set the stage for the children's experiences and how these relate to the critical issue of grave risk in Hague Convention cases.

Parental Abduction

The definitions of *parental abduction* vary, and some are so broad as to include keeping a child for one night longer than permitted on a visit. For the purposes of this study, however, we adopted Finkelhor, Hotaling, and Sedlak's (1991) policy-focused and narrower definition. Using this definition, parental abductions occur when one of three conditions is met: "(a) an attempt was made to conceal the taking or the whereabouts of the child and to prevent contact with the child; or (b) the child was transported out of state; or (c) there was evidence that the abductor had intended to keep the child indefinitely or permanently affect custodial privileges" (p. 808). Abductions are sometimes labeled *family abductions* because extended family members, such as grandparents, often help in the process of removing or retaining children. In Hague Convention cases, because international borders are crossed, the separation from a left-behind parent may be permanent, with only periodic visits possible.

The literature on parental abduction is limited to a series of case studies and surveys of parents, most of whom were left-behind and not taking parents. These studies are fraught with methodological problems, and many are now two decades old, but they do shed some light on how abducted children and left-behind parents are affected by abductions, as we will briefly summarize here.

Effects on Children

The effects of parental abduction on children can vary, based on the nature and length of the abduction, age of the child, whether siblings were also abducted, and children's awareness of the abduction (Cole & Bradford, 1992; Greif, 2009). For example, a study of 20 Canadian families with 37 children abducted by mostly male, non-custodial parents (Cole & Bradford, 1992) found few differences between abducted and non-abducted, control children. However, the abductions in this study were often very brief (65% were less than a week), siblings often were abducted together, and one-third of the children did not know that what happened to them was an abduction. Other research has included longer abductions, often of only one child. For example, Forehand, Long, Zogg, and Parrish (1989) studied 23 abducted children in 17 families by asking left-behind parents to complete several questionnaires after the return of their children. Of 48 parents who received the mailed questionnaires, only 17 returned completed surveys (a low 35% response rate). These left-behind parents retrospectively rated their children on a 48-item Parent Rating Scale, with subscales focused on conduct and learning problems, psychosomatic complaints, impulsive hyperactivity, and anxiety. Parents rated their children as showing significantly more problems post-abduction when compared to pre-abduction on all four subscales, and improving to somewhere in between pre- and post-abduction levels at the time of the survey (between 3 and 26 months after the abduction; mean was 10.8 months post-abduction). The authors point out, however, that even at the worst point (post-abduction), parents' ratings indicated their children showed only slight problems. In other research from the same period, Sagatun and Barrett's (1990) study of 43 abductions in northern California is one of few in which mothers were the majority of abductors studied (25 mothers versus 18 fathers). According to the coauthors, professionals who had worked with the children reported varied impacts of the abductions:

> Some [children] longed to remain with the abducting parent, while others were happy to return to the victim parent. Some children had been severely traumatized by the abduction or concealment, and many will be unable to recover from the loss of a long separation from one parent. Some were terrorized or tortured through the lies they were told and by the manipulation of their identities in the process of concealment. In some cases their childhood had been stolen from them by parents who severely over-identified with them. A few children weathered the abduction experience relatively unscathed, these were usually children whose

separation from their other parent was short and whose removal was nonviolent. (p. 440)

Greif and Hegar's (1993) study found similar varied effects of abduction on children. They mailed surveys to 2,666 left-behind parents, of which 371 parents of 519 children completed and returned the survey (a return rate of 15% to 27% depending on estimates of how many duplicates were included in the original mailing). The researchers concluded that "not all children are irreparably damaged" (p. 140) by the abduction, and the impacts appeared to vary based on the protective or buffering factors in each child's experience. Left-behind parents reported that 54% of the children had experienced a decline in functioning between pre- and post-abduction, 21% had remained the same, and 24% of the children had improved. Functioning focused on behavior at home and at school, overall health, and grades. The great majority of left-behind parents believed the time spent with the abductor was very upsetting (48%) or somewhat upsetting (45%) to the child.

Perhaps the most systematic and well-designed study of parental abductions was Finkelhor et al.'s (1991) analysis of the first National Incidence Study of Missing, Abducted, Runaway, and Thrownaway Children (NISMART-1) survey. NISMART-1 was conducted in 1988, achieved an 89.2% response rate, and surveyed 10,544 randomly selected households in which caregivers were asked about the experiences of their 20,505 children aged 17 or younger. A total of only 59 children among this sample were confirmed to have been abducted in the prior 12 months using the narrower, policy-focused definition provided earlier in this chapter. Of the 59 children, none was reported to have been sexually abused, 5% were physically abused, 8% were reported to be injured or harmed, 17% were said to have suffered serious mental harm, and another 35% were reported to have suffered mild to moderate mental harm as a result of the abduction. The authors state that "most of the children, it would appear, did not suffer serious harm as a result of the episode" (p. 814), but it is clear that some did suffer from injury and serious to moderate mental harm.

Effects on Left-Behind Parents

The taken children are not the only perceived victims in parental abductions in the published literature. In a very limited way, the literature on abductions also discusses the effects on both left-behind parents and siblings. Spilman (2006), in a study of 146 families that had experienced abductions including 42 that had experienced abduction by a family member, found that parents whose child was abducted by a family member showed similar levels of anxiety, interpersonal sensitivity, and depression compared to parents whose child was abducted by a nonfamily member. Similarly, Janvier, McCormick, and Donaldson (1990) surveyed 283 left-behind parents, of whom 65 completed the survey (a 23% return rate). Twenty-six of these left-behind parents had children taken to other countries. The left-behind parents reported negative personal effects such as sleep disorders, anxiety, and depression. Janvier and colleagues found that mothers whose children were abducted internationally reported the highest number of negative effects (20) when compared to fathers with children taken internationally (8) and mothers (17) or fathers (14) who had children abducted domestically. Chiancone, Girdner, and Hoff (2001) conducted one of the first studies focused solely on international parental abduction, interviewing 97 left-behind parents. One of five left-behind parents reported using prescription drugs to cope with stress during the abduction period, 85% relied on family and friends for support, and just less than one-half reported using professionals for counseling related to emotional difficulties.

Overall, the small body of research on both domestic and international abductions points to varied outcomes for both children and the left-behind parents. Some children are profoundly affected by the abduction experience, while others show few negative effects depending on specific characteristics of their abductions. The view that taking parents have committed a wrongful act has resulted in little research attention to the consequences of abduction on taking parents. As noted in the global survey of Hague cases (Lowe, 2007), the majority of taking parents are mothers who are the primary caregivers of their children. Our focus in this book is, in part, to help fill this gap in information about the effects of abduction from the perspective of taking mothers who were victims of adult domestic violence.

Overlap between Domestic Violence and Child Abduction

Domestic violence is a serious problem for women internationally. Although cross-national studies have focused on measuring serious physical and sexual violence, domestic violence is more broadly understood (as described in chapter 1) to consist of a pattern of coercion and intimidation in which violence is used as a means to the end of controlling a partner and other family members (Dutton & Goodman, 2005; Stark, 2007). Domestic violence can be inflicted primarily on the partner, but research on child abuse has found that in approximately one-half of families in which a partner is physically violent to the spouse (typically the father to the mother), the children in the household are also physically or sexually abused, often by the father (Hamby, Finkelhor, Turner, & Ormrod, 2010). Many children physically intervene to protect an abused parent, further endangering the child (Edleson, Mbilinyi, Beeman, & Hagemeister, 2003). In these families, fear and intimidation is used to control all family members, not just the spouse.

Domestic violence frequently plays a role in parental abduction cases. For instance, Greif and Hegar's (1993) book on parental kidnapping provides important insight about the frequency of domestic violence in cases of parental abduction. Their survey of 368 parents and three grandparents in 45 states and six countries is one of the largest and most frequently cited in the literature. The authors constructed five types of parental child abductions, three of which include taking or left-behind parents who were violent toward their partners. Overall, the majority (54%) of all the marriages in which abductions occurred involved parent-to-parent domestic violence, and 30% of the left-behind parents either admitted to being violent toward other family members or had been accused of it.

Similarly, Johnston, Sagatun-Edwards, Blomquist, and Girdner (2001) studied 634 abduction cases in two California counties. Although these were primarily domestic abductions (only 7.5% were abducted out of the United States), the authors found that "mothers who abducted were more likely to take the children when they or the children were victims of abuse, and fathers who abducted were more likely to take the children when they were the abusers" (pp. 2–3). Regardless of the mother's role in the abduction, children in this study were more likely to be placed with their mothers at the end of the case. In a study of 93 left-behind parents whose children were abducted to other countries, Chiancone et al. (2001) found that 84 of the 97 left-behind parents reported that the abductor had threatened their lives or those of other family members before the abduction. Taking parents were equally divided between mothers and fathers. Of those left-behind parents reporting threats, 60% said their lives had been threatened, 21% reported that their children's lives were threatened, and 42% reported that the abductor had also threatened the lives of others. Domestic violence was not a focus of this work and was treated briefly in one table and one paragraph in the report. The study's results, however, suggest that violence and threatening behavior characterized these families in which international parental abduction occurred.

The results of these three studies appear somewhat unclear when trying to understand who are likely victims and perpetrators of violence among taking and left-behind parents. Chiancone et al. (2001) found that most of the taking parents were reported to have used violent threats against those left behind, but the authors do not report the gender of those making threats. In their study, mothers and fathers were roughly equally likely to be the taking parent, but threats were not reported by gender. Johnston and her colleagues (2001) found differing motives among mothers and fathers who abducted their children, with mothers fleeing for safety from abusive partners and fathers using the abduction as part of their coercive control of the left-behind parent. While it is difficult to come to a conclusion about whether taking or left-behind parents are more likely to use violence in the relationship, it is clear that patterns of domestic violence characterize a significant portion of the families involved in parental abduction cases.

Finally, Reunite International (2003; Freeman, 2006, 2009) has undertaken a series of international child abduction studies in Europe. Reunite's 2003 study of 22 families in which 33 children were returned to another country within Europe revealed that the great majority of children abducted were either living solely with their mothers or with both parents at the time of the abduction, that mothers were the primary abductors and caregivers of their children, and that taking parents primarily identified either abuse of themselves or their children as a reason to leave the country where they were residing. In Reunite's study, 12 of the cases involved undertakings (voluntary agreements) that were to be implemented by the left-behind parent on return of the child to the other country, one-half of which involved protection from violence. Yet in two-thirds of these cases, undertakings were not implemented in the other country. More worrisome is the fact that undertakings focused specifically on child safety on return were not carried out in *any* of the six cases in which they were made. Ten of the 11 taking mothers in this study felt that both she and her children were harmed as a result of their return to the other country. In the end, the majority of taking mothers gained custody of their children despite having abducted them, as was also found by Johnston et al. (2001) in California.

Children's Exposure to Domestic Violence

In only a few Hague Convention cases have judges accepted that children's exposure to their mothers' victimization at the hands of an abusive partner represents a grave risk of harm to the children and denied the fathers' petitions for their children's return (see chapter 7). In contrast, a burgeoning social science literature points to significant risks of harm to children exposed to domestic violence, and US child custody legislation and rulings recognize these harms. In this section we review some of the social science literature on children's exposure to domestic violence and its potential harm.

Several different terms have been used to define children's exposure to adult domestic violence. The terms *witness* or *observer* of violence have frequently been used (Fantuzzo & Mohr, 1999; Kitzmann, Gaylord, Holt, & Kenny, 2003), but these terms are being replaced with an expanded terminology referring to child *exposure* to domestic violence. Exposure usually refers to a wide variety of experiences of children in homes where one adult is using violent actions to control another adult (Edleson, 2006; Fantuzzo & Mohr, 1999). For example, Kitzmann et al. (2003) expanded the definition of witnessing violence to include hearing the violence and observing the aftermath of abuse, for example, bruises on the mother's body or moving to a shelter. In some instances of exposure, children may respond by becoming involved in the violent incident. Child involvement may vary from physically intervening in the conflict to distracting his or her parents (Garcia O'Hearn, Margolin, & John, 1997; Peled, 1998). For example, children in homes in which violence was occurring were nine times more likely to verbally or physically intervene in parental conflicts, compared to children from homes in which no violence occurred (Adamson & Thompson, 1998). Similarly, based on the reports of 111 battered mothers, Edleson et al. (2003) found that 36% of the children frequently or very frequently yelled to stop violent conflicts, 11.7% frequently or very frequently called someone for help during a violent event, and 10.8% frequently or very frequently physically intervened to stop the violence. Analyzing the same data, Mbilinyi, Edleson, Hagemeister, and Beeman (2007) found that over 26% of the children were reported to have been intentionally hurt and 38% unintentionally hurt during an incident of adult-to-adult violence. Almost 49% of the mothers reported that they were hurt when trying to protect their children from abuse.

Incidence of Child Exposure to Domestic Violence

The degree to which American children are exposed to domestic violence events in their homes has only been recently established through a national representative survey. The 2008 National Survey of Children's Exposure to Violence (NatSCEV) interviewed 4,549 parents (for children under age 14) and youth (aged 14 to 17) and found that 6.2% of American children were exposed to domestic violence in the past year. The same survey found 16.3% of children of all ages were exposed to domestic violence since birth, but when asking youth directly—those aged 14 to 17—over one-quarter (27%) reported that they were exposed to domestic violence in their lifetimes (Finkelhor, Turner, Ormrod, & Hamby, 2009). Parents may tend to underreport or not recognize when their children have been exposed to violence.

A study of police responses to domestic violence in five US cities found that younger children are more likely to be present than older children when police arrive at homes where domestic violence has occurred (Fantuzzo, Brouch, Beriama, & Atkins, 1997). Children of all ages may be exposed to extreme violence. For example, a study of intimate partner homicides and attempted homicides involving 237 children in ten US cities found that children were frequently present during these extremely violent events. Of 146 children whose mothers were murdered, 35% witnessed the mother's death and 37% found their murdered mothers. Of 91 children in families with an attempted homicide, 62% witnessed the violent event and 28% found their mothers afterwards (Lewandowski, McFarlane, Campbell, Gary, & Barenski, 2004).

Children exposed to domestic violence may also be direct victims of physical and sexual maltreatment. Reviews examining the co-occurrence of documented child maltreatment and adult domestic violence revealed a 41% median co-occurrence of child maltreatment and adult domestic violence (Appel & Holden, 1998) with the majority of studies finding a 30% to 60% overlap (Edleson, 1999; Holden, 2003; Lee, Kotch, & Cox 2004; McGuigan & Pratt, 2001). Using more recent NatSCEV data, Hamby et al. (2010) found that over one-third (33.9%) of children and youth who had been exposed to domestic violence in the past year had also been direct victims of maltreatment. Over a child's lifetime, this rate of co-occurring exposure and victimization rose to over one-half (56.8%).

Similar data are not available on overseas Americans and their children, but there is little reason to think that overseas children's exposure would be substantially different. It does appear that large numbers of children are exposed to domestic violence each year and over their lifetimes, which raises serious concerns about the impact of this exposure on their child and adult development.

Effects of Child Exposure to Domestic Violence

Children can be significantly harmed by exposure to violence even when they are not themselves direct targets of physical or sexual violence (see, for example, Carlson, 2000; Rossman, Hughes, & Rosenberg, 2000). Studies of children who are both victims of violence and exposed to parental violence show that each experience uniquely contributes to behavior problems among children (Litrownik, Newton, Hunter, English, & Everson, 2003). Children's experiences and expectation of consistent safety and care may be disrupted and replaced by instability among caregivers (Gewirtz & Edleson, 2007). This disruption can lead to serious developmental difficulties, including emotional and behavioral problems and academic difficulties (Skopp, McDonald, Jouriles, & Rosenfield, 2007; Turner, Finkelhor, & Ormrod, 2006; Bogat, DeJonghe, Levendosky, Davidson, & von Eye, 2006; Carlson, 2000; Scheeringha & Gaensbauer, 2000; Fantuzzo et al., 1997). A recent study of 3,572 children in one state found that children exposed to domestic violence showed the poorest math and reading achievement and attendance when compared to directly abused children, those *both* abused and exposed to domestic violence, and those with no reported exposures (Kiesel, Piescher, & Edleson, in press).

The specific effects of exposure to domestic violence have been well documented. For example, the frequency of adult domestic violence in a home is highly associated with children's behavioral problems, including externalizing behavior such as aggression and disobedience, and internalizing behavior such as depression, sadness, and lack of self-confidence (Jouriles, Norwood, McDonald, Vincent, & Mahoney, 1996). In general, children exposed to domestic violence demonstrate lower cognitive functioning (Rossman, 1998) and reduced skills for resilience, including lower capacity in the areas of social competence, problem solving, autonomy, and self-efficacy (Appel & Holden, 1998; Graham-Bermann & Edleson, 2001). In a review by Margolin and Gordis (2004), the consequences of being exposed to violence in a child's home included both short- and long-term impacts on the child. Short-term effects were aggression and delinquency; emotional and mood disorders; post-traumatic stress symptoms such as exaggerated startle, nightmares, and flashbacks; health-related problems and somatic symptoms such as sleep disturbances; and academic and cognitive problems. Long-term impacts included an increased likelihood that a child would become either a victim or perpetrator of aggression later in life.

Several meta-analyses drawing from studies over more than two decades have shown children exposed to domestic violence to exhibit significantly greater social and behavioral problems than children not so exposed (Chan & Yeung, 2009; Evans, Davies, & DiLillo, 2008; Kitzmann et al., 2003; Rhoades, 2008; Wolfe, Crooks, Lee, McIntyre-Smith, & Jaffe, 2003). A key point in this literature is that exposed children were not significantly different from children who were physically abused or who were both physically abused and exposed to violence (Kitzmann et al., 2003). Thus, the research to date indicates that exposure to domestic violence may create negative outcomes for a child similar to those of direct child abuse victimization. These negative effects would seemingly constitute a "grave risk" of harm to the child.

American Courts and the Recognition of Child Exposure to Domestic Violence

Over the past two decades, significant change has occurred not only in the social science knowledge base, but also in US laws concerning child exposure to domestic violence. These new laws focus most often on criminal prosecution of violent assaults where children are present, on custody and visitation decision making, and on the child welfare system's response (Dunford-Jackson, 2004; Lemon, 1999; Mathews, 1999; Weithorn, 2001). We will focus on legislative changes concerning custody, as these are most relevant to determinations of grave risk and intolerable situations that a child might face on return to his or her country of habitual residence and probable residence with the violent father. We recognize that a decision in a Hague Convention case is not a custody decision, but the Convention's opening lines and the exceptions it incorporates are clearly focused on child well-being as one major goal of the treaty.

Most US states now include the "presence of domestic violence" as a criterion that judges may use to determine custody and visitation arrangements when disputed. In most jurisdictions here and in other Western countries, there has been an assumption that both parents have the right and ability to share custody of and access to their children (Eriksson & Hester, 2001). In approximately two dozen US states, however, this presumption has been reversed in what are commonly referred to as *rebuttable presumption* statutes. Domestic violence rebuttable presumption statutes generally state that when domestic violence is present, it is against the best interests of the child for the documented perpetrator to be awarded custody until his or her safety with the child is assured.

California Family Code provides an example of a rebuttable presumption statute. Under § 3044, "there is a rebuttable presumption that an award of sole or joint physical or legal custody of a child to a person who has perpetrated domestic violence is detrimental to the best interest of the child." California's code outlines six factors to consider in assessing whether a perpetrator of domestic violence has overcome this presumption, including no new violence or violations of existing orders and successful completion of assigned services. In perhaps the strongest rebuttable presumption statute passed to date, the state of Wisconsin's legislature established that guardians *ad litem* have the responsibility for investigating all accusations of domestic violence and reporting their conclusions to the judge. Wisconsin's law instructs judges to make domestic violence their top priority by stating that "if the courts find . . . that a parent has engaged in a pattern or serious incident of interspousal battery [as described in statutes], or domestic abuse, the safety and well-being of the child and the safety of the parent who was the victim of the battery or abuse shall be the paramount concerns in determining legal custody and periods of physical placement" (Wisconsin Act 130, § 25, 767.24[5]).

Many changes have occurred in us courts regarding how domestic violence is considered when children's well-being is at stake. Perhaps one of the largest federal efforts in this area is known as the Greenbook Initiative (see www.the greenbook.info). This initiative evolved from a national discussion over a decade ago. The National Council of Juvenile and Family Court Judges (NCJFCJ), supported by the David and Lucile Packard Foundation, convened a national working group in the late 1990s to focus on the fragmentation of services provided to families with children where adult domestic violence was occurring. These families' children may have been direct victims of child abuse and neglect and/or exposed to the violence by adults against other adults in their homes. The result was a set of best practice guidelines published in 1999 as *Effective Intervention in Domestic Violence and Child Maltreatment: Guidelines for Policy and Practice* (NCJFCJ, 1999). This document has become known as the *Greenbook*, deriving its name from the color of its cover. Dissemination and implementation of the *Greenbook* recommendations was the subject of a multi-pronged effort by eight federal agencies starting in the fall of 2000.

The *Greenbook* recommended best practices focused on three primary systems: (1) child protection services, (2) domestic violence prevention services, and (3) the juvenile and family courts. It identified practice and policy changes necessary both internally and between systems to reduce fragmentation and increase cooperation toward a goal of improving the safety of all victims in a family—whether adult or child—and holding perpetrators of violence accountable.

A key policy recommendation in the *Greenbook* was that children should remain in the care of their non-abusive parent or parents, whenever possible. As stated earlier, Hague case decisions are *not* custody decisions, but several of the allowable defenses or exceptions, such as Articles 13(b) and 20, do allow judges to consider the possibility of further harm if the child is returned to his or her country of habitual residence. Although judges hearing Hague cases are not to decide on custody arrangements, these new state laws and suggested policies and practices do shed light on factors that judges may consider when deciding whether to uphold or deny a petition for a child's return based on grave risk of harm, intolerable situations, and violations of a child's human rights.

Mother's Reports of Their Children's Exposure to Domestic Violence

We turn now to the participants in our study, and discuss how the mothers we interviewed described the types of violence their children experienced. When analyzing these mothers' stories, we looked at a number of markers. To determine if direct child abuse occurred, we focused primarily on physical or sexual acts against children, again recognizing that these forms of violence are generally accepted markers of abuse in legal and clinical settings. In some cases, these acts were intentional efforts to physically harm the child through hitting, through excessively harsh "discipline," or through sexual abuse. In other circumstances, the father's physical harm to the child occurred because he was assaulting the mother, and the child was possibly an unintentional part of this encounter, as in incidents that women reported in which they were holding a young child in their arms while their husbands were beating them. Although the fathers' violence was directed at the women, the potential for (and actual) harm to children was often present. In those families where the mothers reported that their children were not intentionally or unintentionally physically harmed, we examined the exposure of the child to the father's violence, familial intimidation, and humiliation of the mother. We focused on the effects of the exposure to domestic violence, for the children who witnessed physical attacks on their mothers, or in families where high levels of emotional terrorizing occurred but where the children were not themselves the direct victims of their fathers' violent behavior.

We created a typology of exposure to violence and, based on each mother's report, identified the children as belonging to a particular grouping. We have ordered this typology to flow from acts that caused intentional or unintentional physical injury to the children, to acts where the children were not the direct victims, but were exposed to the domestic violence and psychological harm occurred. Three cases did not have sufficient information to categorize them in the typology, so these are labeled "unclear."

Intentional Physical Child Abuse

In four of the families, the children were themselves an intentional target of the father's physical violence. These children lived in environments of violence perpetrated by the father against all family members. Kayla's story illustrates the kinds of physical abuse experienced by the children in these families:

> It must have been Christmas day, or just after Christmas. My older son did something to my daughter's doll and it got [my husband] into such a tirade that he went to go beat [my son] with that doll. I got in between him and [my son], and kept trying to push [my husband] away from [my son], and [my husband], then, beat me, beat [my son], made [my son] go get me some ice out of the freezer, and looked at me and told me that I would never, ever get in between him and his son, ever again. He [said he] was going to take [my son], find a job up in [another European city] . . . and [he would] take [my son] away, and I would never see [my son] again.

In this excerpt, Kayla described the ways that her husband's abuse of her and the children were intertwined to such an extent that the entire family was affected by these experiences. Here the father intended to physically harm his son, apparently as a punishment for his son's behavior. The mother's efforts to protect her seven-year-old child resulted in her being attacked as well, similar to the findings in Mbilinyi et al.'s (2007) study. The father used his physical violence in an effort to control Kayla's parenting behavior, and used threats of abduction to stop her efforts to protect her child.

For Marta*, the fact that her oldest daughter was not biologically related to her second husband seemed connected to the abuse that he inflicted on her. Similar to Kayla's experience, Marta's* daughter was the intentional target of her husband's violent behavior. She notes,

> He would call my daughter a dummy, would hit her upside the head, and would chase her. [. . .] Since before we went to the United States, she, too, had many problems in school because he also mistreated her. Sometimes, he beat her. [. . .] He mistreated her. He offended her. He would call her dumb and stupid. When my other two kids were born—his kids—he started to belittle her. He didn't want her to come into our bedroom. He didn't want her to touch the kids. He didn't want her to play with them. Therefore, she began to feel neglected. [. . .] I [ended up sending] her to the United States [to live] with my parents.

As the two previous examples illustrate, men in these four families intentionally targeted young children for physical violence. These children were not hurt accidentally, but by conscious and deliberate attempts on the father's part to punish or control the child.

Physical Harm to Child during Abuse of Mother

The cases just described demonstrate how men who were abusing their wives also intentionally and directly targeted the children in their households for physical harm, sometimes in the same incidents and sometimes in separate ones. In other families, men targeted their wives for abuse, and were indifferent to the fact that their violent behavior toward their wives might also harm their children. In four families in our study, the children were not intentionally targeted for abuse, but nonetheless became indirect victims during the fathers' physical attacks on their mothers. The following experiences of Jennifer and Kendra are remarkably similar in their descriptions of how the husbands, in their efforts to punish their wives, ignored the danger they were causing their children. These examples typify the experiences of children in the four families in this category. As Jennifer recounts,

> You know, he had [physically injured me] and, you know, even then I didn't even really realize how much trouble I was in. I would just curl myself around my three-year-old and lay on the floor, you know, up against the wall, and he would kick the crap out of me. I figured out finally one night, just reading an article . . . that it was domestic violence and I was in horrible trouble. [. . .] My son had physical . . . you know, he was just sobbing and [saying] "My tummy hurts right here where he kicked me." [. . .] Yeah, [he] did have—and I'm sure still does in some way—have a recollection of what happened to him in being, you know, beat up and kicked by a big man with a beard. He still hates big men with [beards].

This incident was one of several times in which Jennifer's husband attacked her while she had her toddler or infant son in her arms. Mostly she was able to successfully shelter her sons from her husband's violence, even though that violence inflicted serious injury on her. However, on at least one occasion, her husband's violence toward her injured their son. In these cases, it was not important to the fathers that their children were also being hurt.

Kendra was also placed in the position of having to protect her son from violence that her husband was intent on inflicting upon her. One memorable example is the following event Kendra describes:

I had my son in my arms, and I started walking across the room. And he grabbed me—and they have marble floors there. Everything is marble, it's all hard. Hard and cold. And he grabbed me and my son and actually threw us across the room on the marble. And I protected my son with my body, but I got pretty badly hurt . . . And I just—that was—for me, was the breaking point.

As both these cases illustrate, these men were not intentionally targeting their children for violence, but their efforts to harm the mothers exposed their children (and the mothers) to the possibility of life-threatening injuries. For Kendra, as for several of the mothers, the possibility that her son could be seriously hurt became a "breaking point," a moment that finally forced her to begin the arduous task of planning her escape from her husband.

Child Witnessing Physical Attacks on the Mother

In six families, the children witnessed the father physically attacking the mother, but the children were not themselves either the intentional or unintentional victims of physical harm. However, the terrifying effects of these violent attacks by the fathers in these families clearly frightened the children and left lasting psychological traumas that the children reportedly continue to experience.

For example, after many years of marriage, Lara separated from her abusive husband. Ending the relationship, however, did not end the abuse—her husband broke into her house and physically assaulted her on more than one occasion. Her very young son was present during one of these encounters. Here, Lara recounts the following experience and then explains the effect she believes these events had on her two children:

When I couldn't take it anymore, I went to the authorities, when things got too ugly in front of my son. I felt really bad because my son was so small. He was only about a year-and-a-half. So, [my husband] came in breaking the door down, as it was his custom, and he started to hit me in front of my son. My son tried to defend me. He tried to get his dad off me. He was crying and screaming. I said, "This can't be." I ran for the phone to call the police and [my husband] left immediately. [. . .] That's what they felt, fear. My daughter even threw up one time we were with the psychologist [after they left the other country]. She had a few physical reactions when she remembered those things. She was, and still is, a bit introverted. [. . .] They were very scared, because of how they saw me. During [the time they were living in the other country], I was constantly crying and they would see how worried and scared I was. I tried not to let it show, but it was impossible because I would get phone calls from [my husband] and they noticed. So they were very scared.

This story illustrates how even very young children can be aware of the domestic violence happening to their mother, and may attempt to intervene to stop it. In Lara's case, a child less than two years old was attempting to stop his father from hitting his mother. These events took a psychological toll on Lara's children, clearly showing that the events were momentous in their lives. Even after fleeing to the United States, Lara's children were still coping with their memories of their mother's victimization.

Fiona's* daughter was also very young when she witnessed her mother being assaulted by her father. Like Lara's children, Fiona's* daughter continued to experience psychological distress as a result of her mother's abuse. Fiona* describes an event her daughter witnessed, and then explains her daughter's current difficulties after their return to her husband's country:

> She [my daughter] witnessed him hitting me and kicking me, and at that point, you know, and I turned around and saw her looking there . . . I don't know . . . you know, I don't know . . . she was only two-and-a-half years old. I don't know how much a two-and-a-half-year-old can remember of that. I have no idea. [. . .] But my daughter [. . .] she's very clingy. [. . .] When I get up in the morning, and if I'm not there—it's almost like she panics . . . and she, I can hear her, like, jump out of bed and then rush to see where I am. And even at night she'll call out to me, "Mommy?" It's almost like she, you know, and I've told my mom this before, too—it's almost like she is afraid when I'm not there.

Sometimes the memories surrounding the attacks on their mothers persisted for many years in a child's memory. Tamara's* son remembered vivid details of the night his father attacked Tamara* after being served with the divorce papers. At the time of this event, her son was five years old; five years later, after the children were returned to their father through the Hague proceeding, as Tamara* reports,

> He still remembers. I mean, he was there that night that it got really bad, and he was five, but he still can tell me the exact details of where I was hit and where my head hit the wall, and you know, different things like that. He'll still talk about those things. So, I guess they don't forget.

In Megan's* case, both her son and daughter witnessed her husband's attack in which he choked her and beat her head, saying he was going to kill her. Her daughter was a young child at the time, and Megan* recounts the following conversation with her:

> She had seen these things, you know, this is a six-year-old who's asking questions like . . . before we left [his country], she would ask me questions like, "Why does Daddy call you 'fucking bitch' all the time?" You know, and we would go to a wishing well, and she would throw in her penny, or you know, the equivalent in [the other country's currency], and she'd say, "Mommy, my wish is that Daddy would be nicer to you."

Consistently, the children in families where they were not the intentional or unintentional victims of their fathers, but where they saw his attacks against their mothers, experienced significant levels of fear, even long after they were physically separated from their fathers. The mothers reported that their children had long-lasting emotional reactions to these events. Even though these children were not directly victimized by their fathers, the mothers noticed ongoing emotional difficulties and fearfulness in the children. The mothers attributed these reactions to their children's witnessing of the violence and of the mother's emotional response to the abuse. In these cases, the children's behavior was similar to that of children who were the direct physical victims of their fathers.

Emotional Terrorizing without Child Witnessing Physical Violence

In some families, physical violence either did not occur between the parents, or mothers believed that their children did not witness the physical attacks that did occur. However, the children in five families were aware of the atmosphere of tension and fear in the household, and may have been exposed to violence when their mothers were not aware. In fact, the research literature on domestic violence supports that children are more aware of the violence than parents assume. For example, Johnson, Kotch, Catellier, Winsor, Dufort, Hunter, et al. (2002) found that 77.2% of children reported exposure to moderate-high levels of domestic violence, whereas only 46% of parents reported such exposure of their children, a surprising 31.2% discrepancy. The children's awareness of family tension in our study sample provoked significant distress among them. For example, Sandra's husband never hit her, but he frequently physically threatened her. Sandra recounts the effects the high level of tension in the household produced for her son:

> I think my son is an anxious kid, and I think some of that anxiety happened . . .
> well. Again I think it's a result of an abusive situation, but I think that your children
> are always more aware of it than you think they are . . . Umm . . . I thought my kids
> had no idea because [my husband] tended to come home late at night . . . He was
> around so little that I actually didn't think they were as aware of his personality and
> what was going on between us as they ended up being . . . My daughter, in the first
> grade, they asked her to draw a picture of her family and she drew a picture of her
> father with his fists over me. I was like, "How did she know that?"

Sandra tried to remove the couple's conflicts to rooms away from the children, and she believed that they were not aware of what was happening until her six-year-old daughter drew a disturbing family picture. This story revealed the toll these experiences took on Sandra's children, as well as the level of awareness they had about what was happening between their parents, even when Sandra was trying to protect them from conflict.

Similarly, Belinda's daughter was also aware of the tension between her parents, even though she was quite young. Belinda was beaten up on multiple occasions by her husband, but she reported that he never harmed the children and that they didn't see these attacks. After she relocated to the United States, she would ask her daughter if she wanted to return to the other country:

> I used to ask her if she wanted us to move back to [Latin American country] and
> she would say, "No. I don't know why my daddy yells at you. I don't know why he
> yells at you." Imagine that. She was very young. She was five years old.

Belinda's 15-year-old son was also aware of the conflicts between his parents, and he repeatedly asked his mother to leave his father, saying that he would get a job and help support the family, but Belinda was unwilling to burden him with this responsibility. This example again demonstrates that children are aware of the conflict happening in the household, even when they are as young as Belinda's daughter and even when parents don't think the children have witnessed the violence.

Amanda ended up in an altercation with her husband in which she was seriously cut by a knife that he held (she was unsure if this was an accident). She was in the hospital for several days following this. Her husband abruptly moved the family from the urban area in which they were living to a small, isolated village after the incident. Amanda reports the effect this had on her nine-year-old son while they lived in the other country:

But my son, he was like a nervous wreck, 'cause he knew everything that was going on. I didn't really say anything, but kids can feel it. [. . .] He didn't hear exactly everything that was going on, but he was old enough to kind of put everything together . . . He came back [to the United States] very nervous. I mean, for the first year that we were here, and even the time that we were in [his father's country], he couldn't sleep at night. He had a lot of anxiety; a lot of stomach problems. And all that is part of, like the psychologist told me, we had . . . what's it called? Post-traumatic stress?

As was the case for the children who witnessed physical violence against their mothers, the children in families where overt physical violence was not occurring, or who did not witness the attacks against their mothers, also had significant emotional distress as a result of the abuse. Even when mothers thought their children were unaware of the problems in the relationship, children were more perceptive than their mothers knew. The tension in these families manifested in the children as anxiety, worry, nervousness, and sleep disorders. Clearly, even in families where there was the least direct exposure of the children to the violence, the consequences for them continued to be profound.

Exposure to Domestic Violence Constitutes a Grave Risk of Harm to Children

We started this chapter with a review of the literature on both abduction and children's exposure to domestic violence. The results of our interviews with mothers indicate that the children in our study often faced severe and sustained exposure to domestic violence prior to the mothers' decision to flee the other country, consistent with the literature on both domestic and international abductions. For the majority of the women we interviewed, this violence included serious physical assaults against them, coupled with a degree of threatening behavior that led the women to believe that their lives and/or their children's lives were in danger. In families where women were being physically assaulted, children were also physically harmed by the father, whether as his intended or unintended victims, in eight (36.6%) of these cases. In an additional six families (27.3%), mothers reported that their children were firsthand witnesses to violent attacks against them, even if the father had not physically harmed the child. Sometimes, children saw fathers assault mothers in ways that could have resulted in serious injury or death. Children in five families (22.7%) were aware of domestic violence, but mothers reported that their children did not directly witness abusive actions. Based on current definitions of children's exposure to domestic violence (including physical harm to the child, and witnessing or awareness of the violence), 86.4% of the children in this sample were exposed to domestic violence. These results are consistent with studies of the overlap between domestic violence and child abuse (Jouriles, McDonald, Slep, Heyman, & Garrido, 2008).

These violent events had profound effects on the children. Mothers reported that their children experienced night terrors, intrusive memories, separation anxiety, depression, and increased aggression. The literature on child exposure to domestic violence indicates that even without direct physical harm to the child, being an eyewitness to their mother's abuse or even experiencing the events before and after abusive incidents in a family can result in profound emotional distress for children (Evans et al., 2008; Kitzmann et al., 2003; Wolfe et al., 2003). In these contexts, the father's abuse of the mother is harmful to the child. It is important to be clear that this harm stems from the father's actions and is not a reflection on the mother's parenting. It is also important to note that the child's exposure may create psychological harm to the child equivalent to the harm suffered by children who have been physically abused themselves.

The effects of domestic violence on their children played an important role in creating the circumstances that led these women to leave the country where they were living with their children. As reviewed earlier in this chapter, previous research on child abduction suggests that over one-half of families where parental abduction occurs experience domestic violence (Greif & Hegar, 1993). Although we cannot estimate the number of mothers facing Hague petitions who are experiencing domestic violence, it is evident from the data reported here that when women identify as domestic violence victims, the abuse they are experiencing is, in most cases, severe and constitutes a "grave risk of harm" for their children.

5 | Hague Decisions and the Aftermath

Basically there are three choices in these situations: (1) You stay there in those conditions and you survive as long as you can. (2) You walk away from your child and you walk *away*. (3) You run, with your child. So there's three. That's it.

—*Mother involved in a Hague Convention case*

Despite the evidence we have presented of the seriousness of the abuse these mothers faced, and despite the larger social science literature on the effects of adult domestic violence exposure on children, over one-half of the women in this study had their children returned to the other country—and most of the time, this meant return to the abusive husband. In particular, in determining whether the children could remain in the United States with their mothers, judges seemed to rely solely (but not always) on whether a child had been directly physically or sexually abused by the father. Children consistently remained in the States only when they were directly exposed to their fathers' physical violence as his intended target, or were unintentionally physically hurt during attacks on their mothers. Witnessing or being exposed to the father's physical violence and emotional terrorizing toward the mother, in the absence of physical abuse of the child, was not a sufficient justification for having the child remain with the mother in the United States.

In this chapter we review the judicial decisions made in each woman's Hague petition. But one of the important lessons we learned from listening to these women's stories was that the Hague process was, in fact, just one among several legal struggles that both preceded and persisted after the judge's Hague decision. What happened after the Hague petition sheds further light on the continuing nature of the abuse and difficulties these women face.

US Judicial Decisions in Response to a Hague Convention Petition

After women relocated to the United States, usually within a few months, their (ex-) husbands filed a petition under the Hague Convention to force the prompt return of their children to the other country. In a few instances, the serving of the Hague petition was a traumatizing event for the entire family, as US Marshals or other law enforcement officials would, with little notice, remove the children from the mother's care. Sometimes the children would be placed into some sort of out-of-home care and/or they were immediately turned over to their father's custody until the Hague petition could be decided. Marta* (who did not speak English) describes what happened when she was served with the Hague petition:

> When I got home, the police were waiting for me. They gave me a legal document about 200 pages long, perhaps longer. Then, they told me they had to take the kids. Without further notice, the police went into the house and asked my family where the kids' room was, and they packed some of their clothes and shoes in some boxes my kids stored their toys in. There were about six policemen; two went into the bedroom for some clothes and shoes. [crying] This part is very hard for me [. . .] So, my kids didn't know what was happening. The police said they had to take my kids. [. . .] The kids were still small. [. . .] They clung on to my legs, and the police yanked them away. The kids were crying when they left. [. . .] I couldn't do anything because they told me they had to take them. My kids didn't speak English well, so they didn't understand what was happening.

In this case, Marta's* children were removed from her care, and she was not told where they were going. Marta's* court appearance for the Hague petition was scheduled four hours after her children were taken. She had an attorney helping her with her divorce proceedings, so she was able to delay the hearing for a day, but within two weeks her children were returned to her husband in the other country.

Marta's* experience of having her children returned to the other country was the more common outcome for the women in the study. Table 5.1 shows who had her children returned to the abusive husband and who was able to remain in the United States, along with the reason for denial (if the Hague petition was unsuccessful) and who the children were returned to (if the Hague petition was successful). Overall, 12 women (54.5%) had their children returned to the other country. In seven of these cases, the return to the other country

Table 5.1 US Judges' Decisions on Hague Petitions

Hague Petition Denied; Children Remained with Woman in US (reason for denial)	Hague Petition Granted; Children Returned to Other Country (who children were returned to)
Kendra (settled with ex-husband)	Fiona* (husband)
Jennifer (ex-husband acquiesced to children's relocation)	Tamara* (husband)
Kayla (denied on appeal; reason unclear)	Ruth* (husband)
Pamela (no decision made; husband has not pursued the petition)	Katie* (daughter with Katie*; sons with husband)
Lara (denied on appeal; reason unclear)	Megan* (husband)
Marina (father not credible; domestic violence considered)	Rebecca* (unclear)
Sandra (settled with ex-husband)	Marta* (husband)
Belinda (settled with ex-husband)	Ellen* (with Ellen* and her mother)
Amanda (not their habitual residence)	Stephanie* (with Stephanie* because of husband's abusive behavior)
Ilana (had custody and valid passports)	Kelsey* (husband)
	Austin* (husband)
	Caitlin* (unknown)
TOTAL: 10	12

meant return to the father. In three remaining cases, the judge ordered the women to return with the children, and for the children to remain with their mothers in the other country; in two cases, it was unclear who had physical custody of the child after the return.

For Ellen* and Stephanie*, the judge found evidence that the father may be a danger to the child, but did not consider this sufficient reason to prevent the return of the child to the other country—in other words, the judge did not find that a "grave risk of physical or psychological harm" would befall the child if returned. Stephanie* explains that in her case, the judge made the following ruling:

> The female judge that decided on my case called the abuse "common." Can any type of domestic abuse be "common"? I don't know, and I have the transcript. She called it "common." She was presented with documentation; medical documentation, and the translations of it, of course. She was presented with other documents. She was presented with testimony, my testimony. But, unfortunately, she decided to rule in my husband's favor. And even though she said, "I find a risk in placing this child under his father's custody, so I am ordering the mother to return with the child."

In this case, the judge clearly acknowledged that there was evidence of domestic violence. For Stephanie*, this included physical violence in which her husband would beat her while she was holding her infant son. As she described it, she would hold her child in one arm and try to fend him off with the other. The abuse was severe enough that she was injured and required medical care, the documentation of which was presented to the judge. The judge was concerned enough to order that the child not be returned to his father in the other country. The judge ordered the mother's return to the other country, a remedy that is not provided for within the Hague Convention, but which this judge sought to impose.

Finally, in three cases, custody of the children was split, or it was unclear who had custody after the return. For example, Katie's* sons had remained behind in her husband's country when she had come to the United States with her daughter to help care for her relative. She agreed to return to his country with her daughter, and because of this negotiated agreement, she was allowed to keep custody of her daughter, but she has had no contact with her sons. In Rebecca's* and Caitlin's* cases, it was not clear who had custody of the children once they were returned to the other country.

Stephanie's* case was unusual in that the judge acknowledged the domestic violence in the ruling. In the other cases where the Hague petition was granted and the children were returned, the women reported that either their attorney did not present the domestic violence evidence, or the judge did not find the evidence compelling. Judges who returned the children, from the mothers' point of view, appeared to prioritize the nation-to-nation relations over the issues that were occurring in the family (as we discuss further in chapter 6). When these judges mentioned the domestic violence, they would note that the other country should be able to address these concerns.

For women who were able to keep their children with them in the United States, a similar pattern emerges—the women reported that domestic violence was not a reason mentioned in these decisions. In only one case did the judge appear to base his ruling on the domestic violence evidence that was presented. Marina's lawyer documented the serious domestic violence perpetrated by her husband, including his multiple threats to kill her, the time he put an unloaded gun to her head and pulled the trigger, her children's witnessing of the violence, and the ongoing emotional terror he instilled in the family. The father was asked to testify about this information during the Hague proceedings, and, based on his demeanor in court, Marina reports that the judge did not find him credible. It appeared that this judge based his ruling on the possibility of harm to the children because of the father's repeated attempts to harm Marina.

The other women whose children stayed in the United States did not recall judges commenting on the domestic violence of their husbands, but it was not always clear if evidence about the violence had been presented. For example, three of the ten cases were settled, usually with some arrangement in which the women gave up any monetary claims from the marriage in exchange for being able to remain in the United States with their children. As Sandra notes, "it boiled down to trading money for kids." In these cases, settlements occurred before judges were able to make rulings on the Hague petition, so the judges' evaluations of the situation were not known.

The other reasons that the children were allowed to remain with their mothers varied. When Jennifer's husband threw her out of the house, the judge interpreted this action as acquiescence—that the husband had agreed to let the woman and children leave—which is an available exception to return under the Hague Convention. In Amanda's case (as discussed previously), the judge did not feel that the other country was the habitual residence of the children, primarily because they had been there for a relatively short time (just a few months), and there was evidence of continued intent to live in the United States. For Ilana, the judge agreed that she had been given custody and the right to move from the other country in her divorce proceedings. He found that she had valid passports for herself and her children, so the removal was not wrongful, and he therefore dismissed the husband's petition.

Relationship of Domestic Violence to the Hague Outcome

To understand the relationship of domestic violence to the decisions judges made regarding the Hague petition, we compared mothers using a combined typology of mother and children's exposure to violence. By arranging cases in this way in table 5.2, it is possible to document a distinct pattern—*women who reported that their children were the intentional or unintentional victims of the husband's violence were likely to be allowed to remain in the United States.* Judges were most likely to return the children to the other country (usually to the father's custody) when serious domestic violence had occurred and the child was exposed to it, but the physical abuse was directed only toward the mother and not the child. Judges were also less likely to allow the children to remain in the United States with their mother when emotional terrorizing in the absence of physical violence occurred, and in cases where the abuse situation was unclear.

This pattern demonstrates that judges were either unaware of or ignored the seriousness and pervasiveness of domestic violence exposure in these families. In all but one of the situations of the women we interviewed, the women presented multiple instances of psychological, physical, or sexual abuse. Although judges responded to protect children in situations where there was evidence of direct physical harm to the child, they were less likely to do so when the harm was of a psychological nature, that is, when the child witnessed the domestic violence, or lived within a climate of emotional terrorizing characteristic of coercive control.

Table 5.2 Hague Decisions Compared to Abuse Types

	Mother and Child Both Physically Harmed	Mother Physically Harmed; Child Witnessed Attack	Mother Physically Harmed; Child Did Not Witness Attack	Emotional Terrorizing with No or Minimal Physical Violence	Unclear
Judge Allowed Children to Remain with Mother	6	1	2	1	
Judge Returned Children to Other Country (usually to father)	2	6	1	2	1

The mothers of children who were returned to the other country did not appear to differ from other women who faced similar abuse. For example, the violence experienced by Stephanie* and Marta* (the two situations in which both mother and child were physically harmed, but the judge returned the child to the other country) appeared similar to that reported by the six other mothers whose children were allowed to remain in the United States. Likewise, Lara's children witnessed comparable violent attacks on their mother, but unlike six other families where children also witnessed an attack on their mother, Lara's children were allowed to stay with her in the States. Although we see a pattern in how mother and children's abuse was related to the decision on the Hague petition, our point here is that no consistent use of the distinction we discerned occurred by the judges making decisions on these cases.

For the large number of battered women whose children were not the intentional or unintentional targets of their husbands' aggression, but who witnessed their fathers' violence, this direct exposure to violence was not a sufficient reason to prevent their return to the other country, and to the fathers. These children were eyewitnesses to their mothers' victimization, and as reported in chapter 4, they suffered serious psychological harm from observing these actions. Despite the severity of abuse happening in these families and scientific evidence of the serious impact of such child exposure to violence, judges in these Hague Convention cases did not acknowledge that these dynamics could constitute a grave risk of possible physical or psychological harm to the children and, therefore, a reason to deny their return to the other country as provided in Article 13(b) of the Convention. Finally, in cases where there was a clear pattern of emotional terrorizing, but in which physical violence had not occurred, judges typically returned the children to the other country. In Sandra's case, she came to a financial settlement with her husband in exchange for her custody of the children and the ability to live in the United States. If this agreement had not been reached, it seems likely that her children would also have been returned to the other country.

Other Legal Process Involved in the Hague Petition

In the unfolding of the Hague petition in us courts, several factors were important in these cases. The experiences women had in the legal process surrounding the Hague Convention are summarized in table 5.3. These areas include (1) whether the woman faced criminal kidnapping charges in the other country; (2) factors related to her attorney's experience and provision of expert

Table 5.3 Legal Processes Involved in the Hague Petition

Woman	Criminal Charges Filed against Her in Other Country	Attorney Had Previous Hague Experience	Case Heard in Federal Court	Expert Testimony Offered	Undertakings Ordered	Time Frame in Months	Estimated Cost or Legal Assistance Provided Pro Bono
Belinda					n/a	<1	Pro bono
Amanda			◆	◆	n/a	24	$70,000
Ilana					n/a	6	$10,000
Fiona*			◆	◆	◆	2.5	$80,000
Lara					n/a	9	Pro bono
Ruth*	◆		◆	◆	◆	13	Pro bono
Megan*			◆			1	$30,000
Pamela					n/a	No decision	
Marina		◆		◆	n/a	9	$37,500
Ellen*		◆				12	$7,000
Kendra	◆		◆		◆	2	$7,000

Name						Duration	Cost
Jennifer	◆			n/a		6	$100,000
Kayla		◆		n/a		36	$250,000
Rebecca*	◆	◆				48	$300,000
Stephanie*	◆		—a			4	Pro bono
Austin*	◆		◆			<1	
Marta*	◆		◆			<1	Pro bono
Tamara*			◆		◆	13	
Katie*			—b		◆	<1	
Kelsey*			◆	◆	◆	3	
Sandra	◆	◆	◆	n/a		12	$48,000
TOTAL	7	7	11	4	5	Avg. 10.13 (12.61 SD) Median 6	Avg. $62,166 ($92,808 SD) Median $30,000

Note: Information on Caitlin's* case is unavailable.

a The judge refused the mother's request for a psychological evaluation of her child, saying that the child was too young.

b Katie* had petitioned for undertakings, but her husband's attorney had them deleted because Katie* was not returning to live with her abusive husband.

testimony; and (3) aspects related to the overall case (which court heard the petition, whether undertakings were ordered, and the time frame and costs associated with the woman's defense).

Criminal Kidnapping Charges

Seven of the women were facing both a civil suit in the United States and criminal prosecution for kidnapping in the country they had left. Five of these women had their children returned to the other country, and they faced added legal difficulties in being able to return safely with their children. For instance, Marta* could have been immediately arrested when she returned to the other country because of the kidnapping charge her husband had filed against her. As she explains,

> Once he brought the kids [back to the other country], I wanted to come back immediately, but my parents talked me against it. [. . .] They told me I'd be put in jail if I came back. Because he had . . . there were two hearings; the civil hearing for the kids' custody, and the federal hearing, for the kidnapping. So they told me that as soon as I set foot in [the other country], I was going to be detained, and I would have to be in prison for ten years. So I sought help [and I found] an attorney from [the other country], and she offered to file for immunity so that I could enter [the other country] and not be detained by the police there. So she filed for immunity, and I was able to enter [with immunity for three days until I could go to court and present my information to the judge].

For Marta*, her children were returning to a man who had beaten her on multiple occasions and physically abused his stepdaughter, although he had not directly physically abused the children sent back to him as a result of the Hague proceedings. Instead of being able to return immediately to initiate legal proceedings related to custody and visitation in the other country, Marta* had to remain behind in the United States because she faced criminal prosecution and the threat of a serious prison sentence if found guilty of kidnapping. No provisions for Marta's* return, such as an undertaking or court stipulation requiring the dismissal of the criminal charges in the other country, were made in the US Hague proceedings. Through her own tenacity, while in the States, Marta* found an attorney who practiced in the other country and could help her to return safely. Marta's* case highlights the dual civil and criminal issues that faced one-third of the women in this study. The issue of undertakings and related *mirror orders* (undertakings entered as court orders in both countries) is discussed more fully in chapter 6, which covers the results of the attorney interviews.

Attorney Experience

Only 22% of the attorneys who represented women in Hague petition proceedings had prior experience in litigating Hague cases. In this sample, five women found attorneys who had actually worked with a Hague petitioner or respondent previously. Interestingly, in all but one of those cases, the women's children were sent back to the other country, so it is not clear from these data whether having an experienced attorney led to a safer outcome for the women and children. Only one of the four women who had an experienced Hague attorney felt that the attorney had not represented her interests well. In the other three cases, the women reported that the attorney had presented information about the domestic violence, but the judge had not seen these experiences as sufficient to find grave risk of harm to the children on their return.

Most women found the attorney who represented them through family connections, and they typically sought out these attorneys to initiate divorce proceedings, so most had a divorce or family law practice. Five women reported that their attorneys were experienced in working with domestic violence victims, even if they did not know specific issues related to the Hague Convention. However, in many cases, women felt that their attorneys were not knowledgeable about the Hague Convention and also did not understand dynamics related to abuse. For instance, Ilana, who had fled her ex-husband in Europe after he repeatedly stalked and threatened her, including breaking into her apartment, reports some of her struggles with her attorney:

> She was more of an attorney for divorce. She was thinking really . . . she was really a believer in counseling. The problem with my kind of case, you can't do counseling. It's not working. [. . .] you really need to be careful about the lawyer, and be sure that you can trust your lawyer. And I saw in the Hague Convention case, there are many lawyers, they take your case for to make money. They really, you are the bad person, anyway. They are not going to tell you that. But they are going to act like that, and you're not going to win your case. And I think it's terrible to say that. But, you really need to be careful when you choose your lawyer. You need to take somebody who really will believe you, and most of the time, it's not the case.

Ilana's experience points to concerns shared by other women in the study. For Ilana, her attorney was more interested in a mediation approach to the continued conflict Ilana was having with her ex-husband. Ilana had not been able to achieve a successful end to her ex-husband's abusive behavior in her home country, even after both police and informal interventions with the husband. She was understandably skeptical of taking a "counseling" approach to changing her ex-husband's behavior. She further reflected on the stigma she experienced as a taking parent, that she had already been defined as the "bad person" by choosing to relocate to the United States, even though she was unable to stop her husband's behavior and ensure her own and her children's safety in the other country. These experiences led her to wonder about the integrity of an attorney representing women in Hague petitions, a sentiment shared by other women who felt that they had been poorly represented in their cases.

Expert Testimony

One-half of the women we interviewed obtained expert testimony from psychologists or social workers, who provided an evaluation of the relationship of the child with both the mother and father, and the current emotional health of the child. In several cases, the mental health professional testified that the child was afraid of the father; in one case, the children had been diagnosed with post-traumatic stress disorder (PTSD) as a result of the violence they had witnessed. In addition, in three cases the court appointed a guardian *ad litem* attorney to independently advocate for the children. In Megan's* case, the judge refused her attorney's request that a guardian *ad litem* be appointed for her children (see the section "Undertakings"). The provision of expert testimony seemed to have some relationship to the judges' decisions: in 60% of the cases where the child remained with the mother in the United States, expert testimony was given; expert testimony was offered in a smaller percentage (41.7%) of the Hague petitions in which judges decided to return the child to the other country.

Court of Jurisdiction

A substantial number of the women did not know or report which court (state or federal) heard their Hague case. As we will discuss further in chapter 6, the court in which a Hague case is heard can influence the unfolding of the Hague petition processes. Among the 11 women who did know the court, seven cases were heard in federal court and four cases in state court. From the women's perspective, the venue for their case was not an important consideration. It also appeared that the type of court was not a significant factor in determining the outcome of the Hague petition. In three cases heard in federal court, the Hague petition was denied and the children remained in the United States; in four cases the petition was granted. In state court, one-half of the petitions were denied and one-half granted.

Undertakings

Undertakings are a voluntary agreement between the parents as to expectations of conduct in the relationship going forward (Hoegger, 2003). For example, the women who had criminal charges of abduction waiting to be heard on their return to the other country could ask their husbands to agree, as part of an undertaking, to drop the criminal charges. Undertakings were entered into the record of the US court, but were usually left in the hands of the abusive husband to implement in the other country. Undertakings were structured to address several different concerns, including lifting criminal charges and travel restrictions in the other country against the mother, giving access to the children, and providing psychological support to the children. In all four cases where undertakings were agreed to by the parties in the US courts, none of these agreements was carried out in the other country by the left-behind parent.

Judges also refused to order the left-behind parent to carry out steps that would possibly increase the mother and child's safety on return. Fiona* had asked the judge to order that the father agree to end the violence against her, and that he would provide a separate residence and child support when they returned, but the judge rejected these requests. Megan* had decided to return to the United States after her husband choked her and beat her head against a bathtub in front of her children. The judge, in deciding to grant the petition for the children's return to the other country, denied that grave risk existed and rebuffed Megan's* efforts to obtain court orders that could be used to ensure her safety in the other country. Megan* remembers the judge's reasoning in this way:

> And she said, "I'm not sending those kids to a war zone. I'm not sending them to Bosnia. They're going back to [European country]," and then we asked could we get a guardian *ad litem*? And she said no. And her reasoning, which I mean, there is some legal background to this, is that the Hague Convention is *not* supposed to address issues of custody. But, still, I think it's unconscionable to send a six-year-old girl home, you know, to a man who may be abusing her. You know? And she said, "Well, let the [other country] court handle it." And then, my attorney said, "Well, what about [Megan*]? And she said, "I don't care what [Megan*] does. She can stay

or she can go. Whatever she wants." And [the attorney] said, "Well, are there any safeguards for her protection if she goes back to [the other country]?" And the judge said "No, that's none of my business. That's her problem."

This excerpt illustrates several ways in which Megan's* safety on her return was compromised by the judge's reasoning. The judge noted that she would not send the children to Bosnia, implying in contrast that the country Megan* had come from was a safe place, so she rejected any grave risk argument. The judge dismissed the attorney's request for an undertaking to appoint a special advocate for the child, and she refused Megan's* request for orders that would enhance her safety on her return. In this case, the judge clearly believed that Megan's* safety concerns for herself were not within the judge's powers to assure, and that the other country would be able to address Megan's* safety concerns for her child.

Time Frame and Cost

Finally, although these cases were usually decided in a relatively short time, they tended to be expensive for the women. In four cases, judges made decisions in less than a month, while five cases went on for more than a year; the majority of cases took between 1 and 12 months to conclude. Over one-half of the cases were resolved within 6 months. In terms of payment, only five women obtained *pro bono* legal representation; three out of four of the women from Latin America were served by legal aid attorneys who specialized in work with the Latin American community. The average cost of a case for those who did not receive legal services was over $60,000, with mothers reporting costs ranging from $7,000 to $300,000. Most of the women reported that they were paying small monthly sums to their attorneys to cover these charges, while a few had access to significant financial resources (usually from their parents) and were able to pay their legal fees. More detail on the costs of these cases appears in chapter 6.

Children's Exposure to Domestic Violence and Grave Risk

Studies of the effects of adult domestic violence indicate that children who are exposed to it—even when this exposure consists of hearing or being aware of, but not seeing, the violence—have levels of emotional distress, depressive disorders, academic problems, and acting out similar to those of children who are the victims of physical abuse (Bogat et al., 2006; Carlson, 2000; Fantuzzo et al.,

1997; Kitzmann et al., 2003; Scheeringha & Gaensbauer, 2000; Skopp et al., 2007; Turner et al., 2006). The drafters of the Hague Convention provided for exceptions to the child's return if that return (a) posed a grave risk of physical or psychological harm to the child, or (b) represented an intolerable situation for the child, or (c) violated the child's human rights. Many judges appeared to take a narrow view of these exceptions, refusing a return only in those situations where children were physically harmed by the father, despite the extensive social science evidence that a father's violence toward the mother may also seriously harm a child.

In the assessment of the women whose children were returned to the other country, judges prioritized comity among nations and other countries' courts, or the respect nations have for one another's laws, over the safety needs of the abused women and their children. The issue of the role of international law and domestic violence has been discussed among legal scholars, and is also discussed in chapter 6. Jaffe and Crooks's (2004) cross-national comparison of domestic violence and child custody laws in four countries indicates that nations have differing views on how abuse should be addressed when parents separate. In addition to differences among nations, analyses of a similar international treaty, the United Nations Convention on the Rights of the Child, also finds that tensions exist between respect for children's rights and the rights of nations (Daiute, 2008). In this example, nations are more likely to agree on preventing harmful treatment of children, but less likely to agree on a child's right to self-determination or to safety within his or her own family. These issues are relevant to assessing the relative weight given by judicial authorities to the rights of battered women and children to live free of physical threat and intimidation, as opposed to the rights of nations to expect the speedy return of resident children in these cases.

What Happened after the Hague Decision

The judge's decision on the Hague petition could be likened to a snapshot in an ongoing movie of these women's and children's lives. Both for women whose children were returned to the other country, and for women whose children remained with them in the United States, issues related to the abuse, and the legal struggles it entailed, continued. To date, no available research traces what happens to women and children after a Hague decision. In this section, we review the experiences of women whose children were returned to the other country, and those who stayed with their children in the United States.

The children of 12 women were ordered back to the other country as a result of the Hague petition. Six women lost custody of their children (50% of the women whose children were returned), and in the case of the three mothers who had returned to the United States, they also lost contact with their children. Both Austin* and Kelsey* continued to engage in legal efforts to regain access to their children. After many years of trying to maintain contact with her children, only to have the father refuse to comply with visitation orders from courts in the other country, Megan* decided that she could no longer fight for contact with her children because of the emotional and financial costs. Five women either maintained custody after being returned to the other country by the US court, or they regained custody of their children through legal action in the other country. Two of the women returned to the United States with their children with the permission of the legal system of the other country. One had returned with the children without court permission.

Experiences of Abuse and Economic Hardship on Return to the Other Country

In addition to the custody and contact arrangements for these 12 families, women reported on three other areas: (1) whether their children had experienced physical child abuse after the return to the father in the other country, (2) whether the woman herself had been re-victimized after the return, and (3) the level of economic hardship some of the women faced as they returned to live in the other country.

In the case of Tamara*, Kelsey*, and Ruth*, each reported that their children had experienced physical abuse by the fathers who now had primary custody. As an example of the kind of situation facing the children in these three families, Tamara* reports on the serious levels of physical harm her children faced on their return:

> My oldest daughter, [she and her father] had fought a lot. [. . .] and [. . .] the police had been there [because the daughter had called them]. She'd gone to the hospital once with scratches and bruises on her neck. So, he got tired of it; of the police and the hospital visits. So he kicked her out. Thank goodness for me. And so I got her. So, I did get the order. She's [. . .] been with me for almost exactly two years. She doesn't see her father at all. Well, she sees him only when we're in the car to pick up the other kids on my four days and four hours a month [. . .] It's pretty bad. They . . . they . . . they live in constant . . . especially my son, he lives in constant

fear, and he's always calling me because his dad has hit him, or screamed at him and told him he's going to kill him, and told him he's a stupid asshole. [. . .] The kids are both very afraid. [. . . My son . . .] he keeps saying, "What if Dad hits me 'til I'm dead?"

Tamara's* children experienced an escalation of the emotional abuse their father exhibited prior to Tamara's* decision to flee with the children to the United States. Before they had left the other country, the father had terrorized the entire family to the extent that the mother slept in the same room with one of her children, and all of them locked their doors at night because of the father's erratic behavior. When the children were returned to Tamara's* husband as a result of the Hague petition, two of the three children reported physical abuse by their father. In addition to this physical harm, the son is afraid enough to wonder whether his father will kill him. Tamara* has fought for custody of her children for two years in the other country's courts. She has faced an uphill battle because her husband has been able to cast her as a child abductor, due to the US court's agreement to return the children because of his Hague petition.

Ruth* and Kelsey* relate similar stories of continued violence once the courts returned the children to their husbands in the other countries. Ruth* (after many years of physical abuse against her) managed to escape her husband and return to the United States. Once she arrived, her husband served her with a Hague petition, and the children were eventually returned to him in the other country. In their father's custody, they became the targets of his abuse.

These cases demonstrate one of the possible consequences of returning children to domestically violent fathers. Tamara* and Ruth* had each been physically harmed by their husbands, but the children had not been the victims of his violence prior to the women's decision to flee the other country, although the fathers in both cases had subjected the families to high levels of emotional terrorizing. The violence both these fathers inflicted developed to include direct abuse of the children after they were returned to the other country, but now these children do not have day-to-day support, protection, and assistance from their mothers.

In addition to abuse suffered by the children, four of the women reported new domestic violence committed against them by their abusive husbands once they returned to the other country. Ellen* attempted to reconcile with her husband when she and the children returned after the Hague petition. The couple reunited for a year, and during this time, she gave birth to another child. After her youngest child's birth, her husband's abusive behavior began to escalate again, and she filed for a divorce. When we last spoke with Ellen*, she was in court attempting to get permission to move the children back to the United States where they have supportive family members who can assist in their care.

Fiona's* children were very young when they were sent back to live with their father, an American citizen, in another country. Initially, he wouldn't let her see the children, but after a few weeks, the judge ordered the children returned to her custody because she was still breastfeeding her youngest child. Once in the other country, Fiona* and the children's situation rapidly deteriorated, as she reports:

> I thought, [the us judge] is sending me back, you know, to a potentially violent situation. I have no protection. I have no lawyer. I have no money. Nothing. Where am I supposed to go? [. . . My husband] also told my friend that he was going to have my passport revoked. [. . .] I was frightened that once I got back to [the other country] if he had my passport revoked that somehow I'd be a person without a passport. But, it's just one of the threats he made. [. . . After having nowhere to live] my friend drove me to the next village over [to] a shelter for domestic violence victims. [. . .] I lived there for eight months. [. . .] And at one point—another thing he did was he accused me of breaking into the basement and stealing some of his documents [. . .] And the police raided my room, looking for these documents, and as a result, my husband [. . .] found out the address of the shelter. Then he . . . he started stalking me. And, I was so scared. [. . . My friend] saw my husband's car . . . in front of the shelter, and he dropped [a friend of his] off [. . .] further down the street. [. . .] In the meantime, I had the kids, and I was walking back towards the shelter and she intercepted me. She said, "Get in the car right away." [. . .] She said, "Your husband—he knows where you're living." And that just, that scared me. I mean, right through the roof. Because now I was terrified. He had my address and he was playing this game of . . . I don't know what he was trying to do. [. . .] I told the judge, "Look, you know, he's not paying child support. He's now jobless. [. . .] My future is in America. I'm an American citizen. The children are American. That's where our family is." [. . .] So it was pretty—it was getting costly to the [other country's] taxpayer. [The judge] finally said enough is enough, and he issued deportation orders for me and the kids. [. . .] My husband found out that we had left [. . . and after we returned to America], I got the papers that he had filed another Hague against me.

As Fiona* reports, she had no viable means of financial support—she was the only care provider for her young children, she couldn't work in the other country, and her husband was not paying child support. She eventually moved to a domestic violence shelter with the children, but once he found where she was, he began stalking her. Eight months later, the judge in the other country ordered that she and the children be deported back to the United States. Once she arrived, her husband tried to use the Hague petition again to force the return of the children, but he was unsuccessful this time because of the deportation order from the other country.

Fiona's* case illustrates the complexity of return for the women and children. Katie* similarly reported that her husband renewed his stalking and threatening behavior on her return to the other country. Austin* also experienced more domestic violence when she returned to the other country to petition for custody of her daughter. Her husband was supposed to bring her daughter for a visitation, but he didn't. Austin* reports that she confronted him about this outside of his apartment, and the following occurred:

> [My daughter] was starting to look uncomfortable, as you can figure, because she thought there was going to be an argument, you know, and . . . so I looked down to comfort her. The next thing I knew, I was on the ground. He just punched me. Just punched me. So I got up, [. . .] I tried to hit him back, because I just thought it was outrageous. I mean, you just don't understand. Now that he has this child, he feels that it's just sort of open season, where before, all the abuse was behind closed doors. Now that he has [our daughter], he can do whatever he wants. I went to the police station with a black eye that night. He told me, "Go right ahead. Nothing's going to happen to me." [. . . A psychologist] interviewed my daughter. [My ex-husband] was coaching my daughter to say "Mommy started that fight." And [the psychologist] wrote to the court: "I asked this child and she started to give me all these details. I asked this child how she knew all that. She said, 'Because Daddy told me to say that,' and she said, 'I'm really concerned that Mommy will be dead if Daddy continues to hit her like that.'"

In this situation, Austin's* ex-husband continued to physically assault her with impunity. Austin's* daughter saw this attack and worried that her mother might die as a result of the father's abuse. Unfortunately, this information was not sufficient to change the custody arrangements. Because of her escalating health problems, Austin* ended up returning to the United States without her daughter. Her husband was supposed to send the daughter for visitation with the mother, but after Austin* bought the airline tickets for him and her daughter, he refused to bring her. Austin* is still trying to negotiate an alternative custody agreement in the other country, but feels that she has been unsuccessful because her precarious health status is being used against her. At the time of the interview, she had not seen her daughter in more than a year.

These four cases illustrate a similar dynamic faced by some of the women prior to leaving the other country, namely that ending the relationship doesn't end physical violence by the husband. For each woman, having the children returned to the other country meant that she was once again vulnerable to his abusive behavior. As Austin* noted, having the US court decide in favor of returning the child to the other country—and most often to the father—was interpreted by her abusive husband as "open season" on her. Because the judicial process did not take into account the safety of the women, men had no reason to think they would be held accountable for continuing to victimize the women.

Several of the women who returned to the other country to be near their children after the Hague petition was granted reported great difficulty in being able to live in the other country. Fiona's* experience, recounted earlier, demonstrates some of the difficulties women had in caring for their children in the other country while separated from their husbands. Many women also had difficulty finding work because of their immigration status. In Stephanie's* case, she fled to the United States after incidents of physical violence from her husband that injured her and in which her child was an unintended victim. The judge ordered the child's return, but stipulated that Stephanie* would remain as the primary caregiver because the judge believed that the child might be at risk for additional harm if returned to the father. Once in the other country, Stephanie* reports,

> I was [initially] able to stay with these two ladies, through my former co-worker.
> [. . .] But my husband started to threaten, "If I don't know where you are staying, if
> I don't know the address, I'm going to go to the police and charge you with this and
> that." And actually, at that time, he could [. . .] have, and the ladies got so scared,
> and so they were afraid, and so they said, "We don't want any problems. We are
> sorry for what you're going through. But we have to have you out of here." So,
> within four days of that happening, of him threatening, we were out on the street.
> We landed on the street, with less than fifty euros in my pocket. [. . .] I landed on
> the doorsteps of the American church with my bags, and I said, "Please help me."
> And they did. They took us in. They paid for five days of hotel. [. . .] I was able
> to contact my parents, then. From then on, my parents started to pay for a little
> [room]. I don't have legal papers to be here. Right now, I'm here as a tourist, and I
> can't get a job. [The US judge] was presented with all these things, and yet, she sat
> there and she said . . . "As I sit here on this bench, there are many, many wonderful

Christian organizations around the world that can help you, especially in Europe, and I would imagine that [the other country] is one of those countries that provide a lot of support for people in your situation." [. . .] I had been doing my own research and [. . .] all I heard was, "You will not get help from anybody; not the government, or any association or organization because you're not a citizen, and you are not a refugee." We presented this to the judge. We presented an email from the American Embassy directed to my attorney, where they directly told us that I did not qualify for any help because of this; I was not a refugee, and I'm not a citizen. Still, [the judge] didn't care. [. . .] So now, we are in [city in other country]. [. . .] My husband is not helping me with my papers [or child support . . .]. We have no health insurance, no health protection at all. I am living on money from my family. They send me whatever little they can for food and to make the rent.

Stephanie's* situation highlights the difficulties many of the women faced once they returned to the other country. As she reports, she is unable to support herself there because she does not have the legal status to work. Her husband is not paying child support, and she is not eligible for support from the other country's government. As a result, her parents are providing a small amount of money each month to pay for rent and food. Stephanie* supplements this small allowance with food donations from the church that has assisted her. She reports that her attorney said that her husband is trying to force her to return to the United States without her son by withholding child support payments. At the time of our interview, she remained in the other country in these circumstances, trying to obtain sole custody of her son and the right to return to the United States.

Returning the children to the fathers resulted in continuing physical harm for 7 of the 12 women and their children who were forced back to the other country as a result of the Hague petition. In addition, many of the women had difficulty providing for themselves financially when they lived in the other country and tried to pursue a legal resolution to their situation in the other country's courts.

Women and Children Who Remained in the United States

In ten cases, husbands' Hague petitions did not result in the return of the children. Mothers and children who remained in the United States had three general outcomes: (1) no contact with the abusive ex-husband (three families), (2) resolution of custody and visitation such that he had exercised his visitation rights (four families), and (3) continued legal or domestic violence from the husband (four families). It is this third group that faced the significant difficulties that we will examine here in greater depth.

In the four cases where the custody and visitation issues had not been settled, husbands either continued attempting to intimidate the women directly, or made further legal efforts to have the children returned to them. Jennifer described one example of the persistence of some of the men in harassing the women, even months or years later. The incident she relates here happened six months after the divorce was finalized, and about a year after his Hague petition had been rejected:

> He was [nearby] . . . it was after the divorce . . . all I know is it was summertime. And he was . . . threatening us. He was calling us drunk on the phone. [. . .] I was terrified. Oh God. Oh God, he was calling, he was so drunk. And it was the middle of the night. [. . .] He sent a box that had [. . .] my dirty clothes that must have been left somewhere. [crying] And . . . the . . . and I just was so scared. [. . .] I called the police and I said, I don't know what to do. [. . .] And I had some emergency cash in a safe in the house, and I said, "Can you guys just stay? [crying] I'd pay you." And I went and I got my money out. And I just put it on the table, and I'm going, "Can you please stay?" Anyways, the police were wonderful. They said, "Lady, put your money in your pocket. Of course we'll stay." And they stayed. And they stayed in the house all night, [crying] with all the lights on while I was sleeping. [. . .]

Jennifer had been seriously physically assaulted by her ex-husband on multiple occasions in the other country, attacks that resulted in injuries requiring medical attention. She fled to the United States after a particularly vicious assault, after which he threw her, along with her three-day-old and three-year-old children, out of the house. Yet even after returning to the States, reestablishing herself, succeeding in asserting her defense against the Hague petition, and obtaining a divorce, she continued to cope with threatening and intimidating behavior from her ex-husband. Jennifer's case represents the most direct way that the husbands continued to harass the women. Three other women reported prolonged legal cases related to custody and visitation rights for their children.

The resolution of the Hague petition in the woman's favor did not necessarily produce an equivalent sense of closure for her emotionally. In the two excerpts that follow, Kendra and Pamela both discuss how they feel their lives have been permanently touched with a depth of uncertainty and trepidation about the future.

I think the bottom line is, there's never an end to this thing. And I think that's something I didn't realize. [. . .] And I still know I made the right decision—but I never understood that it would literally take over my life completely, forever. Um, as I said, I—my son is happy. He's graduating and stuff. But it—it took over my life. It's—it just—there's nothing left of the life that I had envisioned before this whole thing hit. (*Kendra*)

Because I felt that I couldn't be, because I was like, how can you be happy? It's sort of like when someone dies. This is how I explained it to one person. I said, "Imagine if a doctor comes to you and he says, 'We have found a tumor in your stomach. We don't know if it's cancerous. We don't know if it's not. But we really don't want to go in there and look at it right now. We could, but we're not going to. We're going to let it sit there for a certain amount of time; years even.' But, perhaps, one day it will be cancerous, or maybe you'll go on with your life and it won't be. But that tumor is still going to sit there." And that's how the Hague is to me. (*Pamela*)

For Kendra, the events that led up to the Hague petition and the continued legal conflict she has experienced since the Hague decision was made (more than four years later at the time of our interview) created a sense of timelessness. Her old life, the life she had envisioned for herself and her family, had been ended by these events. Pamela also related the idea that a death has occurred, that someone has died. But for her, the uncertainty created by the lack of resolution of her ex-husband's Hague petition is like a potentially fatal cancer—it could kill the new life she has established if the petition is reactivated in time, or it might lie dormant beyond the one-year deadline, and he may never cause her any more trouble. For her, the difficulty is in the uncertainty of which outcome will emerge.

Ending the Hague Process Did Not End the Abuse

To date, only one other small study has been done that investigated what happened after children were returned to the other country via a Hague petition (Reunite International, 2003). This study did not report on issues related to domestic violence. As a result, our research presents some of the first evidence about what occurs for battered women and their children after a Hague decision is made.

Women and their children faced great hardship when they returned to the other country. For seven of the families whose children were returned (58.3%), the women experienced renewed violence by the fathers, or children who had not previously been the targets of the men's physical violence became direct victims of physical abuse. By not recognizing the gravity of domestic violence against the women during the Hague petition process, courts returned children to situations that posed for them a grave risk of physical harm, and in three of these families, that risk became a reality. Although the Hague Convention has no focus on the effects of return for parents, it seems a travesty that the legitimate safety needs of the mothers in these situations were not considered in any part of their legal experience.

It was not just the mothers who followed their children back to the other country who were affected after the judicial decision on the Hague petition. Even mothers who succeeded in retaining their children in the United States faced continued threats and extensive fear that their abusive (ex-)husbands would hurt them or their children. Separation, either within the other country or across borders, does not end abusive behavior by persistent men, a fact well documented by the social science literature (Brownridge, 2006; DeKeseredy, Rogness, & Schwartz, 2004).

Domestic Violence Matters in Hague Convention Cases

Given the evidence presented regarding the domestic violence experiences of the women in this sample, the lack of resources that could ensure their safety in the other country, and the effects of exposure to domestic violence on their children, one could reasonably expect that *all* the children in these families would be allowed to stay with their mothers in the United States. But that is not what happened—the majority of the children were returned to the other country, which meant they usually went back to live with their fathers. As we will show in our analysis of published judicial opinions on Hague cases involving domestic violence (in chapter 7), the proportion of children returned to the other country among the families in this sample is similar to the decisions made in published legal rulings. The similarities between these two data sources suggest that domestic violence is not consistently recognized as a serious issue that should be considered when deciding where and with whom children will reside.

Strikingly, not a single judicial decision in the cases of mothers in this study (even those allowing the children to stay with their mothers in the States) found that the child was at "grave risk" of physical or psychological harm as a consequence of the domestic violence, despite the availability of this ruling to judges. We can only speculate on possible reasons for the lack of application of the Article 13(b) provision for grave risk in these cases. Because we did not have extensive access to the court proceeding records for the cases of mothers in our study, we could not verify whether domestic violence was directly presented to the judge in each case. In some cases, neither the woman's attorney nor the judge may have been privy to information about what was happening in the family, so domestic violence could not be factored into the decision. For judges who ruled that children could remain in the United States, it may be that they recognized and were concerned about domestic violence in these families, but they felt that a different legal avenue offered a stronger rationale for refusing to return the children to the other country. In those cases where the judges recognized that domestic violence was occurring, but returned the children to the other country anyway, it may be that the judges had misplaced faith in the availability of voluntary undertakings or social services to help protect battered mothers and children in the other country. Other judges indicated to the women that they felt it was more important to respect the capacity of each nation to protect children from harm, and to let the custody decisions be made there, than to ensure the safety of the women and children by allowing them to remain in the States. Unfortunately, some judges did not seem to believe that the domestic violence the women reported was serious enough to warrant a denial of the Hague petition.

The aftermath of Hague decisions illustrates the unintended consequences of these rulings. Although the Hague Convention is clearly understood to deal with the issue of court selection (that is, determining the habitual residence) and not the merits of child custody, the fact that children were usually returned to fathers in the other country meant that these decisions acted as de facto custody rulings. Some fathers in the other country used the fact that the children were returned by a US judge as proof that the mother acted illegally in fleeing with the children. US judges may not have been making custody rulings, but their Hague decisions were used to support the father's contention that he was the aggrieved party and that the children should be returned to him.

Decisions in Hague cases that involve domestic violence should be made in the context of understanding abuse as an ongoing pattern of emotional terrorizing and coercive control. As the women's stories attest, the Hague process can be used as a tool of abuse, rather than for its intended effect to ensure a remedy for child abduction that is seen as harmful to the child. Unfortunately, the Hague Convention can be used as a form of "procedural stalking" of victims (Miller & Smolter, 2011, p. 637). If the Convention is to be a policy that responds to the real needs for the safety of children, then processes must be developed that require assessment of and response to domestic violence in these cases.

6 | How Attorneys Litigate Hague Domestic Violence Cases

The literature reviewed in earlier chapters focused on domestic violence as an issue in abduction cases. There is also a small literature on litigating Hague Convention cases, but little in this literature directly addresses the issue of domestic violence. There are three primary published resources focused on the litigation of Hague cases. Two of these were published over a decade ago: one is *The Hague Convention on International Child Abduction* by Beaumont and McEleavy (1999) and the other is *International Child Custody Cases: Handling Hague Convention Cases in U.S. Courts* by Garbolino (2000). More recently, a guide for attorneys titled *Litigating International Child Abduction Cases under the Hague Convention*, by the law firm of Kilpatrick Stockton, LLP (2007), was published and widely distributed with the support of the National Center for Missing and Exploited Children.

Beaumont and McEleavy (1999) review the Hague Convention, examine the global case law to the late 1990s, and explore the various issues that have arisen around the world when Hague cases are filed and litigated. There is little direct mention of adult domestic violence in their scholarly review, but in a case involving a left-behind father in Colorado and a taking mother in Wales, UK, the authors describe a young child who was exposed to "random acts of violence witnessed by and directed to the child, together with intimidation and other inappropriate behavior" (p. 150). The four-year-old exhibited many trauma symptoms when living with his father, but then did not show these symptoms when the mother left him to live with her parents in Wales. The judge in Wales denied the father's petition for the child's return based on this evidence of psychological harm to the child.

The two other texts focus on litigating Hague cases solely in US courts. Garbolino's (2000) text, written for and distributed by the US National Judicial College, reviews the basic elements of Hague Convention cases and how these are handled under ICARA and in US courts. There is scant mention of domestic violence in this volume, except the description of a case to illustrate the use of undertakings by the court to insure that children are safe on return to their habitual residence.

Finally, the Kilpatrick Stockton (2007) manual is clearly written for attorneys representing left-behind parents. There is little mention of domestic violence except in suggestions for information gathering from left-behind parents. There is an extensive discussion of grave risk, and at least one case in this discussion involves parents whose "discord and alleged abuse" was a reason for a US judge to deny a petition for the return of a child to Australia.

The Beaumont and McEleavy (1999) and the Garbolino (2000) texts are more descriptive than prescriptive as to the actions attorneys should take in representing clients in Hague convention cases. The Kilpatrick Stockton (2007) manual is much more prescriptive, and advises attorneys to keep the Hague case focused on the narrow jurisdictional issue of habitual residence, that is, which country's court should be hearing and deciding custody and access issues. It argues that attorneys should make every effort not to allow these cases to be turned into a hearing on the merits of custody and access, but rather to stay focused on *where* such evidence should be heard and decided on. Not surprisingly, the approach advocated in the Kilpatrick Stockton (2007) manual is not instructive to attorneys for taking mothers who are *responding* to a Hague petition in US courts.

The International Child Abduction Database (INCADAT; www.incadat.com), maintained by the Permanent Bureau of the Hague Convention, provides another excellent source of information on judicial opinions, but tells us little about how attorneys for parents in these proceedings strategized on behalf of those they represented. The studies conducted by Reunite International in Europe are another source of information on Hague litigation. These studies, mentioned earlier, shed light on litigation of European Hague cases that may or may not include domestic violence. For example, the parents interviewed reported that agreements, or undertakings, by petitioners to implement changes in the other country were issued in just over one-half (57%) of the cases. The 2003 study revealed that two-thirds (67%) of the undertakings issued—including all focused on a child's safety upon return—were not implemented in the other country (Reunite International, 2003). Even when judges issued mirror orders (undertakings entered as court orders in both countries), only one in five of those mirror orders was implemented as planned. These findings by Reunite International are directly relevant to the US cases and the experiences of attorneys we interviewed, as we will discuss.

As this brief review illustrates, there is little information available on how attorneys represent respondents to a petition. We now turn to focus on the results of our interviews with both mothers' attorneys and those representing the petitioning fathers of their children, and highlight how a litigation approach on behalf of a taking mother differs from one on behalf of a left-behind father.

Our interviews revealed that the existence of domestic violence allegations raises unique issues for attorneys representing either respondents or left-behind petitioners, but particularly for those representing taking mothers who had to respond to the Hague petition. Six key dimensions in these Hague cases appeared repeatedly throughout the attorney interviews and are reviewed here. These included

(1) extensive resources required to defend against or pursue a Hague petition;

(2) aspects of the Hague Convention on which attorneys placed greatest importance;

(3) how attorneys on each side assessed the truthfulness of domestic violence allegations;

(4) extent of an attorney's effort to gather and bring evidence regarding domestic violence to bear in court proceedings;

(5) evaluation of whether to pursue a case in state or federal court; and

(6) ineffectiveness of undertakings, court orders, and mirror orders in assuring the safety of the child and mother on their return to the other country's jurisdiction.

Resources Required to Defend Against or Pursue a Hague Petition

Article 26 of the Hague Convention instructs Central Authorities or other agencies of states to provide for representation of petitioning parents. The United States invoked a reservation to this article and does not directly cover the costs of representation for petitioning left-behind parents (see Beaumont & McEleavy, 1999; Garbolino, 2000). Most other countries do, however, provide legal representation for left-behind parents. For example, both the UK and France appoint legal representatives for petitioning parents. In the UK, cases are heard by a limited number of High Court judges, who often have experience with prior Hague cases (see Beaumont & McEleavy, 1999, for more detail). This disparity between the United States and particularly the UK was known to the attorneys we interviewed, and the UK was seen as providing a better model. For example, two attorneys point to the UK as a model:

> You know, the British [system] is the best at that . . . They appoint counsel and they have competent counsel, so they know the Hague Convention, go right to court . . . they have wonderful compliance. (*Petitioner attorney*)

> And the High Court is the court that hears the treaty cases, and they have specialized judges who are experienced in it. In addition, and here's the big deal . . . UK provides legal services to the parties. The cases that are litigated before the High Court, for experienced judges . . . you have the most experienced attorneys, specialized attorneys who get paid if not 100% of their normal billing rate, an awfully close percentage of it by the government to do what they do best. (*Attorney who has represented both respondents and petitioners*)

Among the attorneys we interviewed, the concerns regarding the costs of representing a Hague case in US courts focused on three areas: (1) the overall costs for representation and the ability of clients to pay for this, (2) the resources and support provided to petitioning parents (usually fathers) that are seldom provided to respondents, and (3) the kinds of evidence that are required to effectively argue for exceptions to return of the child. We turn to each one of these now.

In the United States, the costs of representing Hague cases are met in a number of ways. These cases tend to be more complex than typical family law cases involving domestic violence, and they also tend to be expensive. The costs estimated by attorneys for both sides ranged from $35,000 to $200,000. This is somewhat similar to the mothers' estimates of case costs that ranged from $10,000 to $300,000, with a median of $30,000 and an average cost of $62,166. This is also fairly consistent with Chiancone et al.'s (2001) study a decade ago, in which left-behind parents estimated US legal costs of up to $200,000 with a median of $12,000 and a mean of $25,724.

Parents from other countries (the fathers in this study) often had access to many resources to meet these cost challenges. Although the United States invoked a reservation to the Hague Convention regarding public representation of left-behind parents, the US State Department did provide funding to the American Bar Association and NCMEC to establish the International Child

Abduction Attorney Network (ICAAN). ICAAN has now evolved into the US Department of State Attorney Network. The Network (and ICAAN before it) consists of a list of attorneys nationwide who are willing to act on a *pro bono* or reduced-fee basis for left-behind parents from other countries. The Network is specifically designed to provide "legal assistance to an eligible left-behind parent" (see http://travel.state.gov). The State Department also provides legal assistance to these attorneys representing left-behind parents in the form of translations, court orders, relevant legal documents, possible location of the child, helpful articles, model legal forms, and other assistance. According to Garbolino (2000), only the states of Washington and California have directly provided for representation of petitioners through their states' attorneys general or local prosecutors. US implementing legislation (ICARA) awards attorney costs to the left-behind parent if the petition is successful. The reverse is not true for taking parents, the mothers in this study.

These public, *pro bono*, or low-cost resources were systematically made available to left-behind fathers and their attorneys in our study. As one father's attorney notes,

> I wrote off a ton of time, but, for me . . . luckily my firm was paying me as an associate. I mean, we got paid, somewhat, but probably for half of what I did. (*Petitioner's attorney*)

Over two-thirds of the attorneys representing petitioning fathers came from law firms whose primary practice was litigation of corporate matters, and where undertaking a Hague case was more likely to be supported by the firm's *pro bono* resources. Only two of the eight petitioner attorneys interviewed were fully reimbursed for their work by the client or his family.

The same systematic help from ICAAN or the Attorney Network and the resources of larger firms were mostly absent for the taking mothers or their attorneys. Taking mothers are often perceived as the party committing an offense against their children and the left-behind parent, and thus were usually left on their own to find legal representation. Most of the respondent mothers found attorneys who were sole practitioners, part of small firms, or legal aid attorneys with few resources. This sometimes resulted in an imbalance that worked against the taking mothers, as the following statement by a mother's attorney indicates:

> Having three hundred lawyers at your disposal, free Westlaw, a network, a database, the whole thing, it was just David and Goliath; a total setup, surprised, the element

of surprise. Did they really have to have the federal marshals come in and swoop the children? I mean, it just reeked of abuse of power. (*Respondent's attorney*)

In 8 of the 15 cases where we interviewed mother respondents' attorneys, the mothers were able to secure *pro bono*, reduced-rate, or legal aid representation in their cases. In the 7 other cases, the mother and/or her family paid the full costs of litigation. Because many of the mothers' attorneys were sole practitioners or worked for small firms or legal aid offices, the costs of providing *pro bono* representation were often seen as more burdensome by mothers' attorneys. For example, an attorney who represented mothers in a number of Hague cases notes the difficulty in receiving payment for Hague defense services and the impact this had on her law practice:

> The most I've ever been paid is maybe $5,000, something like that, for something that I put literally hundreds of hours into and also took off, put my practice on hold, had to pay for hotel rooms, to travel outside of my city, stuff like that . . . as a small practitioner, for me it was—it's very burdensome and it's definitely not for the money that you do it. It has to be a labor of love or social consciousness. (*Respondent's attorney*)

Defending mothers in Hague proceedings was difficult for many attorneys. And these cases often move on short timelines. Yet it takes time to retrieve from foreign institutions the documentation needed to support grave risk and other exceptions, locate witnesses and hard-to-find records, translate witness interviews and records into English for the court, and then possibly provide translators during court sessions. The costs involved in Hague cases create hesitancy among attorneys to represent mothers. When asked for her advice to other attorneys considering representing a respondent in a Hague Convention case, one attorney replied, half in jest,

> Run for the hills! Close your practice, retire now. Go away, open an espresso stand, and move on with your life. What advice would I give them beyond that? I would say be sure that you understand that this is going to consume your law practice, if you do it properly, and so be very sure that you are financially capable to sustaining that, that you are prepared to take on that burden, dumped into your lap over night, because it's all done on an emergency basis. (*Respondent's attorney*)

This comment is emblematic of the expense that Hague cases represent, and of the ambivalence of some attorneys to accept these cases in the face of the resources required to provide adequate legal support to both mothers and fathers.

Judicial Comity among Nations versus Children's Interests

While the concerns for litigation costs were shared across both mothers' and fathers' attorneys, a difference emerged based on the weight each side gave to various provisions in the Hague Convention. Specifically, this difference focused on how they balanced the requirements of judicial comity among nations, as briefly mentioned in the introduction, with sometimes competing interests in the treaty's exceptions to allow for considering the safety and interests of the children involved in these cases. A major theme, primarily among attorneys who represented fathers, was that mutual respect among nations' judicial systems required upholding the treaty and keeping any exceptions narrow so as to accomplish a prompt return, despite reservations the attorney may have had about the other country's cultural norms or legal and social systems. For example, one attorney who has represented primarily petitioners but also respondents expresses sympathy for the plight of mothers in these cases, but nonetheless takes a strict line on treaty enforcement:

> [T]hey go to a country where their custody laws are male centered, dominated, and the father tends to be a naturalized citizen of that country, and they're Americans, and they feel like, and I'm sure legitimately so, that they're not going to get a fair hearing on custody in the country they're in. And so, they leave to avoid that. And while I totally understand that and can only imagine what they're going through, the law, as far as I'm concerned, just doesn't support that.

The same attorney continues:

> But, if we're going to have the treaty, we have to enforce it, and I think that we need to keep the exceptions to the narrow circumstances that I think they are originally intended to cover, and maybe there needs to be some redrafting of things, if that's what it's going to be. But the ideal outcome is that generally, the people would return to the country where they were living and try their custody cases there.
> (*Attorney who has represented both respondents and petitioners*)

An alternate view among attorneys was that while the treaty's intent for prompt remedies is to be respected, the goal of protecting the interests of children should be front and center. This stance was most often adopted by mothers' attorneys, referring to the purposes of the Hague Convention as stated in the first line of the Convention's preamble: "Firmly convinced that the interests of children are of paramount importance in matters relating to their custody"

(Hague Conference on Private International Law, 2010). The intention of the Hague Convention clearly was and is to protect children from harm, albeit with an emphasis on the harm that abduction may cause in children and their families. It was this focus on protecting children where many of the attorneys, particularly those for the mothers, placed their attention, in contrast to others who focused on enforcing the return of children. For example, an attorney who had represented several mothers who were respondents states,

> There should be some remedy for the non-offending parent [petitioner], but I just don't see how it's appropriate to allow the children to suffer even more by being taken away summarily from someone [respondent] that has been their sole custodian for years sometimes. (*Respondents' attorney*)

There has been considerable discussion in the literature about the use of the Hague Convention's exceptions or defenses, especially Article 13(b). Some have viewed attempts by mothers' attorneys to invoke these exceptions as an effort to thwart or undermine the effectiveness of the Hague Convention (see Hilton, 1997). However, a clear focus of mothers' attorneys was to view exceptions or defenses as valid elements of the Hague Convention and reasons for denying petitions. Mothers' attorneys sought to expand the original formulations of exceptions with arguments based on the growing social science literature on children's exposure to domestic violence. For example, an attorney who had represented several battered mothers as respondents in Hague Convention cases states her view that even though the treaty expects the prompt return of children, the grave risk exception should be invoked in cases of adult domestic violence to deny petitions for the children's return:

> Well, in every case, I tried to make the domestic violence against the mother central, and I used the exception for return, which is called grave danger to the child. And I argued that domestic violence against the mother posed a risk of great danger to the child were the child to be returned; both because the mother would have to return with the child to protect the child, and then, she would be subjected to danger, because a parent who subjects another parent to abuse is, you know, by definition not fit to be a good parent to a child. I argued that domestic violence frequently co-occurs with child abuse. (*Respondents' attorney*)

It is not surprising then, given this tension between international obligations and the protection of children's interests, that the legal strategies of petitioners' and respondents' attorneys subsequently focused on discrediting or accepting allegations of domestic violence and arguing that these allegations be given a lesser or greater weight in the case hearing.

Assessing Allegations of Domestic Violence

Attorney views of domestic violence allegations were very divergent. In particular, attorneys disagreed about how to assess whether an allegation of domestic violence was truthful. The major points of divergence in opinions were in four key areas: (1) the attorney's frame of mind, (2) the issue of report fabrication, (3) the evidence necessary to substantiate a claim, and (4) the importance of cultural differences.

The mothers' attorneys evaluated the women when they first met, and performed a typical screening to discover patterns of domestic violence and other corroborating evidence. It was neither assumed that there was domestic violence, nor was it assumed that the woman was making false allegations. As one attorney relates,

> They come in and they describe a level of fear that you can just tell what they've been going through . . . normally they're pretty . . . I don't know how to describe it except to say that they are really shaken. I mean, many times, there are not 911 calls, you know, and there are not pictures of bruises. (*Respondent's attorney*)

The views of the fathers' attorneys differed markedly from those of the mothers' attorneys. Because they did not interview the woman alleging the abuse except on the witness stand, these attorneys were frequently suspicious of her allegations. One fathers' attorney, for example, says this:

> I'm . . . you know, I'm suspicious. I want to be able to prove it to a court. So, I would say suspicious in that I doubt it. But, I gotta have something, you know, preferably some corroborating evidence like a medical record, a police report, you know, something. (*Petitioners' attorney*)

Because evidence of abuse is not often readily available, especially without the opportunity to talk to the victim, a suspicion of false allegations often existed among the fathers' attorneys. The abuse was viewed as an allegation that could be used by mothers as a defense against the return of the children, and at the very least, it painted fathers in a bad light. Therefore, the fathers' attorneys viewed these allegations by mothers as immediately suspect, as charges to be discredited and countered.

The mothers' attorneys, on the other hand, largely disputed the idea that women fabricate domestic violence allegations in order to allow the children to stay with them. Some claimed that the fathers' attorneys are suspicious because they rarely meet with the women to assess the signs of abuse; others suggested this is a vestige of a sexist society that views claims of domestic violence as frivolous. No matter the reason, however, most mothers' attorneys agreed that women fabricating reports of domestic violence was not a major problem. As one notes,

> I think that is an argument based in sexist viewpoints to view that women will make things up to gain custody. That argument is just old and tired and repeated all the time. I'm just offended by it. (*Respondents' attorney*)

The fathers' attorneys, on the other hand, viewed the issue of fabrication of evidence as a significant problem. For example, one fathers' attorney even suggests that a respondent self-inflicted severe wounds that she attributed to abuse by her husband:

> Obviously, obvious physical injuries can be, obviously, a proof. Although in one case, I'm certain the physical injury was self-inflicted. But, the claim was made that the father had done it. (*Petitioners' attorney*)

Another difference in how mothers' and fathers' attorneys assessed the truthfulness of claims is the evidence they demanded to make a determination of credibility. The mothers' attorneys claimed that evidence of one violent episode was enough to equal abuse, and that even if only one event resulted in physical harm, it almost never occurred without other forms of abuse and coercive control being present over a long period of time. The mothers' attorneys argued that evidence of an abusive personality—for example, obsessively calling the respondent—could be used to show evidence of abuse to the court and to assess their clients' credibility.

In contrast, the fathers' attorneys stated that evidence of one episode of physical domestic violence, especially if it had occurred years before, would not be valuable evidence of domestic violence. These attorneys stated that in order to really have a credible claim there needed to be physical evidence, photographs, police reports, or hospital or similar records of repetitive action. Although both sets of attorneys agreed this evidence was valuable, the fathers' attorneys suggested that it was a prerequisite to having a valid and credible claim. One attorney for a father even stated that he believed the mother should be forced to take a lie detector test in order to determine if her claims were credible, despite such evidence not being admissible in court.

Despite all these differences, the mothers' and fathers' attorneys did look at some aspects of domestic violence in the same way. Both agreed that domestic violence was not really considered when drafting the Hague Convention, and thus does not fit easily into an exception. They also agreed that substantial evidence is needed to make a successful claim that domestic violence could pose a grave risk to the children. The differences between the two kinds of attorneys, however, were fundamental in how each framed the case, and the legal representation each client received.

Attorney Effort in Hague Cases

How clients were represented in these cases varied greatly. Seven of the mothers' attorneys and two of the fathers' attorneys had never before represented a client in a Hague case; three others on both sides had represented clients in 2 to 4 cases. Only three attorneys had represented clients in 30 or more cases, and these attorneys overwhelmingly represented petitioners, usually fathers, in their practices. Inexperienced practitioners emphasized the intensive preparation Hague cases required; while all attorneys noted the significant effort needed to retrieve evidence from other countries, to secure witness testimony, and to obtain expert witness evaluations for their cases.

Preparation Needed to Present Hague Defense

Sometimes attorneys with no Hague experience had only hours in which to research the Hague Convention before appearing in court with their respondent clients. Substantial preparation was needed to mount these cases effectively and required effort by the attorneys, their clients, and sometimes expert witnesses. Attorneys reflected on their lack of knowledge about the Hague Convention and how much new preparation was involved to ensure their clients were well represented.

The concept of *lawyering* was posed by one attorney as a major aspect of her success representing clients. In his essay on good lawyering, Robinson (1994) states that a good lawyer "will be a powerful advocate for his or her clients" (p. 38). Four of Robinson's pillars of good lawyering are enthusiasm, effort, attention, and research. These themes of good lawyering were evident in our interviews, as shown in this statement by one attorney who had represented both types of clients:

> [T]he reality really needs to be brought out, I think in terms of, not necessarily changing the language of our treaty, but in looking at how we lawyer, and looking at how we advise clients, what we do about mirror orders, what we do about international comity, how we address the mutual enforcement of those orders. I mean, that's really where the protection lies. (*Attorney who has represented both respondents and petitioners*)

The effort attorneys made to collect evidence and witness testimony from the other country despite distance and language barriers, and to secure the participation of well-prepared expert witnesses on child well-being and local laws appeared to be major markers of powerful advocacy by both mothers' and fathers' attorneys. Each of these three domains of good lawyering is reflected in the sections that follow.

Retrieving Evidence from the Other Country

An important, time-consuming, and expensive element of lawyering on behalf of a mother was the collection of documentation to substantiate her claims of abuse at the hands of her husband. Attorneys for both sides stressed the importance of backing up mothers' claims of abuse with evidence from the other country. Attorneys took very different views of the feasibility of such an effort, as reflected in the following two statements. The first attorney clearly sees the effort needed to find supporting testimony to be beyond his ability or resources to perform, and in this case, perhaps unnecessary as a petitioner's attorney. The second attorney takes the opposite tack, emphasizing the importance of obtaining evidence from the other country.

> I don't know what else I could do. I mean, to do discovery in [the other country]? Go down to [the other country] and interview witnesses and . . . you know, forget it. You know what I mean? (*Petitioner's attorney*)

> I think it was *really* important in this case that we be able to document with something other than merely the words of my client, and the words of the children, that this had actually occurred, and it wasn't a one-time event, but it was a pattern, and it had occurred on many occasions. (*Respondent's attorney*)

Attorneys who were more experienced in Hague cases developed strategies to manage the unusual labor these cases required. One strategy of mothers' attorneys was to secure more time in US courts, to allow them to obtain the evidence needed from the other country to mount an adequate defense. Some attorneys also hired an investigator or attorney in the other country to assist in collecting this evidence. Hiring an expert familiar with the other country was seen as particularly important in interpreting the laws and legal system of that locale. However, these strategies were expensive and not necessarily easy to implement, as these two attorneys suggest:

> Well, it's lack of access to the evidence . . . You are kind of fighting with one arm behind your back in that regard . . . hire some kind of private investigator in the other country. You need someone who is familiar with the legal system, someone who [speaks] and [reads] the language, of course, someone who is reliable and would be able to do some investigation, so if you had a client who, you know, had some money, that would be one thing I would suggest an attorney should do, is hire an investigator. And also, you need additional time to gain access to the records that are pertinent. (*Respondent's attorney*)

> So, you really need someone in the other country that you can contact that can help you find out what actually happened there, or who can advise you on, for example, what the law of custody is in those countries, and it's very hard if you're in the US to find somebody willing to do that, again, on sort-of a *pro bono* basis in those other countries. (*Respondent's attorney*)

Securing Witness Testimony from This and the Other Country

It was not only documents from the other country that required extra effort by the attorneys, it was also identifying and presenting the testimony of witnesses. These witnesses were not only relatives and friends of the parties to the case, but also country experts who could shed light on the local culture as well as legal protections and social services available to both the mother and child if they were to return to the other country. As one respondent's attorney states,

> [W]e did put in evidence about a number of things in [the other country] about general cultural attitudes, about the legal system and how it addressed domestic violence, the resources available in terms of domestic violence counseling, and the

facilities and some cultural things. We were able to get a woman who was a human rights worker in [the other country] to put an affidavit on some of these things, and she was extremely convincing. So in that case, we did put in country-specific evidence. (*Respondent's attorney*)

A creative way of presenting live witnesses was to present them in court via telephone or videoconference calls connecting the two countries. One petitioner's attorney describes a complex but inexpensive mechanism for presenting witness testimony, a mechanism suggested by the judge in the case:

There's kind of a logistical challenge . . . 'cause you have to do a deposition with somebody overseas, and you have to get a translator. That is a challenge. I was, in both cases, impressed with how easy it was to conduct the depositions over the phone, with the translator . . . Another challenge is just simple, and this has turned into an issue in my second case. It's when you have witnesses in a foreign country. The man from [the other country] flew up here. But he could not afford to bring in four or five [witnesses from the other country]. And in the [other] case the woman, she was pregnant with the couple's second child at the time of the hearing. So she could not travel. As a result, at [the judge's] suggestion . . . in the first case he said that he wanted the [witnesses in the other country] to testify from someplace that was official, like an American Consulate, and there was an American Consulate . . . The consulate was extremely helpful in facilitating the use of the phone and the facilities at the consulate, so it just worked flawlessly having the [witnesses from the other country] go to the consulate at the particular time they were let in. They were taken to a waiting room. Then they were taken into a room and sworn to testify one by one, and the same thing was done with the American Consulate [in the other case]. And these are the sort of logistical things in a case that can just be a nightmare. But in both of these cases it was the best cooperation that I ever had from any consulate in the United States government. They were just real helpful. (*Petitioner's attorney*)

Securing Expert Witness Assessments and Testimony

The final of the three domains of lawyering that emerged as themes in our interviews was the preparation and use of expert witnesses to testify regarding the well-being of the children involved in these cases. Experts usually focused on the physical and psychological risk that might occur if the children were returned to the other country, an Article 13(b) defense. Some attorneys, however, were skeptical of using experts because they felt that experts were appointed by one side or the other, and thus were more likely to have biased views based on who had paid for their consultation. As this attorney notes,

> I try to avoid expert witnesses because the whole nature of these cases is that they're supposed to be summary . . . I'm very suspect about experts and the use of experts in America—because each side gets its own experts . . . And although the federal rules allows for the court to appoint an expert, they tend not to do that . . . Almost every other civilized country in the world has come to the view that you can't have that . . . the court must appoint an expert and the expert's oath and duty must be solely to the court. America takes the opposite view, that everyone's entitled to their own experts who are paid to say whatever the person wants them to say. I'm—as you can hear—very cynical about experts. (*Attorney who has represented both respondents and petitioners*)

Most attorneys on both sides of these cases did not take such a cynical view of using expert witnesses. The importance of expert testimony is evident in the three attorney statements that follow.

> Getting some really good forensic psychologists to do a psychological evaluation. That's the best thing that we, as human beings, have in a human court of law. (*Petitioner's attorney*)

> [T]he court originally started out not at all sympathetic to our position, particularly since there were allegations that the mother and children were not here legally. And we were really able, I think, to convince the court, to educate the court and give the court an understanding of the real picture—the real negative effects it would have on the psychological makeup of the child if they had to go back, and what it would be like for the child to be returned to a place and sort of re-live the domestic violence that had occurred there. So I think experts can be extremely important if you're able to get one. (*Respondent's attorney*)

> [T]ry to get those psychological evaluations, and all the things you need to show as much objective evidence. I mean, the problem with DV [domestic violence] is always the lack of evidence . . . Especially if they're talking about a foreign country, where, you know, getting a police report or even having the police take a report would be impossible. So it basically comes down to credibility and if the kids are young, and they can't really testify, so you have to do as much as you can to bolster the case. The psychological reports for us, helped. (*Respondent's attorney*)

Each of these three attorneys discussed the need to obtain an outside evaluation of the psychological issues that could be present for children in these cases. For respondents' attorneys, finding experts who could also report on the effect of domestic violence on the child was an important reason to use expert testimony.

The presentation of expert testimony was not always helpful in cases, and seemed to depend on how well the expert was prepared to testify. As one father's attorney points out, the expert hired by the mother's attorney in this particular case was not well prepared:

> There was nobody from [the other country who] was called as a witness to corroborate that [the children were exposed to domestic violence] . . . there was nothing, except for she did go to see a psychiatrist here in town, very well respected, who . . . ultimately in his deposition said that it would be in the child's best interest to stay here in the States. But he never got to the level which the Hague requires of saying . . . substantial harm. And since he could not get to that level . . . And unfortunately, to be honest, I'm sure that her expert hadn't been properly informed about what the level was, because if he was, I'm sure that there may have been some other testimony. (*Petitioner's attorney*)

It appeared that in one case, the expert testimony was discounted by the judge because the father never came to the United States, and thus the expert had no opportunity to either interview the father or see him interact with his children.

Overall, attorneys for both fathers and mothers mostly valued the role that experts played in these cases, and felt that, when possible, experts should be used to provide information in support of their cases. These attorneys were in less agreement on the court in which these cases should be heard, the next issue we will consider.

Federal and State Concurrent Jurisdiction in Hague Convention Cases

The federal system in the United States provides two different forums in which a case may be brought: state court or federal court. The petitioner initially decides the forum by choosing where to file the claim. If there is concurrent jurisdiction, as there is in Hague Convention cases, then the respondent may challenge the initial forum selection. Concurrent jurisdiction is provided in ICARA and, therefore, Hague cases may be filed by the petitioner in either federal or state court. If the respondent wants to change the forum, his or her attorney will have to follow the rules of civil procedure to petition for removal to the other court.

Preference for State or Federal Court

Mothers' attorneys were split on the preference for state or federal court, and were equally convinced of the appropriateness of their selected forum for the clients they represented. At times, it appeared that the preference for a particular court was based on local contextual factors, such as which sitting judge seemed more favorably inclined to allow a full hearing of evidence or to consider the physical and psychological harm that the impact of adult domestic violence may have had on the mothers and children involved.

Most of the 15 mothers' attorneys argued that state courts should be the preferred forum for several reasons. They argued that federal court judges would either be unfamiliar with family matters, especially the dynamics of domestic violence, or have little desire to explore them. These attorneys also viewed the state courts, where family matters were commonly heard and where judges may have been better informed on issues of family violence, to be a friendlier forum for their clients and the children involved. For example, here are statements by two mothers' attorneys:

> [Y]ou don't become a federal judge to do these kinds of cases, and they just don't want to deal with domestic violence. (*Respondent's attorney*)

> Most judges in federal court either haven't had to deal with them [family matters], or just don't like them. (*Respondent's attorney*)

Despite these arguments for state court hearings, several mothers' attorneys we interviewed were equally clear that they preferred to have Hague petitions heard in federal rather than state court, sometimes for the very same reasons just expressed. First, one attorney suggested that due process may be more available in federal than in state courts because federal courts do not have expertise in family matters, and judges would want to take more time to understand the issues. The experience of this attorney was that the federal judge, who was less knowledgeable about family matters, was actually more willing than the state court judge to seek a full hearing of the evidence in a trial, including hearing the opinions of expert witnesses. Second, a few mothers' attorneys also expressed the opinion that because federal courts commonly handle international law cases, they might also be more comfortable with Hague Convention cases and more careful to fully examine the treaty's provisions, including allowable exceptions to return, such as grave risk. Finally, it was also pointed out that the Hague Convention was originally designed with a

Central Authority and central court in mind, as is the practice in the UK and elsewhere. One attorney even suggested that ICARA be revised to exclude state courts from hearing cases arising from international treaties such as the Hague Convention.

The eight attorneys who had represented petitioning fathers in these cases were consistently in favor of using the federal courts for petitioning parents and state courts for respondent parents. They believed that federal courts not only had different philosophies regarding these cases, but also had more resources to enforce rulings for the petitioning parent. For example, two petitioning attorneys sum it up this way:

> It was my decision to file it in federal court, and . . . the reason I did it at the time, I know exactly why, . . . because I knew I was going to face a best-interest argument, and I was concerned that the state judges would look at it on a best-interest level versus really looking at the significant harm, and that they would decide it as a custody case. And I was going to lose a custody case. I wanted it in front of a federal judge who would really look at the substantial harm argument and was not used to deciding custody cases on a—you know—best-interest standard. (*Petitioner's attorney*)

> The federal court . . . they're much more powerful. When we were trying to get a child back, we had an emergency order, and the US Marshals grabbed that kid, no questions. It was just done. Getting the sheriff to do it, it was like, well, we'll pull resources from our child protection cases. You know, which is the priority? It seems like the US Marshals, they just did it. There was not a hesitation. They had a court order. They just did it. So, there's the power of the federal government to pull a kid out of a dangerous situation, versus the lack of resources at the state or county level . . . I guess the decision making, why you go federal or state, is important to me. If I represent a victim of domestic abuse, I'd almost certainly go with the state courts. I mean, frankly, even if they're wrong . . . I mean, even if the law isn't on your side . . . Say mom pulled the kids, is alleging abuse, but that should be decided in [the other country]. You know, the family courts here are a little more sympathetic to things, whereas I think a federal court would just say "Nope, [back to other country]." (*Petitioner's attorney*)

In summary, the mothers' attorneys were of two minds regarding a preference for one court forum over another. The fathers' attorneys, however, consistently identified the federal court as the preferred venue for their clients and saw disadvantages to petitioners facing a hearing in state family court. The partiality of attorneys on both sides led to efforts to maneuver their clients' cases into the preferred forum.

Removal of Cases to the Other Court

As one might imagine, securing the venue most advantageous to your client is an important strategy, and one that often created tension between the counsel for the fathers and mothers.

Although the fathers' attorneys chose the forum in which to file the Hague petition, at least some respondents' attorneys were clear that they could move to have the case heard in a different court if their client desired. For example, in one case, the two sides fought to move the case back and forth between state and federal court, with the federal court finally granting the mother's request for removal of the case to federal court. Many of these motions are emergencies that play out minute by minute, as this description by a mother's attorney reveals:

> [W]hen I told [co-counsel] about the federal court sending it back, he said that was absolutely wrong, and they immediately filed this emergency stay, and motion to reconsider the decision of sending it back to state court. So, the thing is that state court had it docketed for the next morning at 9:00 a.m., so they got this motion filed the day before at 3 p.m., the day before the state court hearing at 9:00 a.m. So, it was just a lot of drama. And we went into state court not knowing, you know, calling the federal court judge every five minutes asking has the judge made a decision? Has the judge made a decision? And finally the last phone call was, yes, she was granted the emergency stay, and the motion to reconsider. (*Respondent's attorney*)

In summary, mothers' and fathers' attorneys examined both state and federal courts from a variety of views, seeking the best forum for their clients. In some cases this was the state court, and in others the federal court. Regardless of their preference, there was evidence that many attorneys developed strategies to place their cases before the court that they viewed as most advantageous to their clients' interests.

The Use of Undertakings and Mirror Orders in Hague Cases

Judges' decisions to grant the petitioning fathers' requests for return of their children to the other countries evoked strong views among the attorneys on both sides, particularly on the use of undertakings and mirror orders. Undertakings and mirror orders are mechanisms used in Hague cases in an effort to protect the mother or children when they return to the country of habitual residence. For example, a father may agree to an undertaking stating that he will pay for the return transport of the child and mother, or guarantee the mother visitation with the children (Silberman, 2000). Judges may enter these agreements as orders in the court, but they are only viable within the jurisdiction of the issuing court.

Some judges have sought to arrange mirror orders to provide enforcement in the other country of a US court's orders. In arranging a mirror order, the US judge seeks the cooperation of a judge in the other country, sometimes with the help of Central Authorities, to develop a court order that is acceptable in both countries' courts. This order is then entered in both countries' courts. Mirror orders may be based on undertakings, or may be the result of a judicial determination of necessary conditions for return (Silberman, 2000). These orders are also referred to as *mirror-image orders* (Garbolino, 2000) and sometimes *safe harbor orders* (Beaumont & McEleavy, 1999). One attorney in our study referred to mirror orders as a "safe harbor provision."

The value of these orders depended on the likelihood of enforcement in the country of habitual residence. If the government of the other country did not enforce the orders, they were likely to be useless. Most of the attorneys on both sides agreed that undertakings established in US courts were of limited use in other countries, and that mirror orders issued by both countries when sending children back to their habitual residence was a practice that was preferable but also seldom enforced. As can be seen in chapter 5, the mothers in our study reported that undertakings were not enforced once the mother and children returned to the other country. This is consistent with the findings in a study of European Hague cases cited earlier (Reunite International, 2003). As one father's attorney noted, there is limited usefulness of court orders from the US being enforced in other countries:

> But there is a problem which is also written about, which is that the undertakings in fact are not enforceable according to the other country that takes jurisdiction if it doesn't want to enforce them. (*Petitioner's attorney*)

These doubts about the usefulness and enforcement of undertakings led most mothers' attorneys to avoid requesting them. Even when courts were willing to stipulate specific actions by the father, there were serious doubts among mothers' attorneys about the degree to which these undertakings would provide safety to the children and their mother, if she also returned. Typical of this group of attorneys' statements are the following two:

> There was no specific undertaking. I think the court was concerned that the undertakings would not be enforceable in the other country. (*Respondent's attorney*)

> These undertakings—that are given—are flouted all the time . . . The us courts do not follow through on the undertakings they've given to the requesting countries' courts. (*Respondent's attorney*)

As a result, children in this study often returned to the other country to live with their fathers with few protections, and mothers sometimes faced criminal kidnapping charges or lacked access to their children after their return.

When considering the use of undertakings, the mothers' attorneys were clear that the court orders based on these undertakings must be very specific to the actions that the father agrees to take, and that completion of these actions should be made *before* the child is returned. For example, one mother's attorney states,

> I think the court really has to be detailed with regard to the undertaking. I mean, it's very important that the court takes this into account. You can't just assume that everything's going to be fine once the mother . . . once the respondent returns to the original country. The court should make the largest effort to make sure that for the respondent sent back, that these undertakings have been performed and such, that the petitioner's actually complying with everything they said they were going to do. (*Respondent's attorney*)

Even with strong reservations about the usefulness of undertakings and orders by us courts, some mothers' attorneys asked the courts to issue detailed orders out of concern for both the children and their mother. Sometimes these requests were refused by the judge, as is evident in the following case:

> We argued that the respondent have temporary physical custody of the children, that they return with her to [the other country]. That he [petitioner] would have no contact with my client. That the charges against her for kidnapping be dropped. And we said that in securing the safe harbor, the court would have to communicate and collaborate with the [other country's] court. And she [the judge] refused. (*Respondent's attorney*)

The mother's attorney in this case believed that the judge refused the request for an order because she had made a decision to quickly return these children to the other country and did not want arranging a mirror order with a judge in the other country to slow that process.

Frustration among mothers' attorneys over enforcement led some to go this one step further, and to suggest that the judge hearing Hague petitions should, as mentioned earlier, take steps to find a judge in the country of habitual residence and establish an agreement with the foreign court to follow through on the undertakings being considered, as this mother's attorney states:

> If they're deciding that the respondent should return the child, the court should make sure that the custody proceeding in the other country, they should communicate with the other court in that country to make sure that there will be speedy, a very speedy resolution to the custody proceeding. (*Respondent's attorney*)

This statement implies the use of mirror orders.

An attorney who has represented both mothers and fathers explains the idea behind mirror orders quite clearly, and also believes that US courts currently underutilize this tool:

> In commercial litigation, we have orders that require foreign corporations and foreign entities to do things all the time. There's nothing unusual about that. There is a mechanism that needs to be employed in order to have an order that's rendered in one country, enforceable in another. And, so, if there's an order in the United States and it includes undertakings, what needs to happen is, and typically, particularly if the habitual residence has been determined, there should be no problem in establishing jurisdiction for the entry of a mirror order. What often happens is that that process is either not done; a mirror order is not generated or drafted, the condition of a mirror order is not included in the original orders, and, you know, no action is taken. (*Attorney who has represented both respondents and petitioners*)

This same attorney continues explaining the process of obtaining mirror orders:

> You know, to get a mirror order, you can't just walk into the court with a US order and say I'd like you to sign here. I mean, it's another country. You may have to file an application if one has not been filed. I mean, typically, in a lot of our cases, there's already been something filed in the left-behind country. And so there's a docket number, and so there's an opportunity to be able to use that docket number as a basis without having to file an additional complaint or whatever. But in some cases, you have to file something. And you have to file a consent order, and that consent order has to specify and, typically, what it should have are the factual stipulations, like if it rose to the exercise of jurisdiction by the court, what it is that

you are both agreeing that you're going to do by way of stipulation, 'cause what a mirror order does is it says, "We've been ordered by court X to do this, and we are agreeing that we're going to abide by that in the same place." . . . the idea that you can just take an order from the United States, get on an airplane and *walk* into some police station, or walk to the court and say "I'm an American and here's my order." Well, no! That's never going to happen. And if it does, it's by the grace of some very smart judge on the other side, who's decided to be cooperative. There's a mechanism for things, and for the enforcement of foreign orders, and you gotta figure out what that is. And so, no, undertakings don't work automatically. (*Attorney who has represented both respondents and petitioners*)

In short, attorneys on both sides of these cases viewed voluntary undertakings by the father with great skepticism. The reports of mothers in this study and the analysis of European cases by Reunite International (2003) indicate that enforcement of undertakings is sorely lacking and a major obstacle yet to be overcome.

Recommendations for Improving Practice

Not surprisingly, mothers' and fathers' attorneys differed on some issues, but they also agreed on others. Both sides' attorneys were concerned about the costs of representing Hague Convention cases. They advocated for more support from the Central Authority (the US Department of State) for legal representation for their clients. Though many mothers and fathers received *pro bono* or low-cost legal representation, the avenues to receiving such help differed. Fathers were more often referred to legal representation via the Department of State's Attorney Network or its predecessor, and were represented more often by attorneys in large law firms. In contrast, mothers most often found representation through legal aid agencies or small family law practices, and less often through referral by the Central Authority.

Both sides also agreed that concepts of good lawyering were key to providing effective representation for their clients. Attorneys who made efforts to secure evidence and the participation of witnesses about events, expert witnesses who assessed the impact of family violence on the children, and other experts on the laws and services available in the other country appeared to live up to Robinson's (1994) concept of good lawyering. Others, either due to fiscal constraints or assumptions about the likely outcome of their cases, did not achieve the same level of advocacy for their clients.

Finally, these attorney interviews also led us to question the value of voluntary undertakings agreed on by the petitioning father in US courts. Attorneys on both sides questioned the degree to which such undertakings were enforced, mothers in our study reported that they were not enforced, and European research suggests that skepticism about enforcement is well founded (Reunite International, 2003). This led some to argue that mirror orders, entered in both countries' courts, should be standard practice. However, as pointed out by some interviewed attorneys, this can be very time-consuming, and possibly expensive to carry out effectively; and at least one judge in our study was reported reluctant to engage in the development of a mirror order. Even when mirror orders were in place, there were questions about the degree to which they were enforced (Reunite International, 2003).

The views of attorneys for mothers and fathers diverged on other aspects of the Convention, their cases, and representation of their clients. First, there were clearly differences in the importance that attorneys placed on various elements of the Hague Convention. Not surprisingly, many fathers' attorneys placed greatest importance on the prompt return of children, and viewed exceptions narrowly and their use as undermining the Convention's purposes. Mothers' attorneys largely viewed the safety of their clients and their clients' children as their key focus. They viewed the Convention's exceptions as important components that were intended to allow discretion by a country's courts to decide that concerns for child safety override the goals of prompt return.

It appeared that experts brought in to testify on the grave risk to children were prepared to varying degrees to address the level of evidence required in Hague cases. While establishing habitual residence only requires a *preponderance of evidence*, establishing grave risk of physical or psychological harm requires a higher level of *clear and convincing evidence*. In particular, expert witnesses on behalf of mothers in this study needed information on the criteria for establishing grave physical or psychological harm and how an intolerable situation might be construed under Article 13(b) of the Convention. The term *intolerable situation* was not raised by any attorneys interviewed for this study. When Article 13(b) was invoked, respondents' attorneys focused solely on grave risk terminology. More careful preparation of expert witnesses and clearer assessments of children are called for, given the level of proof required in Hague cases.

When the Hague Convention was developed in 1980, there was no literature on the impact of exposure to domestic violence on children's physical and psychological well-being. The social science research in the intervening three decades has clearly established possible risks to children exposed to domestic violence that may be as significant as those to children who have been direct victims of physical or sexual abuse (Kitzmann et al., 2003; Wolfe et al., 2003). The interpretations of what constitutes a grave physical or psychological risk or an intolerable situation for a child need to be revised based on the current social science available. Even if a narrow definition of grave risk is maintained, the evidence strongly argues that exposure to adult domestic violence be part of such a definition of risk to the child. Only a few attorneys in this study understood and applied this body of literature while arguing their cases. The Swiss government, concerned about the well-being of children in Hague cases, has advocated for changes to Hague Convention protocols, revised its implementing legislation to take "the best interests of the child" into account when determining if an intolerable situation exists, and now also provides for independent counsel for the child (Weiner, 2008).

The attorneys also split on the degree to which they accepted or were skeptical of mothers' domestic violence allegations. The mothers' attorneys had extensive contact with their clients, generally believed their allegations, and sought to support them in court by gathering documentation and using expert assessments of the impact of violence on their clients' children. The fathers' attorneys were very skeptical of such allegations, sometimes questioned the value of expert testimony, and expected extensive independent evidence to be submitted in court to verify such claims. It is clear in these cases that the retrieval of evidence from the other country, the use of expertise on a country's laws and services, and expert assessments of the risk to children were all important elements in mounting convincing defenses for respondents. In some cases, attorneys used innovative methods for bringing testimony into the court from the other country, such as cooperating with American Consulate staff and using existing video- or audioconferencing technology to do so. Of course, collecting, translating, and presenting such evidence required substantial amounts of time and resources, both of which were in short supply for respondents and their attorneys.

Finally, the fathers' attorneys clearly favored having their clients' cases heard in federal rather than state court. Federal courts were seen by these attorneys as more capable of handling international treaty cases and more likely to base their decisions on a narrow interpretation of the Convention's exceptions or defenses. The views of the mothers' attorneys were less clear. Some viewed the state family court judges as being better trained on issues of violence and abuse and more willing to consider the safety of the child over the goal of prompt return. Others viewed federal courts as being more willing to allow longer periods of due process and more confident in dealing with international treaties, thereby allowing their clients a full hearing.

One thing was very clear from all of the attorney interviews: both attorneys and judges were often unfamiliar with the Hague Convention, its purpose, its exceptions, and the case law on it.

with William Vesneski

7 Judicial Reasoning in Hague Cases Involving Domestic Violence

Surprisingly, previous empirical studies of abducted children have not analyzed US court data involving Hague petitions, despite the fact that these data are part of the public record in most cases. We examined published US judicial decisions in Hague cases with three questions in mind: (1) Who are the parties involved in Hague disputes in which domestic violence is alleged? (2) What are the legal outcomes of Hague litigation? (3) How often—and under what circumstances—are the exceptions to return successfully used?

Why We Studied Judicial Opinions

Over the last several decades, scholars have explored the law's complicated role in modern society (Garland, 1990; Hunt, 1993; Calavita, 2001). Traditionally, the law has been thought of as a body of rules and regulations that proscribe behavior and order social relations. This functionalist approach stems from early sociological writings, including those of Karl Marx and Émile Durkheim. Both the Hague Convention and ICARA can be studied from this viewpoint—their provisions and components can be examined in order to obtain a theoretical understanding of how Hague cases should be adjudicated. However, this rather narrow approach to understanding the law provides only a partial understanding of the role that the Convention and ICARA play in the lives of abused women. To truly understand the power of the Convention and ICARA, we must also examine the judicial decisions that give them life. Our research shows that these decisions are, at times, ideologically embedded and reflect a particular set of social attitudes about domestic violence, children, and abused women.

How We Studied Judicial Opinions

The opinions in our sample were identified through online LexisNexis and Westlaw searches. We narrowed our sample to include only published opinions, as is typical of empirical legal research (Chew & Kelley, 2005; Perry, Kulik, & Bourhis, 2004; Choi & Gulati, 2008). A case is *published* in a legal context when it is systematically organized and published in case recorders. Unlike in federal courts—where both trial and appellate court opinions are published— state trial court opinions are not routinely published. Thus, our sample does not include an exhaustive collection of state trial court opinions.

We used published opinions because we were interested in decisions that could serve as precedent in future Hague litigation. *Precedent* refers to the fact that judges and lawyers in the Anglo-American legal system look to past decisions of higher courts for guidance and insight when deciding new cases. In short, these earlier decisions are predictive of future court rulings, and they "shape and constrain" what a court can do in the present (White, 1995). Gibbons (1999) summarizes the nature of precedent in this way:

> [I]f the judgment has any significance in terms of extending or restricting a rule of law, or establishing a rule of statutory interpretation, then it is reported and becomes part of the huge volume of precedents that constitute case law ... it is then a source of law and potentially an originating point for a new trial process with a new set of parties. (p. 15)

Although unpublished opinions are increasingly viewed as precedent, this is a relatively recent development. For example, citations to unpublished opinions are permitted by the Federal Rules of Appellate Procedure only for decisions issued after January 1, 2007 (Rule 32.1). In addition, LexisNexis reports unpublished opinions only for US District Court cases decided after June 21, 2005, with only selective prior coverage. It is difficult to research and retrieve unpublished opinions issued before 2005.

We also consolidated multiple opinions into single "cases" for purposes of analysis. Specifically, in several instances both trial and appellate court opinions were found involving the same pair of litigants. Because we were interested in determining the ultimate outcomes of Hague litigation, these multiple decisions were consolidated into single cases.[1] Once all of the opinions were consolidated

---

1. For example, there are several opinions pertaining to the dispute between Felix Blondin and Marthe Dubois between 1998 and 2000, including decisions made by the US Court of

into cases, we used Shepard's Citations to ensure that we had located all relevant appellate history. The most recent opinion in our sample was issued on March 19, 2009.

Once we had removed cases that did not fit our criteria and consolidated multiple opinions, our final sample was 47 cases. The majority of these cases (35, or 74%) were litigated in federal courts; 22 states and Puerto Rico are represented in the sample. All cases used in these analyses are listed at the end of the references, and are indicated by an asterisk (*) before the case citation.

We used three strategies to analyze these data. First, we completed descriptive analyses to answer our questions about the parties and legal outcomes associated with Hague disputes. Second, to answer our questions concerning the frequency of and circumstances surrounding use of the grave risk defense, we completed a content analysis of the opinions. Third, to assess which combination of factors was most relevant to case outcomes, we conducted a Latent Class Analysis (LCA). These methods are described in more detail in appendix D.

Judges' Rulings on Hague Cases Involving Domestic Violence

Our study of these judicial rulings led to six sets of results that we present in the following sections. The first two sections provide information about the people involved in the cases we studied, and we present success rates for the Hague petitions in our sample. The next three sections are informed by the content analysis. Specifically, we explore the courts' consideration of domestic violence when determining habitual residence, we detail how often the defenses to petitions were asserted and accepted, and we identify the factors the courts relied on when ruling on the grave risk defense. In our final analysis, we present information from the Latent Class Analysis.

Description of Parties

Judicial opinions in the 47 cases examined provided important data about the parties involved in Hague litigation. For example, of the 40 cases where the father's citizenship was identified, the majority were foreign citizens (n = 32; 80%). Foreign fathers were most often citizens of France, Israel, Mexico, Greece,

---

Appeals for the Second Circuit and the US District Court for the Southern District of New York. All of these opinions were consolidated into one case for purposes of our research.

and Italy. In contrast, the mothers in our sample were most often American. Mothers' citizenship was identified in 39 disputes, and of these, 25 (64%) were American (or had dual citizenship).

Setting aside the citizenship data, our analysis also indicated which parents initiated Hague petitions. We found that in our sample, fathers—not mothers—most often initiated the petitions in US courts when allegations of domestic violence were present. Fathers initiated petitions in 44 of the 47 (94%) cases in our sample. More specifically, we found that the most frequent pattern involved non-US fathers petitioning for return of their children after an American mother left the father, took her children, and entered the United States. This occurred in 25 of the cases (53%).

In terms of children, although the Convention applies to youth under age 16, our analysis also shows that the median age for children in the sample was 6 years (ages were reported for 75 of the 79 children in our sample). A slight majority of the children were girls (52.5%). This differs from our interview sample, where almost two-thirds (63.2%) of the children involved were boys.

Petition Success Rates

Of the 47 disputes in this sample of published cases, 22 (46.8%) resulted in the dismissal or denial of a Hague petition (meaning that the children remained with the respondent—usually the mother—in the United States). On the other hand, 20 disputes (42.6%) resulted in the granting of a petition (meaning that the children were returned to the country of habitual residence). In 5 instances (10.6%) the outcome could not be determined because the dispute was remanded to a lower court, and no subsequent opinion could be located. Table 7.1 summarizes these outcomes. Although fewer than one-half of the cases were decided in favor of the mother, these cases tended to have larger numbers of children, so overall, 58.9% of the children were placed in the mother's care at the end of the legal process.

Table 7.1 Outcomes of Petitions

Petition Outcome	Number	Percent
Dismissal/Denial	22	46.8
Granted	20	42.6
Remanded to Lower Court	5	10.6
Total	47	100.0

Habitual Residence and Domestic Violence

One of the first decisions a court must make in a Hague petition case is whether the children have been removed from their habitual residence. We identified three cases (7%) where the court made links between the coercive and controlling attributes of domestic violence and children's habitual residence. First, in *Tsarbopoulos v. Tsarbopoulos* (2001), the court explicitly considered a battered mother's isolation in a country where she was not familiar with cultural norms and did not speak the local language. In its ruling, the court found that there was no habitual residence in Greece—the country from which the children were taken by their battered mother—because the mother had been coerced into living there. The court found that the violent nature of the father's behavior left the children's mother socially isolated, unable to communicate with others (because she did not speak Greek), with only limited access to financial assets, and living in fear of violence. The court wrote that the husband had "control of all major decisions of the couple" (p. 455).

Second, in *Ponath v. Ponath* (1993), the court ruled that the petitioner (father) had prevented his two-year-old son and wife from leaving Germany and returning to the United States "by means of verbal, emotional and physical abuse" (p. 12). The father was also arrested for physically attacking a family member who was trying to see the mother and child. Altogether, the father's abuse history led the court to conclude that the mother and child "were detained in Germany against her desires." The court concluded that the child was not habitually resident in Germany under such circumstances (p. 12).

In the third case, *Ostevoll v. Ostevoll* (2000), the court considered a woman's abuse by her husband in determining habitual residence. The woman argued that at the end of the couple's relationship, she was not permitted to leave her home in Norway without being accompanied by her violent husband. The court also noted that the husband hid the mother's and children's passports, thus preventing them from leaving Norway. Under these facts, the court ruled that for much of the woman's time in Norway, she remained there "voluntarily, albeit reluctantly" (p. 42) and as a result, Norway was not the children's habitual residence.

Exceptions to a Hague Petition

As defined in our introduction to this book, respondents to Hague petitions may argue that any of five exceptions prevents the return of their children to the habitual residence. To review, one exception is premised on Article 13(b) of the Convention. This exception applies when there is a "grave risk" that a child who is returned to the habitual residence will suffer "physical or psychological harm," or an "intolerable situation."

A second exception provided by the Convention is consent. If the parent filing a Hague petition initially consented to a child's removal, then the removing parent can offer that consent as a defense against a Hague claim under Article 13(a). In *Friedrich v. Friedrich* (1996), the court stated that consent needed to be a formal "act or statement," such as "testimony in a judicial proceeding; a convincing renunciation of rights; or a consistent attitude of acquiescence over a significant period of time" (p. 1070). Subsequent cases have differentiated between consent and acquiescence, and indicate that consent can be more informal (*Baxter v. Baxter*, 2005).

Third, the Convention allows a child to remain with the removing parent if the child has been away from the habitual residence and is settled in the new environment, often after one year. This exception is provided for by Article 12 of the Convention. It is important to note that judicial opinions make clear that if a removing parent has hidden a child from the other parent, thus preventing the left-behind parent from contesting the removal, then the one-year exception may not apply. The one-year time limit was designed to prevent a left-behind parent who was aware and in contact with a child from returning to court later to petition for the child's return to the original country.

Fourth, Article 13 of the Convention states that if a child objects to returning, and has attained an age and degree of maturity at which it is appropriate to take the child's views into account, the child's objection may constitute an exception to return (*Ostevoll v. Ostevoll*, 2000). The Convention purposely avoids setting a particular age at which a child's views should be considered because the drafters felt that such a specification was "artificial, even arbitrary" (Perez-Vera, 1981). Instead, the Convention leaves the decision of when to consider children's views up to a court's individual discretion.

Fifth, a child's return is not appropriate when it contravenes "the protection of human rights and fundamental freedoms" (Article 20). This exception has been interpreted to mean that children should not be returned to countries where their fundamental human rights may not be secured.

Overall, the exceptions or defenses available to parents responding to a Hague petition were only occasionally effective in our sample. Altogether, a Hague exception prevented return of a child in only 18 disputes, or 38%, of the cases in our sample. Table 7.2 summarizes how often exceptions were raised and

Table 7.2 Success Rates for Defenses in Published Cases Involving Domestic Abuse

Defense	Asserted		Successful	
	Number	*Percent*	*Number*	*Percent*
Grave Risk	38	81%	12	26%
Consent/Acquiescence	14	30%	1	2%
One-Year/Settled	12	26%	3	6%
Child Opinion	9	19%	2	4%
Human Rights	7	15%	—	—

their success rates. Grave risk was the most frequently asserted exception, but was successful in only one-quarter of the disputes. The other four exceptions available were raised less frequently and were rarely successful in these cases.

Judicial Definition of Grave Risk

As can be seen in table 7.2, the courts in our sample accepted the grave risk defense in only 12 of 38 cases in which it was asserted. So we turned to understanding the reasoning behind their decisions. To accomplish this, we examined passages of court opinions pertaining to grave risk. The results of our analyses suggest that the courts respond to five distinct factors when determining grave risk:

(1) whether children were maltreated by the petitioning parent,
(2) whether the children witnessed domestic violence,
(3) whether the children suffer from post-traumatic stress disorder,
(4) whether the abuser made threats to kill the children or others, and
(5) whether there was expert testimony available.

The key factors that appeared to define the 12 cases in which there was a successful assertion of a grave risk defense are shown in figure 7.1. Many of the successful cases included multiple factors, as can be readily seen in the figure. We discuss each factor in more detail in the following sections.

Child Maltreatment

Of the 12 disputes where the grave risk defense was successful, courts found evidence of child maltreatment in almost all (11, or 92%). Maltreatment nearly

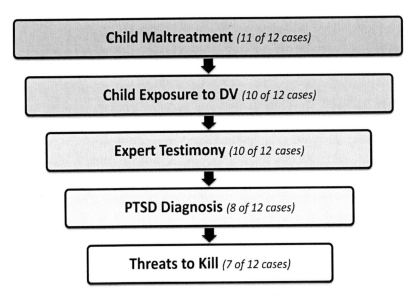

Figure 7.1 Common Factors in Successful Grave Risk Defenses

always consisted of physical or sexual abuse. For example, the petitioner in *Van De Sande v. Van De Sande* (2005) "physically abused" his daughter by spanking her repeatedly, and at "least once" delivered "a sharp blow to the side of [the child's] head" (p. 569). In *Rodriguez v. Rodriguez* (1999), one of the children involved in the case testified that "his father first began to beat him when he was six years old," at which time he was struck "with a one inch belt about the legs, back, and buttocks. The force of the blows, and resulting welts and bruises, were such that [the child] was caused to miss a week of school." The child was told by his father that if he had bruises as a result of maltreatment, "[he] must not tell anyone" (p. 459). Similarly, the court in *Elyashiv v. Elyashiv* (2005) accepted the grave risk defense in a case where the children's father "routinely used his belt, shoes or hand to hit [the children]" (p. 394). The *Elyashiv* court went on to write that "most frequently, the abuse occurred when the children's playing interfered" with their father's sleep. Once, for example, "[their father] became so enraged that he placed a pillow over [his son's] face to quit his crying" (p. 399).

Successful grave risk defenses are not limited to instances of physical abuse, however. In *Tsarbopoulos v. Tsarbopoulos* (2001), the court denied a father's Hague petition because he sexually abused his four-year-old daughter. In this case, the court not only wrote that the child described sexual abuse to her teacher, but that she exhibited behaviors "which were consistent with sexual abuse: masturbation, nightmares during nap times and bedwetting" while at school (p. 1060).

Exposure to Domestic Violence

In 10 of the 12 cases (83%) where grave risk was found, the court indicated that children had been exposed to violent episodes between their parents. In several of these episodes, children had intervened in the violence. For instance, in *Simcox v. Simcox* (2007), the couple's oldest child, a daughter, testified that her father would grab her mother's jaw and "put his finger on her neck, pulling hair" (p. 599). She also described how once while driving, her father had "banged her mother's head against the passenger window of the vehicle," and that she "often had to intervene by placing herself between them." In the same case, another child in the family testified that her father had "held her mother by the neck against a wall," and that her older sister had "tried to stop him but he hit her" (p. 598).

If a child solely witnessed the violence and did not intervene, that too has been enough to justify a grave risk defense. In *Walsh v. Walsh* (2000), for example, one of the couple's children recounted seeing domestic violence in the home. The court noted that the child had told a social worker that "she had memories about her mother being abused . . . that her mother was hit and hurt by her father, and that her father pushed her mother down stairs" (p. 211). She also stated "that her father once became enraged at her . . . over dirty shoes, spitting in her face and calling her stupid . . . She said she was terrified of phone calls from her father" (p. 52). And in *Turner v. Frowein* (2000), the court described a violent incident between a child's parents this way: "the defendant began choking and kicking the [child's mother], inflicting a beating so severe that she subsequently required a hysterectomy. Like the previous violent incidents, the child witnessed this beating" (p. 324).

Expert Testimony

Based on our study, expert testimony that describes the harm children might suffer if they are returned to their habitual residence makes it more likely that a grave risk exception will be deemed meritorious. Expert testimony was offered in 10 of the 12 successful grave risk claims (83%). For example, in *Danaipour v. Danaipour* (2004), a child psychologist who was treating a child involved in the case provided expert testimony that the child had been sexually abused by her father. The court wrote that it "credited the observations" made by the expert that returning the child to Sweden, where her father resided, would amount to returning her "to the place of trauma [and the] location of her victimization" and could "have profoundly disturbing effects on the child" (p. 296). In *Panazatou v. Panazatou* (1997), a child psychiatrist testified that the return of a child to her father supported a finding of grave risk. The psychiatrist testified that the "separation of the [three-year-old] child from the mother's care would cause grave risk of psychological harm to the child, both short and long term" (p. 4). Similarly, in *Turner v. Frowein* (2000), a court-appointed psychologist who examined both the child and the father stated that the father "had a tendency toward aggressive behavior." During the trial court proceedings, which included allegations of both domestic violence and child sexual abuse, the psychologist testified that the "child was anxious and very afraid of [his father] . . . and that the child likely would suffer substantial psychological harm if forced to return to his father's care" (p. 328).

Post-Traumatic Stress Disorder

Post-traumatic stress disorder occurs in people who have been exposed to traumatic stress or stress that involves the threat or actuality of death or injury (American Psychiatric Association, 2000). People suffering from this disorder typically experience a constellation of symptoms, including intrusive reexperiencing of the trauma, avoidance of things associated with the trauma, and higher levels of arousal (such as difficulty sleeping or concentrating). Children were found to have a diagnosis of PTSD in 8 of the 12 cases (67%) where a grave risk defense was successful. In these eight disputes, the courts indicated that returning children to their habitual residence posed a risk of causing a recurrence of stress symptoms characteristic of the disorder. PTSD was brought about in these cases either because the children witnessed domestic violence in the home, or were themselves victims of child maltreatment. The court in *Ostevoll v. Ostevoll* (2000) made this point exactly in a case where a father had physically and emotionally abused his wife and three daughters, ages 8, 11, and 13. In supporting its grave risk finding, the *Ostevoll* court wrote that the children were "suffering from post traumatic stress syndrome, having all experienced the abuse themselves as well as having witnessed their mother's abuse" (p. 48).

Similarly, in *Simcox v. Simcox* (2007), the court wrote that all but one of the children "were suffering from some level of post-traumatic stress disorder" and that their psychological trauma could be exacerbated if they were to be returned to Mexico (their habitual residence) and come into contact with their father

(p. 608). The court in *Blondin v. Dubois* (2001) made an analogous finding. Here, an appellate court accepted the lower court's finding that the children in the case had suffered from PTSD. The appellate court cited the lower court's opinion, which read, "the children face an almost certain recurrence of traumatic stress disorder on returning to France because they associate France with their father's abuse and the trauma they suffered as a result" (*Blondin*, 2001, p. 161).

Threats to Kill

In 7 of the 12 cases (58%) where grave risk was found, the batterer threatened to kill the mother, a child, or himself. Often these threats were explicit, as in *Elyashiv v. Elyashiv* (2005). Here, the court explained that when the children's mother asked her husband for a divorce, he "refused and threatened that, if forced to do so, he would kill [her]" (p. 399). Similarly, the couple's child once reported to a teacher about being physically abused by the father. Upon learning of the report, the father "threatened to kill [the child]" (p. 400). In *Blondin v. Dubois* (2001), a dispute involving more than three years of appeals, the Court of Appeals for the Second Circuit denied the father's Hague petition and cited the child's testimony in the opinion. The court wrote that one of the couple's children "described various instances of abuse and its effects on her, including her father's spitting on and hitting her mother, at least once with a belt buckle; [and] his putting something around [her sister's] neck and threatening to kill her" (p. 167).

Implicit threats of harm also helped justify a grave risk exception. For example, in *Baran v. Beaty* (2007), a mother left her husband in Australia and returned to her parents' home in the United States. During the course of the relationship, the petitioning father had stated that his son "should have been aborted, that [the child] would die if he 'became an American' and that [the mother] could not blame him 'if something happened' to the child" (p. 1257).

Our content analysis indicates that the courts in our sample addressed five distinct factors when determining whether grave risk could be used as an exception to a Hague petition. It is important to note that these factors frequently overlap in the same case. In fact, grave risk was found in all seven cases where five or four factors were present, but very infrequently in cases where one or two factors were found. This pattern suggests that the presence of multiple factors has a cumulative effect that increases the likelihood that the court will find the existence of grave risk.

Table 7.3 Bivariate Analysis of Case Factors by Decision in Published Cases

Case Factor	Case Decision		
	Child Returned	*Child Remained*	X^2
Case Characteristic			
State Court (vs. Federal)	19.1	30.4	.76
Expert Testimony Offered	19.1	47.8	4.05[*]
Preexisting Custody Order	38.1	65.2	3.29[†]
Child Characteristic			
Involved > 1 Child	38.1	65.2	3.24[†]
Involved at Least 1 Male Child	42.9	72.7	3.94[*]
Youngest < 5 Yrs. Old	47.6	73.9	3.20[†]
Abuse/Violence			
Child Witnessed Domestic Violence	38.1	56.6	1.49
Threats to Kill Mother/Others	23.8	30.4	.24
Child Abuse (Physical/Sexual)	23.8	56.5	4.56[*]
Child with PTSD Diagnosis	4.8	34.8	—[a*]

[*] $p < .05$
[†] $p < .10$
[a] Significance is based on Fisher's exact test.

Bivariate Analyses

Chi square analyses are presented in table 7.3. Significant associations were found between the case decision and four factors, and three additional factors trended toward significance. Children were more likely to remain when expert testimony was offered in the case, if there was at least one male child, if child abuse allegations were made, and if the a child was reported to have a PTSD diagnosis. A trend toward having the children remain in the United States was seen if there was a preexisting order that gave custody, even temporarily, to either parent if more than one child was involved, and if the youngest child was less than five years old.

Latent Class Analysis

The final step in our analytic strategy was to consider methods to assess outcomes within a multivariate context. Because many of the factors just mentioned seemed to be interrelated and appearing together, we turned to the statistical technique of Latent Class Analysis (Hagenaars & McCutcheon, 2002; Mc-Cutcheon, 1987). LCA was used to identify case profiles based on the set of interrelated factors that could be present in these cases, and on the case outcomes. LCA is a particularly useful technique for identifying cases that share similarities on a number of factors, such as these cases.

LCA is a statistical method that capitalizes on the multivariate associations between the variables entered in the model, allowing researchers to see how they operate together to create case-centered *profiles*. LCA seeks to empirically identify subgroups (each with its own unique profile) (Magnusson, 1998). Because subgroup membership is typically unknown to the researcher, a latent categorical variable is assumed to exist that reflects an underlying pattern of experience. The latent variable's categories indicate the subgroup, referred to as a *class*, that is most likely for each case. These classes represent subgroups of cases that are similar to each other on the variables entered into the analysis, and different from cases in the other subgroups. For more on LCA and our methods, see appendix B.

Each of the case factor variables were entered into the LCA. A two-class model (BIC 704.9, p < .0001) was found to provide the best fit to the data. The one-class model had poorer model fit (BIC 759.3). A three-class model also showed poorer fit to the data (BIC 727.3, p = .27) and was not a significant improvement over the two-class model, leading us to accept the two-class solution. Additionally, the average class probability was high for each class (1.00 for Class 1 and 1.00 for Class 2). In the two-class model, classification of each case into its most likely class resulted in Classes 1 and 2 having 8 (17.0%) and 39 (83.0%) members, respectively.

Means for each variable used to determine the latent class are shown in table 7.4. For example, the table shows that Class 1 is composed of a subgroup of cases, and in these cases grave risk was established 100% of the time, and the petition was denied (children remained in the States) in all of the cases in this subgroup. In contrast, the children who were often returned to the other country rarely had the defense of grave risk established, and the majority of these children (58.3%) were returned to the other country. In the subgroup where the child always remained, none of these cases was heard in a state court, all had expert testimony presented, and almost two-thirds had evidence of a preexisting custody order. Each of these factors was markedly different in the other subgroup, where one-third of the cases were heard in state court, only 20.5% used expert testimony, and just under one-half had a preexisting custody order.

Table 7.4 Latent Class Analysis of Published Cases

	LCA Subgroup	
Case Factor	Child Always Remains (n = 8)	Child Often Returns (n = 39)
Case Outcome		
Grave Risk Established	100.0	10.3
Child Remains in US (petition denied)	100.0	41.7
Case Characteristic		
State Court (vs. Federal)	0	33.3
Expert Testimony	100.0	20.5
Preexisting Custody Order	62.5	48.7
Child Characteristic		
Involved > 1 Child	100.0	38.5
Involved at Least 1 Male Child	75.0	56.8
Youngest < 5 Yrs. Old	75.0	59.0
Abuse/Violence		
Child Witnessed Domestic Violence	87.5	38.5
Threats to Kill Mother/Others	62.5	20.5
Child Maltreatment (physical/sexual)	100.0	28.2
Child with PTSD Diagnosis	100.0	2.6

These cases also differed in terms of the characteristics of the children, in that the Child Always Remains group involved more than one child in every case, and three-quarters of these cases had at least one male child and at least one child under the age of five. In the Child Often Returns group, the majority of cases involved one child only, and had lower levels of male children and fewer young children than the first group.

The two groups also varied in the report of domestic violence and its effects. In those cases where the Child Always Remains, 87.5% had a child who witnessed domestic violence between the parents; over one-half the cases included threats to kill the mother or others in the child's family; and in all these cases, an allegation of child abuse was also made. In the Child Often Returns group, each of these factors was substantially lower, with only about one-third of the children witnessing domestic violence, few threats to kill the mother or others (20.5%), and less than one-third reporting child abuse. The most dramatic difference between the groups is seen in the fact that 100% of the children in the Child Always Remains group were reported to have a diagnosis of PTSD, but only 2.6% of the children in the Child Often Returns group had this diagnosis.

Discussion

The data presented in this chapter tell us five important things about Hague litigation involving domestic violence. First, early assumptions about who would remove children and seek their return through Hague petitions does not reflect the reality of Hague litigation involving domestic violence; in other words, fathers were not the primary taking parents—mothers were, in our sample of published cases. This is consistent with the worldwide data on taking parents that reveals 69% are mothers (Lowe, 2011). Second, the courts in our sample rarely considered domestic violence in conjunction with habitual residence determinations. It should be noted that this failure may be attributed to the fact that the violence may not have been raised, explicitly and in a legally cognizable way, in pleadings or during litigation. It is unclear why this is true, though women's fear of an uncertain outcome or threatening contact with the batterer may be reasons. Third, on those limited occasions when the courts accepted a grave risk exception, the content analysis suggests that five factors are particularly important as they make their decisions. And finally, a small subset of cases was characterized by these factors, plus structural features of the families.

Altogether, the findings of this published case analysis have important policy and legal practice implications for women who flee domestic violence with their children and cross international boundaries.

Parties in Hague Convention Disputes

Our descriptive analysis indicates that in our sample of 47 cases, men who batter their wives and partners are typically the individuals who bring Hague petitions. These petitions are brought against women who have fled one country with their children and entered the United States. These women must then defend their actions in legal proceedings designed to return their children to the country from which they fled. This finding contradicts early assumptions that helped to shape the Convention, specifically, that fathers would primarily be the taking parent, and that left-behind mothers would seek redress using the Convention (Weiner, 2000).

Domestic Violence and Habitual Residence

One of the first steps in resolving a Hague petition is to determine a child's habitual residence. Despite its significance, the Convention does not define habitual residence, and as a result, US courts have stated that decisions about it are to "remain fluid and fact based, without becoming rigid" (*Levesque v. Levesque*, 1993, p. 666; *Prevot v. Prevot*, 1994, p. 560). Given this ambiguity, US courts have taken conflicting and extreme positions in resolving the argument over the meaning of the term (Weiner, 2000). In our research, we found that the courts rarely considered the presence or severity of domestic violence when determining habitual residence. In fact, in only 3 of the 47 cases (6%) we examined did the court find that domestic violence had a significant bearing on a habitual residence determination.

We recognize that current law does not require courts to attend to or address domestic violence when determining habitual residence. We believe this gap in law falls far short of accounting for the actual, lived experience of battered women and their children as described in earlier chapters. Inherent in domestic abuse is a pattern of coercion that may prevent a woman from participating in decisions about where she and her children live (Stark, 2007). Similarly, controlling behavior is a common characteristic of abusive partners, and this control encompasses family decision making (Barnish, 2004) and household finances (Alvi & Selbee, 1997). The failure of the Hague Convention and its US implementation to recognize these dynamics creates an additional barrier to safety for women seeking to extricate themselves from a violent partner.

Barnish's (2004) summary of prior research on battered women who immigrate to a new country is helpful when considering the Hague Convention. Barnish has explained how batterers ensure that women remain silent about their abuse by misleading them about their rights in the new country, preventing them from accessing language classes, destroying their passports and visas, threatening them with deportation, and restricting their contact with friends and family in their home country. Under these circumstances—which are analogous to the cases we studied—battered women and their children are, in essence, confined to their homes through violence, coercion, and control. Our research indicates that a more expansive legal process for determining habitual residence is needed. Such a process would specifically ask whether a mother has made a decision about where she and her children live under threat of violence. By including a focus on domestic violence, determining habitual residence would more accurately account for the real-world lives of battered women and help ensure their own and their children's safety.

Grave Risk Factors

Because of its particular relevance to domestic violence cases, we were especially interested in understanding how the courts in our study put the grave risk exception into action. That the use of grave risk as a defense had a low likelihood of success is unsurprising, given that US courts have consistently stated that exceptions should be narrowly interpreted. To do otherwise, the courts hold, would undermine the Convention's policy goal of returning children who are wrongfully removed from their habitual residences (*Simcox v. Simcox*, 2007; *Friedrich v. Friedrich*, 1996).

In general, the courts in our study were reticent to use the exception. For example, in *Whallon v. Lynn* (2000), the court wrote that the harm necessary to prove the grave risk defense must be "a great deal more than minimal" and it must exceed that which would "normally" be expected to result from a transfer of custody (p. 92). Similarly, the court in *Friedrich v. Friedrich* (1996) stated that the exception applies only when the evidence shows that children would be placed in an "intolerable situation."

Our research indicates that the courts look to certain factors when determining whether grave risk applies to a case. It is important to note that no matter how violently a batterer may treat his wife or partner, without these factors, this violence is not in and of itself considered harm to children. Two cases in our sample illustrate this finding about grave risk.

First, in *Antonio v. Bello* (2004), the respondent—a mother defending against a Hague petition brought by her child's father—testified that the father had physically abused her during the marriage. However, the court wrote that "she made no claim and submitted no evidence that petitioner had ever harmed" their son (p. 3). Because the child had not been directly harmed, the court ruled that the grave risk exception was not applicable. Second, in *Dallemagne v. Dallemagne* (2006), the father had previously punched the children's mother to the point that she was unconscious, and had tried to run her over with a car. Nevertheless, the court did not find grave risk because "there was no credible evidence that the petitioner has ever physically harmed the children" (p. 1299).

The reticence of the majority of courts in our sample to connect domestic violence with a grave risk of harm to children runs counter to the weight of social science research, as discussed in chapter 4. In addition, research tells us that at least 40% of children of abused mothers are also abused (Appel & Holden, 1998; Edleson, 1999).

Treating domestic violence as if it were separate and apart from other forms of family violence runs counter to recommended family law practice. For example, the National Council of Juvenile and Family Court Judges has written that "judges are now almost universally under a statutory obligation to consider domestic violence as a factor when determining the best interests of children" (Dalton, Druzd, & Wong, n.d., p. 10). At the same time, the council's *Model Code on Domestic and Family Violence* presumes that it is in the children's best interests to reside with their nonviolent parent in a location of that parent's choice, within or outside the state where the family lives (NCJFCJ, 1999).

Generally, courts in our study avoided linking domestic violence with grave risk, but this trend is not universal. For example, in *Ostevoll v. Ostevoll* (2000), the children's father was physically abusive to their mother; he rarely permitted her to leave the family residence, and when she did leave, he accompanied her. She was permitted to take the children outside of the residence only if she went to church. In accepting the grave risk defense, the *Ostevoll* court wrote that although other courts may focus only on whether children have been physically abused, such a view is "myopic," and that considerations of grave risk must also consider whether children witnessed domestic abuse (pp. 52–53).

Unlike other cases we studied, the *Ostevoll* decision relied on social science literature. We found only two other instances where courts looked to social science literature for support in accepting a grave risk defense (*Walsh v. Walsh*, 2000; *Tsarbopoulos v. Tsarbopoulos*, 2001).

Evidentiary standards further limit use of the grave risk exception. The majority of exceptions in the Convention (consent, child maturity, and whether a child is settled in the new environment) must be proven by a preponderance of evidence—the usual standard in US civil proceedings, including family law disputes. However, ICARA requires that the grave risk and human rights defenses be proven by clear and convincing evidence—a significantly greater burden than the preponderance standard. As a consequence, abused women arguing grave risk face a more difficult path to retaining custody of their children than do women arguing a different exception. It should be noted that the Convention does not dictate the use of different burdens of proof; this requirement is imposed by ICARA, the US implementing legislation (42 U.S.C. § 11603[e][2][A]).

Implications for Policy and Practice

The research reported in this chapter contributes to our understanding of how US courts have interpreted and implemented the Hague Convention. By showing that this implementation frequently leads to court decisions against the interests of even severely battered women, our research also adds to the body of legal and social welfare scholarship revealing structural biases against battered women in a variety of official settings (Kohn, 2007; Lindhorst & Padgett, 2005; Buel, 2003; Czapanskiy, 1993). Such scholarship includes studies showing that prosecutors' heavy caseloads are associated with lower numbers of guilty verdicts against batterers (Belknap, Graham, Hartman, Lippen, Allen, & Sutherland, 2000), that family violence was only relatively recently accepted as a legitimate factor in determining custody (Cahn, 1991), that battered women may be arrested for engaging in defensive tactics following an attack by their intimate partner (Henning & Feder, 2004), and that welfare workers do not properly implement procedures for domestic violence victims (Lindhorst, Meyers, & Casey, 2008). In this context, our research also suggests that the legal system's response to abused women and their children is, at times, ideologically fraught and embedded within larger patriarchal social attitudes. Similar observations have been made previously by legal scholars researching a wide variety of legal proceedings (for example, Sarat & Felstiner, 1995; Merry, 2000).

As the weight of social science evidence and US public policy brings about expanded understanding of the welfare interests of children, court rulings in Hague Convention cases may change over time as well. Judicial recognition may increase regarding evidence that exposure to adult domestic violence may pose a grave risk and intolerable situation to many children growing up in homes where violence is present. There is little logic to current legal arguments that exposure to domestic violence in the home does not constitute a potential grave risk to children. A more in-depth understanding of battered mothers' and their children's experiences should provide judges and attorneys with a deeper understanding of these issues in Hague Convention cases and their very real impacts on child development and well-being.

These findings also suggest the need for specialized training focused on international abduction cases involving domestic violence, and the need for technical assistance for judicial officers and attorneys. The development of national and global Bench Guides that incorporate our and others' research findings could address domestic violence and its implications for decisions in Hague Convention cases. The recommendations of the recent Sixth Special Commission of the Hague signatories, meeting in June 2011, supported the development of such documents for judges globally (see www.hcch.net).

Just as important, our results suggest that continued research is needed on child abduction and its relationship to domestic violence. We have little systematic information on the parents who are found to have abducted their children into the United States from other countries, and we have almost no understanding of their motives, their experiences, or the outcomes of their cases apart from official published decisions. The research described in this book focused on parents who brought their children into the United States; it did not address those parents who flee the States and go to other countries after being victims of domestic violence in America. Further research is needed with both types of taking parents to identify key barriers and facilitators to a safe resolution of their disputes.

Finally, although it would be difficult to amend the Hague Convention, this research can contribute to clarifying its proper use in cases where domestic violence is present, and our findings may contribute to a new or revised Hague Convention protocol or a revision of ICARA. Judges hearing these cases have an obligation to be knowledgeable about the Convention and the risks that mothers face both in the United States and abroad. Most important, battered mothers and their children deserve access to attorneys and advocates who can effectively represent them in these complex cases.

8 | Practice and Policy Implications

The Hague Convention was originally intended to protect children from the harm of abduction, and to protect custodial parents from having the other parent unlawfully remove or retain a child in another country. In practice, the Convention is now often used against mothers who are the primary custodians of their children. In cases where women cross international borders with their children to escape abuse, they may be treated as potential criminals rather than as women fleeing from seriously dangerous situations in countries where many barriers to help may exist. Ultimately, this study sought to understand from various viewpoints the experiences of mothers who allege that they have been victims of domestic violence, who come to the United States with their children and then face Hague petitions in our courts.

There are many implications of the findings for work on Hague Convention cases involving allegations of adult domestic violence. As stated in the appendixes, both our interview study and the published case review samples are limited in serious ways. But there are, nonetheless, clear implications of our findings that we have grouped according to each key finding of this study.

1. *Mothers and children often experienced severe violence from the left-behind fathers who filed Hague Convention petitions to have their children returned.*

The implications of this finding are several. Consistent with the recommendations of the National Council of Juvenile and Family Court Judges (1999), children should remain in the custody of a non-abusive parent and not be returned to a petitioning parent if there is evidence of the use of coercive violence against the child or other parent. Best practice would include assessment of all Hague Convention cases for the presence of domestic violence and the delivery of this assessment information to the judges hearing these cases. US attorneys representing both respondent and petitioner parents should assess for the presence of domestic violence, paying particular attention to patterns of coercive control and emotional terrorizing in addition to the presence of physical violence. The Hague's Permanent Bureau and the US Central Authority might also issue interpretive guidelines for judges to clarify when a child's exposure to domestic violence should be considered a form of grave risk or an intolerable situation.

Some preventive steps may also help parents prior to relocation abroad. These would include providing detailed information about the possible outcomes of Hague Convention petitions in cases of alleged domestic violence and resources available to overseas victims of domestic violence. Such information could also be incorporated into online information on international travel provided by the US Department of State. The State Department might also collaborate with other stakeholders to develop online information, particularly to correct a common misperception that US-citizen parents have the right to return their children to the United States without the permission of the other parent, and that they are not bound by the other country's custody laws.

2. *Mothers were unable to access helpful resources in the other country, so they left with their children to seek safety and support of family members in the United States.*

Parents responding to Hague petitions should be offered the same technical assistance as that offered to petitioning parents by the US Central Authority. In addition, US domestic violence crisis line staff and battered women's advocates need to be provided with training on the Hague Convention and its implications for abused parents so that they may more quickly respond when a battered mother and her child reach out to them for help. Further, work is needed internationally to strengthen the basic set of legal and social service domestic violence resources available for US-citizen and other battered parents. Every overseas US citizen should be able to access basic domestic violence services (including emergency shelter and protection orders) regardless of her or his immigration status. US Embassies also need to expand their capacity to provide emergency assistance to battered parents and children attempting to flee from abusive situations. Happily, the Americans Overseas Domestic Violence Crisis Center, located in Portland, Oregon, has undertaken an effort to help start educating embassy staff and others in overseas citizen organizations.

3. *US authorities and courts were not receptive to mothers' safety concerns.*

One of the most troubling findings in our study was the short time that mothers and their legal representatives were given to develop a defense to the Hague petition once it was served. Attorneys need to receive adequate time to prepare a defense and thus ensure that due process is provided to the responding parent. As Hague cases are then heard, US state and federal courts and attorneys need to consider more frequently applying the "intolerable situation" (Article 13[b]) and "human rights violation" (Article 20) exceptions in the Hague Convention, as these are likely to be relevant to the issue of children's harm from exposure to domestic violence.

Mothers trying to defend themselves and protect their children also face unusually high standards of evidence when their attorneys attempt to apply an Article 13(b) exception. The level of evidence required to prove grave risk, intolerable situation, or human rights violation should be changed in ICARA from *clear and convincing* to *a preponderance of evidence* so that mothers and their attorneys may more readily use this defense. In addition, the level of deception, coercion, and threats involved in a family's relocation to another country should be considered in any decision regarding habitual residence of a family, and hence the child.

Finally, as mentioned earlier, mothers reported mixed experiences with US Embassies abroad. Once mothers are living overseas, embassy staff and others need to provide better responses for mothers and their children, as we have just outlined.

4. *Mothers and children faced great hardships after a Hague Convention decision.*

Mothers reported that they faced many challenges after a decision was made regarding the Hague petition. Mothers who returned, following their children back to the other country, faced especially dangerous circumstances. Judges who decide to return a child to a habitual residence for resolution of divorce and custody issues should require that the safety and well-being (both physical and economic) of the child and abused parent be secured *before* ordering the return of a child. Undertakings and mirror orders cannot ensure a child's or mother's safety in the face of a grave risk of physical or psychological harm (Article 13[b] finding) and should not be considered an appropriate remedy to such dangers. It would also be helpful for the United States to ratify the 1996 Hague Convention on Jurisdiction, Applicable Law, Recognition, Enforcement and Co-operation in Respect of Parental Responsibility and Measures for the Protection of Children. Judges could use the 1996 Convention in order to develop protections for children to the extent that the other country is a party to this particular Convention.

Mothers often felt that they faced prejudice in foreign courts after a US judge ordered their children returned. It would help to ensure a more fair hearing if US judges would provide written documentation clearly indicating that a decision to return a child to the country of habitual residence is not an endorsement of custody for the petitioner.

Finally, the circumstances many mothers reported following a Hague decision, *either* in their favor or in the petitioners', indicated that they and their children would benefit from access to mental health services, both in the United States if they remain here and in the other country on return, especially provided by professionals who are knowledgeable about the dynamics and effects of domestic violence.

5. *Legal fees and representation were major barriers for women responding to Hague Convention petitions.*

Battered women faced major barriers in obtaining and paying for legal representation. Assistance in accessing attorneys and obtaining *pro bono* legal representation needs to be made available for abused respondent parents, just as it is by the Central Authority for left-behind parents. The legal costs incurred by the abused parent to defend against a Hague petition should be paid by the abusive left-behind parent when his or her petition is denied. This would act as a deterrent to abusive fathers using the courts to extend their control over their former partners. In addition, in only a few cases we studied were guardians *ad litem* appointed to represent the children. Courts should consider the appointment of guardians *ad litem* whose role would be to represent the child's interests in Hague legal proceedings.

6. *Hague Convention decisions have not considered two decades of research on child exposure to domestic violence when deciding on grave risk.*

Article 13(b) should be interpreted to protect children from the risk of psychological harm and being placed in an intolerable situation that may result from exposure to their mother's physical abuse. To facilitate this, Hague Convention operating protocols and/or ICARA should contain a definition of domestic violence that includes coercive control. Definitions of custody and access should also be changed to deny returns requested by left-behind parents with only visitation or *ne exeat* rights. These changes would uphold the Convention's original intent to protect primary caregivers.

As stated earlier, attorneys representing parents in Hague cases need to evaluate the exposure of children to domestic violence in every case. Children may be direct victims of child maltreatment, unintentional victims hurt in attacks by one parent against the other, or indirectly exposed to violence by seeing or hearing it or experiencing the events surrounding it. In addition, given the findings from successful Article 13(b) defenses, it would be ideal for attorneys to engage specialists who could assess abused parents and their children for the presence of PTSD as a result of the domestic violence. Judges should ensure such evaluations are carried out when evaluations have not been requested by attorneys. Finally, when a 13(b) exception has been found by the court, judges should not have the discretion to return a child to the other country, and any custody hearings should proceed in the United States to further ensure the safety of the child and mother.

7. Safety for battered mothers and their children facing Hague petitions requires training for attorneys and judges on both domestic violence and the law surrounding Hague Convention cases.

This final finding calls for a significant capacity-building strategy with judges and attorneys. First, tens of thousands of judges may potentially hear Hague Convention cases in the United States, and thus judicial training systems need to be developed that are easily and quickly accessible, including the creation of judges' Bench Guides on Hague Convention cases involving allegations of domestic violence. Hague-related training offered by the US Department of State and others should include information about how to assess for domestic violence in Hague Convention cases and how to represent *both* petitioning and respondent parents when there are allegations of domestic violence. Most current trainings and materials focus on how to represent only the petitioning parent.

More generally, judicial and attorney trainings on domestic violence should incorporate information about the Hague Convention. To facilitate better representation and judgments in Hague cases, a national repository with routinely updated information on domestic violence laws and resources available in other countries should be created so that a better assessment can be made of what is available to battered mothers and their children in the other country.

In summary, these findings point to many needed changes, changes that would greatly enhance the safety of children and their mothers in Hague Convention cases where domestic violence is alleged or present. Another direction implied in these findings and our review of the literature is where future research might be helpful. This is the focus of the next section.

Future Research

At the beginning of this book, we laid out a theoretical argument concerning why it is important to pay attention to globalization and the issues surrounding the work of transnational institutions, human rights, and migration and citizenship. We return briefly to each of these subjects now, and end with a discussion of future research focused on the Hague Convention and domestic violence.

Transnational Institutions and Gender

In a world that becomes increasingly smaller because of innovations in transportation, communication, and technology, the boundaries between nation-states become more porous. A variety of international institutions have developed in the past hundred years to address the growing complexity of personal, legal, and financial relationships that exist across multiple borders. The Hague Convention on the Civil Aspects of International Child Abduction represents one of these emerging transnational institutions. At its best, the Hague Convention offers parents who have been unlawfully deprived of the presence of their child a legal avenue for being reunited. This goal is an important one and is central to the interpretation of the treaty. Unfortunately, as we have shown in this research, by framing the Convention in a gender-neutral format, the distinctive issues that face primarily women—in this case, domestic violence—are unrecognized and unaddressed. As a result, the operation of the Hague Convention in the lives of women who have experienced domestic violence becomes an example of the "mischiefs in the law" (Edwards, 2010, p. 40)—places where gender is deeply implicated in legal decision making, but where these differences remain unacknowledged.

The United Nations recognized that policies can be created and implemented that look free of gender on the surface, but lead to troubling, gendered consequences. The UN's solution to this problem was to advocate for gender mainstreaming as a technique to encourage international organizations to analyze policy and organizational responses to locate differential effects for women. In the years since the Fourth World Conference on Women in Beijing, significant efforts have been made, primarily in development-oriented institutions such as the World Bank, to implement a gender mainstreaming approach (Moser & Moser, 2005). A significant critique of gender mainstreaming is its tendency to reify "woman" as a category and to ignore the intersectional nature of human identity and social location (Eveline et al., 2009). As Eveline and coauthors point out,

> Rather than a theory of multiple inequalities, our case study shows the need for a methodology that pays attention to the way in which gender, "race" and other categories are not only conceptualized in the policy process, but also co-ordinated into existence within ruling relations of advantage and disadvantage (Eveline, 1994, 2005). As Smith insists, it is the co-ordinated work efforts of everyday life, rather than static categories or social locations that must be the starting point for understanding the extra-local mechanisms that reproduce injustice and inequality. (p. 214)

The contrasting experiences of Latina immigrants and those of the US-born mothers in our study highlight some of the ways in which gender intersects with ethnicity and class to produce differing "everyday life" experiences with the institutional process of the Hague petition.

Scholars of gender issues in international organizations have suggested that specific mechanisms of accountability may contribute to deeper awareness of and commitment to eradicating institutional gender inequality. For example, Moser and Moser (2005) suggest concrete strategies that could strengthen institutional responses to gender inequality. First, institutions should consider what gender equality means in their context, and set meaningful targets for improvement. Second, international bodies should commit to ongoing gender training and systematic monitoring of processes and outcomes to detect gender bias. Finally, as noted by several authors (Edwards, 2010; Eveline et al., 2009; Rao, 2006), women need to be equally represented as participants and decision makers in international organizations and through the processes invoked by these groups. Because of the complexity of the legal relationships involved in treaties as opposed to organizations such as the World Bank, the implementation of these suggestions would not be straightforward, and would require significant leadership and negotiation. Without a process that directly analyzes the ways in which the Hague Convention has unequal effects for women and men, the treaty is implicated in the production of gender inequality as well as being a legal tool to address inequality.

Human Rights and Domestic Violence

Since World War II, efforts to develop a common framework for the just treatment of all people have focused on the articulation of human rights. As put forth in the 1948 Universal Declaration of Human Rights, all people at all times have a right to life, liberty, and security of person (Article 3) and to be free from torture or cruel, inhuman, or degrading treatment or punishment (Article 5). Although straightforward in principle, the human rights framework has been slow to accept experiences that happen primarily to women (such as domestic violence and rape) as human rights violations. As Edwards (2010) notes,

> Feminist scholars have not only pointed to a number of omissions to argue that human rights law has failed women, but they argue further that existing provisions have neither been recognized as relevant to women nor interpreted to reflect women's experiences. That is, they argue that the operation of human rights law, in structure, process, and substantive content, excludes women's concerns and experiences. (pp. 55–56)

Domestic violence is a widespread phenomenon. International studies have reported rates of physical and/or sexual violence that range from 9% to 71% (Garcia-Moreno et al., 2005; Johnson et al., 2008), while in the United States, two national surveys in the past 15 years have found that about one-quarter of women will experience physical or sexual violence or stalking by an intimate partner (Black et al., 2011; Tjaden & Thoennes, 1998). As we have documented in these women's stories, their experiences of violence were not trivial, but were serious and potentially life-threatening. In comparing the women's stories to the criteria used to define torture, the only thing separating the two is that men who perpetrate domestic violence are not doing so by order of the state. Unfortunately, as we discussed at the end of chapter 1, the fact that domestic violence is perpetrated in the "private" home rather than by a "public" actor has meant that this form of violence has not typically been defined as a human rights abuse, despite its similarity to other forms of torture or terrorism.

Within this context, it is difficult to overcome the "gendered fault-line" (O'Hare, 1999, p. 366) where women's concerns are relegated to the realm of the private and are, therefore, not considered a human right. Although feminist scholars have enjoined international bodies to take seriously the particular concerns of women in human rights discussions (see Edwards, 2010, for a historical review), the application of a human rights framework to domestic violence is not commonly practiced. This study provides further evidence that the public/

private distinction in the human rights debate is a hollow one when it comes to the actual experiences of the victims of violence.

Citizenship in the Context of Global Migration

The Hague Convention is not concerned with issues of citizenship when making a determination of the location of the habitual residence of a child. However, issues of citizenship are central to the experiences of the women and children who are fleeing across international borders because of domestic violence. Citizenship is the formal designation made by nations that allows them to require certain actions by residents, and to distribute rights and services based on legal status (Stasiulis & Bakan, 2003). But, as Stasiulis and Bakan (2003) note, "Citizenship is not reducible to legal status alone. Citizenship exists on a spectrum, involving a pool of rights that are variously offered, denied or challenged, as well as a set of obligations that are unequally demanded" (p. 2).

Underlying the Hague Convention is the premise that the nation in which the child usually resides should be the legal arbiter for matters related to child custody and visitation. Two problems exist with this premise. First, other countries determine citizenship in ways that differ from the United States, such that some women are not able to obtain full legal rights in the other country because of their immigrant status. As we discussed in chapter 2, countries that denied citizenship to immigrant women also restricted these women's access to other resources that might have helped them find safety in the other country. For example, some women were told by domestic violence service agencies in the other country that they were not eligible for services because they were not and could not become a citizen of the country. Second, as we noted in chapter 5, when children were returned to the other country, women who returned with them were often at a distinct disadvantage because they no longer resided with their husbands, and thus might not be eligible to work or live in the other country for extended periods. As immigrants to the other country, their experience of citizenship was "partial, provisional and precarious" (Stasiulis & Bakan, 2003, p. 14).

Similarly, Latina women who came from other countries to the United States to escape the abuse faced issues regarding their citizenship status. They were usually in the States illegally, having stayed past the period of time allowed on the visa, or having smuggled themselves and their children across the US border. They came to the United States for the same reasons that the US-citizen women came—to obtain help from family members in order to find a safer situation for themselves and their children. Currently, US legal resources that are available to immigrant women, such as the VAWA self-petition or the U-Visa, fail non-US-citizen women who are subject to Hague petitions because they rest on assumptions about the citizenship of the husband, or about the location of the abuse. In some cases, the asylum process was available as a transitional status that allowed Latina women and their children to remain in the United States with their children, but this remedy was not always available.

Women who are taking mothers and subject to a Hague petition are in a kind of citizenship limbo. Although US-citizen mothers expected to receive the rights available to women who are abused in the States, this presumption was not the case, leaving some of the women to feel that they and their children were being deported from their own country. Without an international consensus on the fundamental right of women and children to be free from abuse within the home, the exclusions created by citizenship status will continue to limit the ability of battered mothers to ensure their own and their children's safety.

Next Directions in Research

This study provided deeply descriptive information on the experiences of women who were subject to Hague Convention petitions after experiencing domestic violence in another country and fleeing to the United States with their children. Our findings suggest that future research should focus in three particular areas.

First, although this research indicates that women who volunteer for studies on domestic violence in US Hague cases experience serious abuse, it is unclear how prevalent domestic violence is within international child custody cases. The Permanent Bureau of the Hague should coordinate international data collection on the incidence of domestic violence in these cases and the outcomes for children in the aftermath of court decisions. As noted previously, our recruitment techniques required that women already self-identify as victims of domestic violence in order to see the study as relevant to them. Future research might also focus more broadly on the prevalence of domestic violence among US international child custody cases. Studies that attempt to evaluate the frequency of domestic violence should adopt a contextualized assessment approach (Lindhorst & Tajima, 2008) to understanding how violence is experienced and defined within couples' relationships.

Second, children are at the heart of Hague Convention cases, yet we know relatively little about their experiences from their perspective. Information on children in this study was provided by mothers, not by the children themselves (many of whom were quite young at the time of our interview with their mothers). However, children from the first Hague Convention cases in the United States are now adults and could be interviewed to gain further insight into the consequences of decisions in these cases. Although parental abduction has been discussed from the perspective of the negative outcomes for children, little is known about whether these outcomes differ for children when their mothers abduct them to escape domestic violence. Research that allows adult children to tell these stories in their own words would likely provide unexpected insights into their experiences. Comparative research could tease out the question of whether there are long-term negative outcomes for abducted children, and whether these outcomes are a result of the parental abduction, exposure to domestic violence, or family dissolution more generally.

Finally, this research indicates that a decision on the Hague Convention petition does not necessarily end women's and children's exposure to abuse and legal difficulties. More research is needed on what happens after Hague Convention decisions are made when the relationship has been characterized by domestic violence. This research would most effectively look across countries rather than focus on a single jurisdiction, as was done in this study. It may be that some countries have implemented systems that allow for greater safety of battered mothers and children. Cross-national research in this area, led by the Permanent Bureau of the Hague, could illuminate patterns that are both country-specific and shared by battered women regardless of nation of residence.

Conclusion

We pursued this research project after hearing from battered mothers who had been respondents in Hague Convention cases tried in US courts. These cases draw our attention to a growing worldwide concern about how adult domestic violence and child exposure to it are understood in the context of parental custody and relocation. Federal initiatives to address child exposure to domestic violence in juvenile and family court proceedings, in child protection agency practices and policies, and even within organizations focused on preventing and intervening in domestic violence are over a decade old at this point. The most surprising aspect of this study's findings is how Hague Convention proceedings appear to be lagging so far behind these larger changes underway in domestic court and social service responses to children's exposure to domestic violence. The time has clearly come to bring the Hague Convention, ICARA, US

Department of State policies and practices, attorney knowledge and practice, and judicial understandings into line with 21st-century social science information about the effects of domestic violence on children and mothers. We dearly hope that our labor on this project and the voices of mothers, attorneys, and judges contained in this report are part of making this happen.

Sudha Shetty, Esq.

Afterword

It is ten years later that I am now able to see light at the end of the tunnel; the light is still a ways away, but I can see it. I need to reflect on how we began this project and where we are headed in the future. The Hague Domestic Violence Project started at the Seattle University School of Law under the leadership of Dean Rudy Hasl, Professor Dave Beorner, and a wonderful law librarian, Bob Manteaux. In 2002 the initial listing of cases and resources was housed in the Access to Justice Institute, of which I was director at the time. The HagueDV Project would not have gone far if we had not received funding from Pearl Gipson, a program officer at the Washington State Office of Crime Victims Advocacy, who believed the issues surrounding Hague Convention cases were important, and wanted to help this group of battered mothers who, in desperately trying to protect their children, were willing to cross international borders.

The information in this book would not be here were it not for the courageous battered mothers who were able to speak up, the volunteer law students in Seattle and Minnesota who helped locate these mothers' cases, the wonderful Thomson Reuters FindLaw and Westlaw volunteers, the leadership at Seattle University, the Universities of Minnesota and Washington, and of course the team of researchers—Taryn Lindhorst, Jeffrey L. Edleson, Gita Mehrotra, Luz Lopez, and William Vesneski—for being steadfast in their belief that there are terrible, unintended consequences of the Hague Convention that needed to be investigated and now shared with others.

This book is an affirmation to all those mothers who are considered child abductors under the Hague Convention on the Civil Aspects of International Child Abduction simply because they could not take the torture at home and crossed an international border to protect themselves and their children. They often feel alone, terrified, and crushed under the legal and financial implications of their decision.

Much remains to be done, for we have really just started talking about these issues openly. This book goes to press at a critical moment. Several countries with large populations are contemplating joining this treaty. When they do, even more mothers will face Hague petitions if they endure situations such as those described in this book. There is an urgent need to educate lawyers, judges, and advocates in the United States and elsewhere to understand the complications of gender-based violence and its effects in Hague Conventions cases. Professor Edleson and I are fortunate to have recently received a technical assistance grant from the US Department of Justice's Office on Violence Against Women to start this educational process. This grant will allow us to develop new in-person, print, and online learning opportunities for lawyers, judges, and advocates working with or hearing cases involving battered mothers who are respondents to Hague petitions.

The Hague Convention is a very important piece of international law. It creates protocols between countries for the safe return of a child after that child is taken from a resident country to another without the permission of a custodial parent. Something is wrong, however, when a mother and her children are placed in renewed danger by our courts because the Convention and those making judgments based on it are not flexible enough to take the necessary steps to protect these vulnerable adults and children. We hope this book, and our own and others' future work on this issue, will shed new light on these unintended consequences of a well-meaning treaty and provide a path to greater safety for children and their courageous mothers.

Appendix A

If You Need Help

For Attorneys and Judges

Technical assistance, including model Bench Guides, is available through the Hague Domestic Violence Project. Contact the project at www.haguedv.org.

The US Central Authority for Hague Convention cases is the Office of Children's Issues, US Department of State: http://travel.state.gov/abduction

For Battered Women

Women who are outside of the United States and need support around domestic violence concerns can contact the Americans Overseas Domestic Violence Crisis Center. To access the crisis line from overseas, contact your regional AT&T operator and ask to be connected.

Website: http://www.866uswomen.org

National and international toll-free number: 866-USWOMEN
    (866-879-6636)

If you are in the United States, it is helpful to find a domestic violence advocate to provide support and help you develop a safety plan (what to do if abuse occurs). To find an advocate in your area, contact the National Domestic Violence Hotline.

Website: www.thehotline.org

National toll-free number: 1-800-799-SAFE (1-800-799-7233) (también en
    Español)

For deaf, deaf/blind, and hard of hearing (video phone and TTY):
    1-800-787-3224

En Español: www.thehotline.org/en-la-linea-nacional-sobre-la-violencia
    -domestica

Computer use can be monitored and is impossible to completely clear. If you are afraid your Internet or computer usage might be monitored, please use a public computer, or call the hotlines listed here.

Women interviewed in this study offered many concrete suggestions for other mothers who might face similar legal cases under the Hague Convention.

We have grouped these suggestions into categories, presented in the sections that follow.

General Issues

Understand that domestic violence is not a psychological problem. You are not crazy!

Strive for your kids. Be strong and fight for them.

You don't have to take his abuse—you can leave.

Find other moms who know about domestic violence to talk to, so you won't feel alone.

Know you will be afraid at many moments in the process.

Hold onto your faith.

It's not going to be easy, but never give up!

Before Leaving the United States

Know the signs that your husband may be abusing you.

Find out the legal implications of moving to another country with your children.

Know that the Hague Convention applies in the other country even if no one in the family is a citizen of that country (for example, all are US citizens abroad).

Realize that although your children are US citizens, they are still bound by the laws of the country where they live.

Don't go to another country with your children if you believe you are in a domestic violence situation.

If you feel your marriage is troubled, don't go to another country; but if you do, make sure you have a return ticket, and make plans in United States that show you intend to return.

In the Other Country

Retain control of your passport and your children's passports, if possible.

Keep documentation of the abuse if possible.

Go to the US Embassy and try to get help—at least ask the staff to help you find an attorney.

Contact the domestic violence system in the other country (if there is one), even if all you can do is get documentation that the system cannot help you.

Find a lawyer or legal representative as soon as you can, once you realize you may need to leave.

Be wary of calling the police, but if your life is in danger, you may have to contact them.

Double-check what your lawyer or the US Embassy says, especially if they are telling you to leave without permission.

Understand that even if you have custody of your children, this may not give you the legal right to leave the other country.

If You Decide to Leave

Try to go through the other country's courts before you leave.

If you decide you must leave, carefully plan your escape if possible, and get help from others as you can.

If you are going to leave, and especially if you are going somewhere unknown to your husband, don't tell anyone your specific plans.

Realize that sometimes it's "fight or flight," and you may have to flee to survive.

Use every bit of "independent" time to your advantage for your plan.

Be ready to lose everything if you must leave.

US Attorneys

Find a lawyer who believes in your right to leave for your own safety and your children's—don't retain a lawyer who thinks you were wrong to leave.

Have your lawyer prepare you for the kinds of questions your husband's attorney will ask you.

Make sure your lawyer is willing to put in extra time researching the Hague Convention and consulting with other attorneys who have helped battered mothers with Hague petitions.

If you are an immigrant woman, prepare for working with interpreters in court.

Educate your lawyer on how to recognize domestic violence and obtain evidence about it (for example, witness statements).

US Courts

Train lawyers and judges on the Hague Convention and the issues facing battered women living in other countries.

Judges should make explicit plans for children's well-being when returned to the other country—don't just assume they will be okay with the father.

Undertakings should be created and enforced in both countries. Fathers should have to show that they have addressed undertakings before the children are returned to them.

Don't charge women for representation, and don't place special financial
bonds on women.

Judges should take domestic violence into account when deciding what
happens to the children.

Overall Hague Process

Create an addition to the Hague Convention that recognizes domestic
violence as a legitimate reason to leave.

Understand that some women are forced to go to the other country or forced
to stay there against their will.

Make provisions for women who may be exposed to danger if their children
are returned to the other country.

Add more women's voices to the legal system—as judges, lawyers, and
policymakers at national and international levels.

Listen to the children.

Appendix B

Methods for Mothers' Study

This study was guided by an initial conceptual framework based on previous research related to battered mothers' processes and decisions to end an abusive relationship. We examined this literature to develop a framework for considering what might influence a battered woman in another country to leave that country and come to the United States. Previous research has identified three core areas that affect women's decisions to leave an abusive partner: (1) the level of violence experienced (DeMaris, 2001; Kingston-Reichers, 2001); (2) her evaluation of the effect the violence has on her and on her children (Humphreys, 1995; Short, McMahon, Chervin, Shelley, Lezin, Sloop, et al., 2000); and (3) her access to resources, particularly those specifically related to domestic violence (Panchanadeswaran & McCloskey, 2007). In the case of women leaving another country, we considered the role that resources in that country might play, as well as resources in the United States. Once the Hague Convention petition was filed in the United States, we also considered whether a woman's domestic violence experience was addressed in the Hague Convention petition process, and in particular the role domestic violence played in the judge's decision about returning the children to the other country. Finally, with very little prior research available on what happened after a Hague Convention decision was made, we considered what outcomes, regarding safety for children and their mothers, resulted from the court's decision.

Most of our information about battered women who were subject to a petition under the Hague Convention comes from published legal rulings that document only the aspects of the case relevant to the those decisions. As a result, we have only limited knowledge about the experiences, perspectives, and actions of the mothers, attorneys, and other key players in these situations. Therefore, a primary focus in this study was to solicit the stories of battered mothers who had been respondents to a Hague Convention petition in us courts.

Research methods that focus on providing in-depth descriptions and interpretations of phenomena (usually referred to as *interpretive* or *qualitative* methods) are the preferred method for (1) developing knowledge about a phenomenon that is poorly understood (Marshall & Rossman, 1999);

(2) explicating processes involved in interactions between individuals and social institutions around critical events such as legal prosecution (Roe, 1994); (3) accessing a "hidden population," such as women who may be in the United States hiding from abusive partners (Faugier & Sargeant, 1997); and (4) understanding how individuals assign meaning to critical events within their particular historical and social context (McHugh, Livingston, & Ford, 2005). Each of these factors was important to this study.

To understand what has happened to battered women who flee with their children from other countries, we focused on obtaining biographical, chrono-logical, and process-oriented data. A goal of interviewing mothers was to identify commonalities and discrepant areas among the women's experiences, and to examine whether patterns of experiences could be related to the outcome of the Hague Convention petitions.

To obtain information about the processes involved in Hague Convention cases, we also interviewed both respondents' and petitioners' attorneys about their views and responses to the women's stories, including whether they believed domestic violence had occurred and the role it should play in Hague petition decisions. In addition, we interviewed other key informants, such as expert witnesses, a guardian *ad litem*, an advocate, and a paralegal, all of whom had worked on Hague Convention cases involving domestic violence. We attempted to interview judges, but had little success. Judges we contacted suggested that because most judges have heard only one Hague Convention case while on the bench, they may be uncomfortable discussing their views about it; doing so might be viewed as a breach of judicial ethics in terms of giving case-specific information. So instead, we expanded our scope to review all published judicial opinions related to Hague cases in which domestic violence was alleged. Finally, we did not interview the father petitioners for safety reasons we will specify. Nor did we interview the children, because approximately one-half of them were in a father's custody, and because we were focused primarily on the decisions of their mothers and the strategies and opinions of attorneys, judges, and others in these cases.

Human Subjects Approval

This study was reviewed and approved by University of Minnesota Institu-tional Review Board (IRB; No. 0610S93508). The University of Washington agreed to have the University of Minnesota IRB be responsible for the human subjects' concerns in the study. The researchers also obtained a Privacy Certificate from the National Institute of Justice to prevent being forced by subpoena to provide in court any of the information that was obtained in the course of discussions with the mothers, attorneys, and other informants.

Because the interviews occurred via telephone, and because almost one-half of the women contacted were outside of the United States, we obtained permission to gain verbal rather than written consent from the respondents. An Information Statement containing all the same information as in a traditional consent form was sent to each participant, usually by email. At the beginning of the interview, the Information Statement was reviewed, and participants were encouraged to ask any questions. Mothers were offered the option of being anonymous and making up pseudonyms for themselves and other people in their stories, but none chose to do so. All interviews were confidential. Once tape recording began, participants were asked on tape for their verbal consent to participate in the study.

At the beginning of each mother's interview, during the informed consent process, we asked about potential immediate threats to the mother's safety (for example, whether the abusive partner was within earshot). During the course of the interview, if the woman became distressed, she was reminded about the voluntary nature of participation and asked if she wanted to continue. Verbal support was offered during the interview for women who became noticeably distressed. Researchers have an ethical responsibility to respondents that transcends the collection of data. In our research, this responsibility meant ascertaining from the women whether they had safety plans as needed, providing resource and referral information, and ensuring that no harm occurred as a result of the interview. Each mother received a follow-up contact within one and three days of the interview to assess whether she had any concerns after the interview.

Confidentiality of all participants was ensured by keeping all materials relevant to the research project in a locked file in a locked office, or in secure computer locations that were protected by firewalls and passwords. Access to materials was limited to project staff as required for completion of project duties. All staff signed confidentiality agreements.

One of the issues involved in this study is the relatively small number of women who have had Hague Convention petitions filed against them in US courts, and the threats this poses to the confidentiality of these women and their families. For instance, some of the women fled from small countries where their case may have been the only one heard from that country in US courts. Just by knowing the country where the Hague petition originated, the woman could potentially be identified. In another circumstance, one of the principal investigators entered the terms "Hague" and a specific detail about a woman's residential setting into a search engine. The woman's published legal case was listed as the first item generated by the search. As a result, special care has been taken to protect the confidentiality and safety of the women, attorneys, and others who volunteered to be part of this research. The following steps have been taken to ensure the confidentiality of materials presented in this report:

1. Pseudonyms are used in all cases for all persons involved in the case. Where direct quotes are used, information that could identify the woman's case has been deleted or redacted.

2. Individual countries are not identified; instead, regions of the world (that is, North-Western Europe, the Mediterranean, and Latin America) are used.

3. Information presented in this report has been read by external reviewers who were familiar with the Hague Convention or our research methodology. These reviewers were instructed to look for places in the report where they believed that enough information was given that a woman's identity could be discovered. In these situations, the report was revised to maintain the woman's confidentiality.

National Advisory Board

We created a National Advisory Board to help us consider human subject safety, determine interview and recruitment procedures, understand our results, and consider the best methods of disseminating our findings. The National Advisory Board members included:

Hon. Barbara Madsen, Chief Justice, Washington State Supreme Court
Hon. Ann Schindler, Judge, Washington State Court of Appeals
Merle H. Weiner, Philip H. Knight Professor, University of Oregon School of Law
Chad Allred, JD, Attorney-at-Law, Ellis, Li & McKinstry, Seattle, Washington
Barbara Hart, JD, Battered Women's Justice Project and University of Southern Maine

Paula Lucas, Founder/Executive Director, Americans Overseas Domestic
   Violence Crisis Center, Portland, Oregon
Sarah Ainsworth, JD, Counsel Emerita, Legal Voice, Seattle, Washington
Roberta Valente, JD, Consultant, National Council of Juvenile and Family
   Court Judges, Reno, Nevada

Research Design of the Hague Domestic Violence Study

As noted previously, international child abduction cases can be resolved
outside of the legal system, or they may be heard as custody cases within state
court systems without invoking the Hague Convention. In these cases,
decisions are made at a local level. Left-behind parents in other countries have
the right to initiate Hague proceedings if they feel their children have been
wrongfully removed or retained in another country. Such cases in the United
States are split between incoming and outgoing Hague petitions. The focus
of this study was on the *incoming* cases, those that were heard in US courts
and, therefore, raised issues related to the treatment of battered women within
the US legal system.

Reaching Taking Mothers in US Hague Convention Cases

We used three methods to reach women who had been respondents to a
Hague petition in US state or federal courts. First, we established routes by
which women who had heard about the project could contact us directly.
Second, we identified attorneys who had participated in Hague cases, and we
contacted them about whether they had represented an eligible woman. Third,
we worked with an international advocacy organization to provide information about our study to women with whom they were working.

   We anticipated that women who had been involved with legal petitions
under the Hague Convention might be reluctant to talk with researchers and
could be difficult to find because they may be in hiding from or in fear of their
abusive partners. Therefore, our first recruitment task was to create a website
that described the research project and provided information about each of
the researchers, so that prospective participants in the study would be able to
evaluate the legitimacy of the research endeavor. Although we did not track
how women found out about the study, it is possible that some women

discovered the study website while searching for information on the Hague Convention.

The website titled Hague Domestic Violence Research Project was launched in January 2007. A revised version of the website that no longer has recruitment information and is being used for dissemination purposes continues to be available at www.haguedv.org. The recruitment website consisted of six areas:

1. A description of the research study

2. Biographies of each of the research study team members, including links to their university websites where available

3. Information for mothers interested in the study, including a download-able version of the Information Statement

4. A section on privacy and confidentiality of data gathered for the study, including links on addressing Internet browser safety for battered women

5. Information for respondents' and petitioners' attorneys, including a downloadable version of the Information Statement

6. Information for judges, including a downloadable version of the Information Statement

Based on our knowledge of the demographics of international parental abduction cases in the United States, we knew that a significant minority of the involved families had left Latin American countries. In order to recruit Spanish-speaking women into the study, all the materials for the mothers' portion of the website and interview materials were translated into Spanish. The Spanish translations were then reviewed and corrected by Luz Lopez, PhD, assistant professor at Boston University, research consultant to the study, and a native Spanish speaker. Spanish information could be accessed through a prominent link on the home page.

A toll-free number (1-866-820-4599) was also established for the research project and rang directly to a voice mailbox. A recorded message in both English and Spanish instructed women to provide either a phone number or an email address for the research team to use to contact them. Women who obtained information about the study via the website could also contact study personnel via an email address (info@haguedv.org).

Another step in sample construction was to identify attorneys who had represented women in published Hague Convention cases involving domestic violence and heard in US courts. The Access to Justice Institute at Seattle University had previously posted 36 publicly available Hague Convention cases on its website. (This site is no longer online, but the case information located there was transferred to the current www.haguedv.org website.) Our initial attorney recruitment list was constructed through review of the cases on this Access to Justice Institute website. Westlaw and LexisNexis searches to identify additional Hague Convention cases involving domestic violence were conducted by volunteer law students from three law schools associated with the Minnesota Justice Foundation during the first year-and-a-half of the study, and through these searches we identified additional attorneys who were approached about recruitment of mothers to the study. We did not distinguish between respondent and petitioner attorneys at this stage in the recruitment process, expecting that some attorneys may have represented both petitioners and respondents.

Attorneys on this list were contacted by email and telephone seeking their voluntary participation in the study, and also seeking their cooperation in passing information from the research study team to their former clients who were taking mothers and respondents in a Hague Convention case. The research team, following our approved human subject protocols, responded only to mothers' inquiries and never initiated a first contact with a taking mother. We used *snowball sampling*, a technique that relies on contacts between similar people within social networks to identify members of hidden or difficult-to-reach populations (Berg, 1988). Thus, we also asked these attorneys to identify other attorneys who they believed had represented parents in Hague Convention hearings. We further attempted to use snowball sampling with the mothers we interviewed, but we found that none of the mothers was aware of any other women who had been respondents to Hague petitions.

Through these various methods, we identified 102 attorneys who had represented either a petitioner or a respondent in a Hague case. The project was able to speak with 77 attorneys; the remaining 25 did not respond to three or more calls or emails, or they could no longer be located. Of those reached, 51 attorneys reported that they had represented a mother who the attorney believed had experienced domestic violence. Each of these attorneys was given information to mail to the client about our study.

In addition to contact with attorneys, we also provided information to the staff of the American Domestic Violence Crisis Line (now known as the

Americans Overseas Domestic Violence Crisis Center). Women who have experienced domestic violence while in other countries contact this organization, and some of the crisis line's clients had been respondents to Hague petitions. We provided information about the study to this advocacy organization, and asked staff to offer information about contacting the research team to women they thought would be eligible participants.

Constructing the Sample of Battered Mothers

As stated earlier, informational packets about the study were developed in both English and Spanish for battered mothers. Respondent attorneys and staff of the advocacy organization were asked to mail or email these materials to the mothers they had represented, along with information about the study's website. These packets explained the purpose of the study, how the woman's safety would be maintained if she chose to participate, and the risks and benefits to the woman. Women who participated received $100 for completing the telephone interview.

Inclusion criteria for all battered mother participants were as follows:
- At least 18 years of age or older
- Had a petition filed against her for wrongful removal of child(ren) under the Hague Convention in a US state or federal court
- Was not actively under appeal and her Hague case had concluded
- Reported that she was in a situation that could be construed as domestic violence by answering yes to at least one of the following questions:
  Did this partner ever threaten to throw something at you, hit you, or threaten to harm your children?
  Did you or have you ever felt afraid of this partner?
  Have you ever considered yourself to be a victim of abuse from this partner?
- Was able to participate in a telephone interview up to four hours long, and completed on one or more occasions
- Was willing to have the interview taped and transcribed (with all identifying information later deleted)
- Had no medical or psychiatric conditions that would impair participation

In total, 45 women contacted the project to volunteer for an interview. Of these, 14 were not eligible for the study, either because they did not have a Hague case or because their case was outgoing (being heard in the courts of

Table B.1 Data Sources for Multi-Method Hague Convention Study

Data Type	Data Source	No. of Pages
Formal Texts	Hague Convention on the Civil Aspects of International Child Abduction	12
	International Child Abduction Remedies Act	9
	Judicial Opinions (47)	approx. 470
Transcripts of Interviews	Mother Respondents	702
	Respondent Attorneys	316
	Petitioner Attorneys	155
	Other Experts	73

another country). Five women contacted the project but were not subsequently reachable to determine their eligibility. Three women were eligible to be interviewed, but no interview could be scheduled with them, usually because they could not find a time to participate. One additional interview was completed, but in the course of the interview, it became clear that this woman's Hague case was being heard in another country's court, although she also had legal proceedings underway in a US court. In one case, the audio recording equipment malfunctioned, so no transcript was available. The final sample consisted of 22 women (74.1% of those eligible) who participated in an interview with the project staff.

Data Collection Procedures

Our interest in these interviews was to elicit the mothers' stories of their Hague experiences in whatever way they felt comfortable telling us, given that many of the experiences they had to share were traumatic to recall. The interviews focused on obtaining data from participants in a broad, open-ended way, rather than in the closed-ended format typical of survey research. We used an interview guide to ensure consistency across interviews and to incorporate ideas from our initial conceptual framework. The interview guides were reviewed by members of the research team, the advisory board, and experts in social and legal research.

The narrative data collection approach used in this study was conceptualized as a process in which respondents were constructing an account of their experiences to respond to what they saw as the priorities of the interview process. As such, these stories should be understood as partial accounts that are variable across time—the process of telling one's story changes that story, sometimes in subtle and sometimes in significant ways, depending on the revelations contained within the telling (Elliott, 2005). Additionally, the process of telling a story depends on the response of the "audience," in this case, the interviewers. Though similar data may be elicited by any skilled interviewer, the final shape of a particular narrative may not be directly reproducible because of how the telling of a story shapes subsequent narratives and the responses of the interviewer (Hyden, 2008; Riessman, 2008).

Qualitative research emphasizes that the data collection process is flexible and should continually be refined based on information gleaned from interviewees. Once the mother had told whatever aspects of the Hague story were important to her, additional questions were asked if she had not covered key areas in her descriptions. Whenever possible, mothers were asked to give specific examples of events and to provide as much information as possible on the chronology of events. For both the mothers' and attorneys' interviews, the research team discussed the content and revised the interview guide to include additional questions based on information gathered in the first interviews.

The beginning of the interview with the mothers opened as broadly as possible, with the question, "Tell us about the events that led up to the Hague petition being filed against you," and women were allowed to talk until they had provided as much information as they wanted in response. In addition to this opening question, further open-ended questions focused on six general domains: (1) factors in her decision to leave, (2) resources she used in the other country and in the United States, (3) effects of the situation on her children, (4) barriers she encountered, (5) legal processes around the Hague case, and (6) recommendations she might have to improve the situation for other women. These questions were asked if the woman had not spontaneously provided an answer in her opening discussion. Closed-ended probes were developed for a limited number of questions, which were primarily asked at the end of the interview. The interview guide was translated into Spanish and revised by Dr. Lopez.

The mothers' interviews took on average 2.5 hours to complete, ranging from 1.5 to 7 hours in length. More than one interview time was required in three instances because of scheduling and fatigue factors.

Interviews and Transcription

Interview data were collected using digitally recorded telephone interviews. Interviews were conducted by members of the research team: Dr. Taryn Lindhorst, Dr. Jeffrey Edleson, Dr. Luz Lopez, and Ms. Gita Mehrotra. All interviewers were trained social workers with several years of experience in the field of domestic violence, and each had specific expertise in work with trauma or violence survivors. Dr. Lopez conducted all the interviews with Spanish-speaking women.

Respondents were required to initiate the first contact with our research team either by calling the toll-free number or via email. A project research team member then made a preliminary return phone call or sent a reply email to explain the nature of the study, discuss any safety issues, assess the woman's eligibility for participation, and answer questions about the study. Once the woman appeared to meet study inclusion criteria and had consented to participate, the full interview either continued, or the respondent and interviewer made an appointment to conduct the interview at a time that was convenient to the interviewee.

All interviews were digitally recorded as WMA files and transcribed by professional research transcriptionists. Because the interviewers resided in three different parts of the United States, we created a secure website where digital and text files could be uploaded. Three transcriptionists, all experienced in research interview transcription, provided transcription assistance to the study. Each transcriptionist signed a confidentiality statement, and pledged not to keep a copy of the recordings being transcribed. A secure website was created for each transcriptionist, so that each would have access only to his or her files. The digital sound files were uploaded to this site, and the transcriptionist downloaded the sound files and then uploaded the transcript when it was completed. This method was chosen in order to avoid the possibility that emails with the attached files could be intercepted or misdirected. Spanish language interviews were first transcribed in Spanish and then translated to English by a bilingual/bicultural translator. Each transcript was reviewed for accuracy; Dr. Lopez reviewed both the Spanish version transcript and the resulting English translation for accuracy.

During one interview there was a malfunction in the audio recording equipment, so a transcript of this interview could not be produced. Basic information from this case was written down, so it was maintained in the analyses, but no quotations from the interview are included in the results.

Data Analysis

The analyses of the interviews serve two functions: (1) to elucidate the individual and institutional factors that promote or inhibit safe outcomes for battered women and their children, and (2) to support the dissemination of materials for attorneys and judges involved in Hague Convention cases. The first stage of analysis began immediately on completion of the interview with discussion of each mother's situation within the research team to identify key themes and issues. Once interviews were transcribed and all identifying information deleted, they were read multiple times by members of the research team. We constructed summaries of each interview and event chronologies for each mother to capture important sequences of events. We used content analysis (Hsieh & Shannon, 2005; Sandelowski, 2000) and grounded theory analysis (Charmaz, 2006) as analytic strategies to identify an overall theoretical model of decision making by battered women, and to identify factors associated with US court decisions in their Hague Convention cases.

Each interview was entered into ATLAS.ti (Muhr, 2005), a qualitative data management program for coding. Four members of the research team participated in the analysis, which involved an iterative process of reading through the transcripts and coding for substantive themes that were mentioned by a participant in the course of telling the story. For this stage of the analysis, at least two investigators read each transcript for the set of general themes generated by the battered mothers and attorneys. Rather than use line-by-line coding, we coded ideas and concepts as they were communicated through passages or whole responses. The emerging set of themes was discussed during research team conference calls and used to develop a formal coding framework. Codes were generated in three ways: inductively from categories that arose from within the data (Saldana, 2009), deductively based on relevant literature (Marshall & Rossman, 1999), and based on the factors identified in the initial conceptual framework. Each transcript was then coded according to this framework. Quotations exemplifying key themes were identified.

Once the documents were coded, we created matrices to allow for both within-case and across-case comparisons (Meyer & Avery, 2009; Miles & Huberman, 1994). In the mothers' interviews, each transcript was screened for several features, such as types of abuse she reported, whether her children were physically abused by their father, the kind of violence witnessed by the children, and the domestic violence resources she used in the other country and in the United States. In the third stage of analysis, we conducted a within-case and across-case interpretive analysis (Ayres, Kavanaugh, & Knafl, 2003). Within-case analysis allowed us to fully identify the uniqueness created by the individual contexts of each of the women, while the across-case analysis facilitated grouping similar cases together to identify commonalities. We created case-based listings and summarized these in typologies of abuse and processes related to the Hague petition. We then examined how these typologies and other dynamics in the cases related to the judges' decisions to return the children or allow them to remain in the United States.

Limitations

The goal of this project was to create new knowledge about a small and distinct set of people defined through their involvement in a particular set of international legal processes. Although we believe our efforts to recruit and gather information from this vulnerable and hard-to-reach population were sound and thorough, several limitations should be kept in mind.

Our recruitment efforts focused on obtaining the greatest possible inclusion of respondents involved in Hague Convention cases where domestic violence allegations had been made. Recruitment of the study sample relied heavily on contacts between attorneys or advocates and their clients, because no direct method exists for identifying and sampling women who have faced petitions under the Hague Convention. Because of this indirect recruitment process, the sample may be biased in certain ways. First, women had to have enough social and economic resources to obtain representation from an attorney. Women who did not have resources for legal defense were likely not to be found through a sampling strategy that relied on contacts with attorneys. Second, women could be recruited into this study only indirectly, through self-referral. From information provided by the mothers, we have evidence that women came to label themselves as victims of domestic violence at different times leading up to or during the Hague legal process. Because of the dynamics related to self-identification as a victim of abuse, other women may have experienced what we have defined as domestic violence, but they may not have applied this label to themselves, so they did not contact the research team. The experiences of women who did not self-identify as victims of domestic violence might differ substantially from those of women who had already adopted this identity, but their stories are not represented here.

We collected data using a narrative approach that allowed women, attorneys, and others to tell their stories in their own words, rather than using a more tightly structured survey style. This approach resulted in spontaneous and rich descriptions from the mothers of the ways in which they experienced abuse, and facilitated the discussion of a sensitive and traumatic subject for the mothers in our study (Hyden, 2008). In most of the interviews, mothers experienced moments in the recounting of their experiences that were emotionally distressing and that required sensitivity and support to allow the women to continue. Though the narrative approach facilitated in-depth descriptions of traumatic events, we did not exhaustively review each kind of abuse a woman could have experienced in what would be more typical of a survey format. For example, when we document that participants reported being raped by their partners, this information was spontaneously provided by the women, not solicited by the research team. As a result, aspects of abusive behavior toward the women and their children may not have been revealed because specific questions were not asked, and women self-selected the information they considered most salient to report in the interview process. We did specifically ask mothers if they were physically harmed by their partners when their spontaneously provided reports did not include physical attacks, but in terms of categorizing the other forms of abuse that women experienced, these may be underrepresented because specific questions were not asked. Although at the time of our interview, most of the women reported that the Hague petition had been filed within the past five years, some of the women we interviewed had cases that were significantly older. Impressions of what occurred may change with time, and how attorneys and judges approached these cases has also evolved over the period of these cases.

There were additional limitations with the data obtained from sources other than the mothers' interviews. First, the information from attorneys and others varied considerably depending on whether there was case material in the public domain. In some cases, extensive documentation was available, but in others there was no public record. Attorneys were able to speak about only those aspects of their Hague cases that did not violate the privacy of their clients. Second, obtaining reliable contact information about other professionals involved in these cases was difficult, so only five additional informants were interviewed. Although these five participants had valuable information to contribute, it is not clear how well their experiences reflected issues in Hague legal representation, so their interviews are not reported here. Third, because we were not able to speak with judges who presided over each woman's case directly, we had to rely more generally on published opinions, which often were not available for the specific cases of mothers we interviewed. Finally, as stated earlier, due to safety considerations for both children and their mothers, we did not attempt to interview the fathers or children in this study.

We offer this final note on generalizability. Generalizability in quantitative research is the likelihood that research findings based on a study sample can be applied to the larger population. Qualitative research is also concerned about the applicability of study findings beyond the research sample, although the generalizability of qualitative data is evaluated conceptually rather than statistically (Sandelowski, 1997). Qualitative generalization is based both on the richness of contextual detail brought to bear in the presentation of data, and on the evidence for commonalities identified across cases. As Ayres et al. (2003) have noted, ideas that have "explanatory force in both individual accounts and across the sample are most likely to apply beyond the sample" (p. 872). In keeping with these ideas, we have focused on providing rich details from the interviewees, and identified themes that are relevant across more than one research participant. Qualitative research can help show the variations in reasons that women may leave countries with their children, and thus position policy to be more humane in taking into account the differing circumstances of these women and their children.

Appendix C

Methods for Attorney Study

Constructing the Sample of Respondent and Petitioner Attorneys

After conducting interviews with mothers, we went back to our list of attorneys and recruited respondent and petitioner attorneys to participate in the study. Our first efforts were to interview attorneys directly connected to the cases of the women interviewed in the study. Information from each woman's case was used to identify attorneys for interviews. We asked each woman for permission to interview her attorney at the end of her interview.

We interviewed 15 respondent attorneys (in 11 cases the attorneys represented mothers we had interviewed). Respondent attorneys who were not associated with the case of a mother we interviewed were identified from our initial efforts to recruit mothers for the study. We sought to maximize variation among respondent attorneys interviewed, so we actively solicited additional interviews from attorneys who either (1) had participated as respondent or petitioner attorneys in multiple Hague cases, even if they had not represented a mother we interviewed, because the majority of attorneys we interviewed had only had a single Hague case; or (2) had represented a petitioner father's case opposite an already interviewed respondent mother's attorney.

Identifying petitioner attorneys was more challenging, as many of the women we interviewed did not know the name of the left-behind father's attorney. Of the mothers we interviewed, seven had their cases published, so legal documents were available that allowed us to identify petitioner attorneys. In cases where we were able to talk with the mother's attorney, we sought information on the petitioner attorney. In total, we identified nine petitioner attorneys who were associated with a respondent case, and completed interviews with six of them. Two additional petitioner attorneys were also interviewed who were either specialists in Hague cases, or had represented large numbers of clients in Hague-related legal proceedings in the United States. Attorneys who participated either received $100 or were able to direct a contribution for the same amount to a charity of their choice after completing the interview.

Through our initial interviews, we identified that several women had various experts involved in their cases. As a result, we expanded our original scope and conducted interviews with five experts, including two expert witnesses who testified in the court proceedings about the effects of the abuse for the children, an advocate who had assisted a battered woman in a Hague case, an attorney appointed as a guardian *ad litem* in a Hague case, and a paralegal with extensive experience working on Hague cases. Each of these interviewees also either received $100 or was able to direct a contribution to a charity of their choice.

Once attorneys and other experts had agreed to be interviewed, the research team sent them an email asking for basic information about their experience with Hague cases in order to use the limited interview time on more detailed process questions. The interview guide began with the request, "Please tell me about your history and involvement in working with Hague Convention cases." Other open-ended questions focused on the role of domestic violence in these cases (including the interviewees' estimation of the truthfulness of domestic violence reports and how they assessed for abuse), key issues in the cases they represented, advice for policymakers or other lawyers, and their thoughts on how to improve the safety of battered mothers and children in these cases. These interviews lasted from 40 to 90 minutes.

Data Analysis

Attorney interview transcripts were subjected to a coding process similar to that described in appendix B. We read them multiple times, both in their entirety and as reports of subsections of the coded text, to identify themes. We also created a matrix of attorney-provided key variables and extracted supporting quotes that exemplified these concepts.

Appendix D

Methods for Judicial Opinion Study

Judicial opinions that apply the Hague Convention to legal disputes involving both child abduction and domestic violence served as the data for this study. We used judicial opinions because they include detailed information about the parties involved in Hague litigation, and because they are the official records of who prevailed in the legal proceedings.

The opinions in our sample were identified through online LexisNexis and Westlaw searches. Typical search terms included *physical, violence, harm, assault, fight, punch, harass,* and *abuse.* In all, 57 different combinations of terms were used to identify cases where domestic violence might have occurred. All searches included reference to the Hague Convention.

State and federal court opinions—at all court levels—were obtained through our online searches, although no US Supreme Court opinions were located (*Abbott v. Abbott* [2010] occurred after our search). The results of the LexisNexis and Westlaw searches were supplemented by a search of the International Child Abduction Database (INCADAT) for disputes involving domestic violence that were litigated in the United States. INCADAT was established by the Permanent Bureau of the Hague Conference and includes judicial decisions from courts in 34 countries that interpret the 1980 Hague Convention. Search terms mirroring those used in the LexisNexis and Westlaw searches were used for the INCADAT search.

The online search initially yielded 306 opinions. We then took several steps to construct the final sample. First, we reviewed the opinions to determine whether they actually discussed domestic violence and, in fact, litigated the Hague Convention. Opinions that did not meet these criteria were removed. For example, opinions discussing child abuse without allegations of domestic violence were removed, as were those that simply cited or made reference to the Convention without actually issuing a legal judgment about it. It should also be noted that none of the legal opinions in our sample was primarily focused on determining whether domestic violence existed. Domestic violence was regarded by the courts as part of each case's factual background. Second, we narrowed our sample to include only published opinions, as is typical of empirical legal research (Chew & Kelley, 2005; Perry, Kulik, & Bourhis, 2004; Choi & Gulati, 2008).

Data Analysis

To facilitate the descriptive analyses, we developed a coding form to help extract needed information from the opinions in our sample. This form was used to gather demographic information about the parties; information about the disputes, including residence and citizenship of parents and children; children's genders and ages; the severity and frequency of domestic violence; and the presence of child maltreatment. Data were also gathered about key legal issues and decisions, such as the judge's decision on the children's habitual residence, the Hague defenses that were litigated during the dispute, and whether the petition was granted or denied. All gathered data were placed into Microsoft Excel and frequencies were determined.

Our content analysis focused on evaluating the portions of the opinions that addressed the grave risk defense. Content analysis was selected because it is well suited to the empirical study of legal texts (Hsieh & Shannon, 2005). Indeed, it resembles the process of legal reasoning, including the systematic reading of materials, identifying and coding their consistent features, and drawing inferences about their use and meaning (Hall & Wright, 2008; Lens, 2008). Content analysis has previously been used to study a variety of legal phenomena addressed in judicial opinions, such as use of the primary caretaker standard in custody disputes (Mercer, 1998), the admissibility of expert evidence (Merlino, Murray, & Richardson, 2008), and criminal sentencing of youth sex offenders (Bouhours & Daly, 2007).

The content analysis proceeded in two phases. First, we searched for specific terms and phrases that were associated with concepts in our coding sheet, including child maltreatment, the severity and frequency of domestic violence, and whether children testified during the court proceedings. In addition, the research team's understanding of the lethality of domestic violence sensitized it to the importance of an abuser's threats to kill his partner or children. As a result, we searched the opinions for any threats made by abusers. Second, it became clear that the opinions included several key concepts that were not included in the coding form, but which were critical to the courts' decision making. These emergent concepts were recorded as they appeared, and the opinions were subsequently searched for them. An iterative process of identifying and coding key concepts related to the grave risk defense and then returning to the opinions to confirm, refute, or modify them continued until no further concepts were identified (Lens, 2008; Graneheim & Lundman, 2004). Examples of these emergent concepts include whether a child was diagnosed with post-traumatic stress disorder, whether a child witnessed violence in the home, and whether experts testified during the proceeding.

The final step in our analytic strategy was to consider methods to assess outcomes within a multivariate context. Logistic regression was not appropriate for two reasons. First, the dataset for this analysis was small and, as a result, violated some of the more traditional assumptions about the number of cases per independent variable required to create stable beta coefficients (Pedhazur, 1997) Second, many of the variables showed strong intercorrelations, suggesting that some of these factors may cluster together in cases. From a theoretical standpoint, analyzing each factor while controlling for the others would not address the potential interrelatedness of the data, and might obscure meaningful patterns of relationship.

For these reasons, we turned to the statistical technique of Latent Class Analysis (Hagenaars & McCutcheon, 2002; McCutcheon, 1987) to identify case profiles based on the set of interrelated factors that could be present in these cases, and the case outcomes. LCA is a particularly useful technique for identifying cases that share similarities on a number of factors. LCA is a statistical method that capitalizes on the multivariate associations between the variables entered in the model, allowing researchers to see how they operate together to create case-centered *profiles*. LCA seeks to empirically identify subgroups (each with its own unique profile) (Magnusson, 1998). Because subgroup membership is typically unknown to the researcher, a latent categorical variable is assumed to exist that reflects an underlying pattern of experience. This variable is empirically inferred from the data using an approach based on conditional probabilities (Goodman, 2002). The latent variable's categories indicate the subgroup, referred to as a *class*, that is most likely for each case. These classes represent subgroups of cases that are similar to each other on the variables entered into the analysis, and different from cases in the other subgroups.

The LCA was implemented using Mplus 4.2. In LCA, the researcher typically determines the number of classes that exist in a sample by performing the analyses iteratively, each time specifying an increasing number of classes. The solutions are compared, and the one best representing the data is chosen. The selection of the number of classes is based on several factors (Muthen & Muthen, 2000): interpretability of the results given the study purpose, theoretical meaningfulness of the classes, and classification accuracy. The last is the ability to distinguish membership in the latent classes given the model and the data, and is reflected in *average class probabilities* (higher reflect superior ability to accurately classify cases into their most likely class). Another important tool for choosing the optimal number of classes is the Bayesian Information Criterion (BIC; Schwartz, 1978). Lower BIC values typically reflect better fit to the data, and reductions of six or greater are considered "strong" (Raftery, 1995).

References

Abbott v. Abbott. Transcripts of the US Supreme Court hearing on January 12, 2010. Retrieved May 14, 2012, from http://www.supremecourt.gov/oral_arguments/ argument_transcripts/08-645.pdf

Abramsky, T., Watts, C. H., Garcia-Moreno, C., Devries, K., Kiss, L., Ellsberg, M., et al. (2011). What factors are associated with recent intimate partner violence? Findings from the WHO multi-country study on women's health and domestic violence. *BMC Public Health, 11*, 1–26.

Acevedo, M. J. (2000). Battered immigrant Mexican women's perspectives regarding abuse and help-seeking. *Journal of Multicultural Social Work, 8*, 243–282.

Adamson, J. L., & Thompson, R. A. (1998). Coping with interparental verbal conflict by children exposed to spouse abuse and children from nonviolent homes. *Journal of Family Violence, 13*, 213–232.

Alvi, S., & Selbee, K. (1997). Dating status variations and woman abuse: A test of the Dependency, Availability, and Deterrence (DAD) model. *Violence Against Women, 3*, 610–628.

American Bar Association Commission on Domestic Violence. (2004). *Fundamentals of domestic violence*. Available online at www.americanbar.org

American Psychiatric Association. (2000). *Diagnostic and statistical manual of mental disorders* (4th ed., text rev.). Washington, DC: Author.

American Psychological Association Intimate Partner Abuse and Relationship Violence Working Group (2002). *Intimate partner abuse and relationship violence*. Washington, DC: American Psychological Association.

Anderson, D. K., & Saunders, D. G. (2003). Leaving an abusive partner: An empirical review of predictors, the process of leaving and psychological well-being. *Trauma, Violence and Abuse, 4*, 163–191.

Appadurai, A. (1990). Disjunction and difference in the global economy. *Public Culture, 2*, 1–24.

Appel, A., & Holden, G. (1998). The co-occurrence of spouse and physical child abuse: a review and appraisal. *Journal of Family Psychology, 12(4)*, 578–599.

Ayres, L., Kavanaugh, K., & Knafl, K. A. (2003). Within-case and across-case approaches to qualitative data analysis. *Qualitative Health Research, 13(6),* 871–883.

Barnish, M. (2004). Domestic violence: a literature review. Home Office, Inspectorate of Protection. Available online at www.justice.gov.uk

Bauer, H. M., Rodriguez, M. A., Quiroga, S. S., & Flores-Ortiz, Y. G. (2000). Barriers to health care for abused Latina and Asian immigrant women. *Journal of Health Care for the Poor and Underserved, 11,* 33–44.

Beaumont, P. R., & McEleavy, P. E. (1999). *The Hague Convention on international child abduction.* New York: Oxford University Press.

Belknap, J., Graham, D., Hartman, J., Lippen, V., Allen, G., & Sutherland, J. (2000). Factors related to domestic violence court dispositions in a large urban area: the role of victim/witness reluctance and other variables. US Department of Justice grant report (96-WT-NX-0004).

Berg, S. (1988). Snowball sampling. In S. Kotz & N. L. Johnson (Vol. Eds.) *Encyclopaedia of Statistical Sciences, Vol. 8.* New York: Wiley.

Bhuyan, R., Shim, W., & Velagapudi, K. (2010). Domestic violence advocacy with immigrants and refugees. In F. Danis & L. Lockhart, *Domestic violence mosaic: Culturally competent practice with diverse populations.* New York: Columbia University Press.

Black, M. C., Basile, K. C., Breiding, M. J., Smith, S. G., Walters, M. L., & Merrick, M. T., et al. (2011). *The national intimate partner and sexual violence survey (NISVS): 2010 summary report.* Atlanta, GA: National Center for Injury Prevention and Control, Centers for Disease Control and Prevention.

Bogat, G. A., DeJonghe, E., Levendosky, A. A., Davidson, W. S., & von Eye, A. (2006). Trauma symptoms among infants exposed to intimate partner violence. *Child Abuse & Neglect, 30,* 109–125.

Bouhours, B., & Daly, K. (2007). Youth sex offenders in court: an analysis of judicial sentencing remarks. *Punishment & Society, 9(4),* 371–394.

Brabeck, K. M., & Guzman, M. R. (2008). Frequency and perceived effectiveness of strategies to survive abuse employed by battered Mexican-origin women. *Violence Against Women, 14,* 1274–1294.

Brown, J. (1997). Working toward freedom from violence: The process of change in battered women. *Violence Against Women, 3,* 5–26.

Brown, R. (2002). *Roadmaps for clinical practice: Case studies in disease prevention and health promotion—intimate partner violence.* Chicago: American Medical Association.

Brownridge, D. A. (2006). Violence against women post-separation. *Aggression and Violent Behavior 11(5),* 514–530.

Bruch, C. S. (2004). The unmet needs of domestic violence victims and their children in Hague Abduction Convention cases. *Family Law Quarterly, 38,* 529–542.

Buel, S. (2003). Effective assistance of counsel for battered women defendants: a normative construct. *Harvard Women's Law Journal, 26,* 217–350.

Bullard, E. M. (2011). Insufficient government protection: The inescapable element in domestic violence asylum cases. *Minnesota Law Review, 95,* 1867–1898.

Cahn, N. (1991). Civil images of battered women: the impact of domestic violence on child custody decisions. *Vanderbilt Law Review, 44,* 1041–1097.

Calavita, K. (2001). Blue jeans, rape, and the "de-constitutive" power of law. *Law & Society Review, 35(1),* 89–116.

Campbell, J. C., Glass, N., Sharps, P. W., Laughon, K., & Bloom, T. (2007). Intimate partner homicide: Review and implications of research and policy. *Trauma, Violence, & Abuse, 8(3),* 246–269.

Campbell, J. C., Rose, L., Kub, J., & Nedd, D. (1998). Voices of strength and resistance: A contextual and longitudinal analysis of women's responses to battering. *Journal of Interpersonal Violence, 13,* 743–762.

Campbell, J. C., Webster, D., Koziol-McLain, J., Block, C., Campbell, D., Curry, M. A., et al. (2003). Risk factors for femicide in abusive relationships: Results from a multisite case control study. *American Journal of Public Health, 93(7),* 1089–1097.

Carlson, B. E. (2000) Children exposed to intimate partner violence: research findings and implications for intervention. *Trauma, Violence, & Abuse, 1(4),* 321–342.

Chan, Y. C., & Yeung, J. W. K. (2009). Children living with violence within the family and its sequel: A meta-analysis from 1995–2006. *Aggression and Violent Behavior, 14,* 313–322.

Charmaz, K. (2006). *Constructing grounded theory: A practical guide through qualitative analysis.* Thousand Oaks, CA: Sage.

Chew, P., & Kelley, R. (2005). *Unwrapping racial harassment law* (University of Pittsburgh School of Law Working Paper Series, Paper 22).

Chiancone, J., Girdner, L., & Hoff, P. (2001). Issues in resolving cases of international child abduction by parents. Washington, DC: Office of Juvenile Justice and Delinquency Prevention, US Department of Justice.

Choi, S., & Gulati, G. (2008). Bias in judicial citations: a window into the behavior of judges? *Journal of Legal Studies, 37,* 87–129.

Clive, E. M. (1997). The concept of habitual residence. *Juridical Review, 137,* 147. In *Mozes v. Mozes* (1999).

Cole, W. A., & Bradford, J. M. (1992). Abduction during custody and access disputes. *Canadian Journal of Psychiatry, 37,* 264–266.

Copelon, R. (1994). Intimate terror: Understanding domestic violence as torture. In R. J. Cook (Ed.), *Human rights of women: National and international perspectives* (pp. 116–152). Philadelphia: University of Pennsylvania Press.

Crenshaw, K. W. (1991). Mapping the margins: Intersectionality, identity politics, and violence against women of color. *Stanford Law Review, 43,* 1241–1299.

Czapanskiy, K. (1993). Domestic violence, the family, and the lawyering process: lessons from studies on gender bias in the courts. *Family Law Quarterly, 27,* 247–277.

Daiute, C. (2008). The rights of children, the rights of nations: Developmental theory and the politics of children's rights. *Journal of Social Issues, 64,* 701–723.

Dalton, C., Drozd, L., & Wong, F. (n.d.) *Navigating custody and visitation evaluations in cases with domestic violence: A judge's guide.* Reno, NV: National Council of Juvenile and Family Court Judges.

Davids, T., & van Driel, F. (2005). *The gender question in globalization: Changing perspectives and practices.* Burlington, VT: Ashgate Publishing.

DeKeseredy, W. S., Rogness, M., & Schwartz, M. D. (2004). Separation/divorce sexual assault: The current state of social scientific knowledge. *Aggression and Violent Behavior, 9(6),* 675–691.

DeMaris, A. A. (2001). The influence of intimate violence on transitions out of cohabitation. *Journal of Marriage and Family, 63,* 235–246.

Duluth Model (n.d.). Wheel gallery. Available online at www.theduluthmodel.org

Dunford-Jackson, B. L. (2004). The role of family courts in domestic violence: The US experience. In P. G. Jaffe, L. L. Baker, & A. Cunningham (Eds.), *Ending domestic violence in the lives of children and parents: Promising practices for safety, healing, and prevention* (pp. 188–199). New York: Guilford.

Dutton, M. A. (1992). *Empowering and healing the battered woman: A model for assessment and intervention.* New York: Springer Publishing.

Dutton, M. A., & Goodman, L. A. (2005). Coercion in intimate partner violence: Toward a new conceptualization. *Sex Roles, 52,* 743–756.

Edleson, J. (1999). The overlap between child maltreatment and woman battering. *Violence Against Women, 5(2),* 134–154.

Edleson, J. L. (2006). Emerging responses to children exposed to domestic violence. Harrisburg, PA: VAWnet, a project of the National Resource Center on Domestic Violence/Pennsylvania Coalition Against Domestic Violence. Retrieved May 9, 2010, from http://www.vawnet.org

Edleson, J. L., Mbilinyi, L. F., Beeman, S. K., & Hagemeister, A. K. (2003). How children are involved in adult domestic violence: Results from a four city telephone survey. *Journal of Interpersonal Violence, 18(1),* 18–32.

Edwards, A. (2010). *Violence against women under international human rights law.* Cambridge, England: Cambridge University Press.

Elliott, J. (2005). *Using narrative in social research: Qualitative and quantitative approaches.* London: Sage.

Ennis, S. R., Rios-Vargas, M., & Albert, N. G. (2011). *The Hispanic population: 2010.* Washington, DC: US Census Bureau.

Eriksen, T. H. (2007). Globalization: The key concepts. New York: Berg Publishers.

Eriksson, M., & Hester, M. (2001). Violent men as good enough fathers. *Violence Against Women, 7,* 779–798.

Espenoza, C. M. (1999). No relief for the weary: VAWA relief denied for battered immigrants lost in the intersections. *Marquette Law Review, 83,* 163–220.

Evans, S. E., Davies, C., & DiLillo, D. (2008). Exposure to domestic violence: A meta-analysis of child and adolescent outcomes. *Aggression and Violent Behavior, 13,* 131–140.

Eveline, J., Bacchi, C., & Binns, J. (2009). Gender mainstreaming vs. diversity mainstreaming: Methodology as emancipatory politics. *Gender, Work & Organization, 16,* 198–211.

Fantuzzo, J. W., Brouch, R., Beriama, A., & Atkins, M. (1997). Domestic Violence and Children: Prevalence and Risk in Five Major U.S. Cities. *Journal of the American Academy of Child and Adolescent Psychiatry, 36,* 116–122.

Fantuzzo, J. W., & Mohr, W. K. (1999). Prevalence and effects of child exposure to domestic violence. *The Future of Children, 9,* 21–32.

Faugier, J., & Sargeant, M. (1997). Sampling hard to reach populations. *Journal of Advanced Nursing, 26,* 790–797.

Federal Interagency Forum on Child and Family Statistics (2009). *American's children: Key national indicators of well-being, 2009.* Washington, DC: US Government Printing Office.

Finkelhor, D., Hotaling, G., & Sedlak, A. (1991). Children abducted by family members: A national household survey of incidence and episode characteristics. *Journal of Marriage and Family, 53,* 805–817.

Finkelhor, D., Turner, H., Ormrod, R., & Hamby, S. L. (2009). Violence, abuse and crime exposure in a national sample of children and youth. *Pediatrics, 124,* 1411–1423.

Fleury, R. E., Sullivan, C. M., & Bybee, D. I. (2000). When ending the relationship does not end the violence: Women's experience of violence by former partners. *Violence Against Women, 6, 12,* 1363–1383.

Forehand, R., Long, N., Zogg, C., & Parrish, E. (1989). Child abduction: Parent and child functioning following return. *Clinical Pediatrics, 28,* 311–316.

Frias, S. M., & Angel, R. J. (2005). Risk of partner violence among low-income Hispanic groups. *Journal of Marriage and the Family, 67,* 552–564.

Freeman, M. (2006). *International child abduction: The effects.* Leicester, UK: Reunite International. Retrieved May 9, 2010, from http://www.reunite.org/research.asp

Freeman, M. (2009). *Relocation: The research.* Leicester, UK: Reunite International. Retrieved May 9, 2010, from http://www.reunite.org/research.asp

Ganatra, N. R. (2001). The cultural dynamic in domestic violence: Understanding the additional burdens battered immigrant women of color face in the United States. Journal of Law in Society, 2, 109–147.

Garbolino, Hon. JD. (2000). International child custody cases: Handling Hague Convention cases in U.S. courts (3rd ed.). Reno, NV: National Judicial College.

Garcia, L., Hurwitz, E. L., & Kraus, J. F. (2005). Acculturation and reported intimate partner violence among Latinas in Los Angeles. *Journal of Interpersonal Violence, 20 (5)*, 569–590.

Garcia O'Hearn, H., Margolin, G., & John, R. S. (1997). Mothers' and fathers' reports of children's reactions to naturalistic marital conflict. *Journal of the American Academy of Child and Adolescent Psychiatry, 36*, 1366–1373.

Garcia-Moreno, C., Jansen, H. A. F. M., Ellsberg, M., Heise, L., & Watts, C. (2005). *World Health Organization multi-country study on women's health and domestic violence against women*. Geneva, Switzerland: World Health Organization.

Garland, D. (1990). Punishment and modern society: A study in social theory. Chicago: University of Chicago Press.

Gewirtz, A., & Edleson, J. L. (2007). Young children's exposure to adult domestic violence: Towards a risk and resilience framework for research and intervention. *Journal of Family Violence, 22*, 151–163.

Gibbons, J. (1999). Language and the law. *Annual Review of Applied Linguistics, 19*, 156–173.

Gomez, D. (2003). Last in line—The United States trails behind in recognizing gender-based asylum claims. *Whittier Law Review, 25*, 959–988.

Goodkind, J., Sullivan, C. M., & Bybee, D. I. (2004). A contextual analysis of battered women's safety planning. *Violence Against Women, 10(5)*, 514–533.

Goodman, L., Dutton, M. A., Weinfurt, K., & Cook, S. (2003). The intimate partner violence strategies index. *Violence Against Women, 9*, 163–186.

Goodman, L. A. (2002). Latent class analysis: The empirical study of latent types, latent variables and latent structures. In J. A. Hagenaars & A. L. McCutcheon (Eds.), *Applied latent class analysis* (pp. 3–55). New York: Cambridge University Press.

Graham-Bermann, S. A., & Edleson, J. L. (2001). *Domestic violence in the lives of children: The future of research, intervention, and social policy*. Washington, DC: American Psychological Association.

Graneheim, U., & Lundman, B. (2004). Qualitative content analysis in nursing research: concepts, procedures and measures to achieve trustworthiness. *Nurse Education Today, 24(2)*, p. 105–112.

Greif, G. L. (2009). The long-term aftermath of child abduction: Two case studies and implications for family therapy. *American Journal of Family Therapy, 37*, 273–286.

Greif, G. L., & Hegar, R. (1993). *When parents kidnap: the families behind the headlines*. New York: Free Press.

Haas, G. A., Dutton, M. A., & Orloff, L. E. (2000). Lifetime prevalence of violence against Latina immigrants: Legal and policy implications. *International Review of Victimology, 7*, 93–113.

Hague Conference on Private International Law. (2010). *Convention of 25 October 1980 on the Civil Aspects of International Child Abduction.* Available online at http://hcch.e-vision.nl

Hagenaars, J. A., & McCutcheon, A. L. (Eds). (2002). *Applied latent class analyses.* Cambridge, UK: Cambridge University Press.

Hall, M., & Wright, R. (2008). Systematic content analysis of judicial opinions. *California Law Review, 96(1),* 63–122.

Hamby, S. L. (2009). The gender debate on intimate partner violence: Solutions and dead ends. *Psychological Trauma, 1(1),* 24–34.

Hamby, S., Finkelhor, D., Turner, H., & Ormrod, R. (2010). The overlap of witnessing partner violence with child maltreatment and other victimizations in a nationally representative survey of youth. *Child Abuse & Neglect, 34,* 734–741.

Hammer, H., Finkelhor, D., & Sedlak, A. J. (2002). *Children abducted by family members: National estimates and characteristics.* Washington, DC: Office of Juvenile Justice and Delinquency Prevention, Office of Justice Programs, US Department of Justice.

Henning, K., & Feder, L. (2004). A comparison between men and women arrested for domestic violence: Who presents the greater threat? *Journal of Family Violence, 19(2),* 69–81.

Heyman, M. G. (2005). Domestic violence and asylum: Toward a working model of affirmative state obligations. *International Journal of Refugee Law, 17,* 729–748.

Hilton, W. M. (1997). Limitations on Article 13(b) of the Convention on the Civil Aspects of International Child Abduction. *American Journal of Family Law, 11,* 139–144.

Hoegger, R. (2003). What if she leaves? Domestic violence cases under the Hague Convention and the insufficiency of the undertakings remedy. *Berkeley Women's Law Journal, 18,* 181–210.

Holden, G. W. (2003). Children exposed to domestic violence and child abuse: Terminology and taxonomy. *Clinical Child and Family Psychology Review, 6(3),* 151–160.

Hsieh, H. F., & Shannon, S. E. (2005). Three approaches to qualitative content analysis. *Qualitative Health Research, 15,* 1277–1288.

Humphreys, J. C. (1995). Dependent-care by battered women: protecting their children. *Health Care for Women International, 16,* 9–20.

Hunnicut, G. (2009). Varieties of patriarchy and violence against women: Resurrecting "patriarchy" as a theoretical tool. Violence Against Women, 15, 553–573.

Hunt, A. (1993). Explorations in law and society: Towards a constitutive theory of law. New York: Routledge.

Husband guilty of murdering his wife. (2009, May 1). BBC News. Available online at www.bbc.co.uk/news

Hyden, M. (2008). Narrativing sensitive topics. In M. Andrews, C. Squire, &
M. Tamboukou (Eds.), *Doing narrative research* (pp. 121–136). Los Angeles: Sage.

International Child Abduction Remedies Act, 42 U.S.C.A. § 11603 (1988).

International Social Service (2007). *Learning from the links between domestic violence and international parental child abduction.* Melbourne, Australia: Author.

Jaffe, P. G., & Crooks, C. V. (2004). Partner violence and child custody cases: A cross-national comparison of legal reforms and issues. *Violence Against Women, 10(8),* 917–934.

Janvier, R. F., McCormick, K., & Donaldson, R. (1990). Parental kidnapping: A survey of left-behind parents. *Juvenile and Family Court Journal, 41,* 1–8.

Jelinek, L., Randjbar, S., Seifert, D., Kellner, M., & Moritz, S. (2009). The organization of autobiographical and nonautobiographical memory in posttraumatic stress disorder (PTSD). *Journal of Abnormal Psychology, 118,* 288–298.

Johnson, M. P. (2008). *A typology of domestic violence: intimate terrorism, violent resistance, and situational couple violence.* Lebanon, NH: Northeastern Press.

Johnson, R. M., Kotch, J. B., Catellier, D. J., Winsor, J. R., Dufort, V., Hunter, W., et al. (2002). Adverse behavioral and emotional outcomes from child abuse and witnessed violence. *Child Maltreatment, 7,* 179–186.

Johnson, H., Ollus, N., & Nevala, S. (2008). *Violence against women: An international perspective.* New York: Springer.

Johnston, J., Sagatun-Edwards, I., Blomquist, M., & Girdner, L. (2001). *Prevention of family abduction through early identification of risk factors.* Washington, DC: Office of Juvenile Justice and Delinquency Prevention, US Department of Justice.

Jones, A. (1994). *Next time she'll be dead: Battering and how to stop it.* Boston, MA: Beacon Press.

Jouriles, E. N., McDonald, R., Slep, A. M., Heyman, R. E., & Garrido, E. (2008). Child abuse in the context of domestic violence: Prevalence, explanations, and practice implications. *Violence and Victims, 23,* 221–235.

Jouriles, E. N., Norwood, W. D., McDonald, R., Vincent, J. P., & Mahoney, A. (1996). Physical violence and other forms of marital aggression: Links with children's behavior problems. *Journal of Family Psychology, 10,* 223–234.

Kiesel, L. R., Piescher, K. N., & Edleson, J. L. (2011). *Direct and indirect child exposure to violence: Effects on academic performance and disability.* St. Paul, MN: University of Minnesota (manuscript submitted for publication).

Kilpatrick Stockton, LLP. (2007). *Litigating international child abduction cases under the Hague Convention.* Alexandria, VA: National Center for Missing and Exploited Children.

Kingston-Riechers, J. (2001). The association between the frequency of wife assault and marital dissolution in Canada. *Journal of Population Economics, 14(2),* 351–365.

Kitzmann, K. M., Gaylord, N. K., Holt, A. R., & Kenny, E. D. (2003). Child witness to domestic violence: A meta-analytic review. *Journal of Consulting and Clinical Psychology, 71(2)*, 339–352.

Klevens, J. (2007). An overview of intimate partner violence among Latinos. *Violence Against Women, 13*, 111–122.

Kohn, L. (2007). Justice system and domestic violence: Engaging the case but divorcing the victim. *New York University Review of Law & Social Change, 32*, 191–252.

Koss, M. P., Goodman, L. A., Browne, A., Fitzgerald, L. F., Keita, G. P., & Russo, N. F. (1994). *Common themes and a call for action.* Washington, DC: American Psychological Association.

Kury, H., Obergfell-Fuchs, J., & Woessner, G. (2004). The extent of family violence in Europe: A comparison of national surveys. *Violence Against Women, 7*, 749–769.

Lansner, D. (2008). The Nicholson decisions: New York's response to "failure to protect" allegations. *American Bar Association Commission on Domestic Violence e-Newsletter, 12.* Retrieved March 3, 2010, from http://www.abanet.org/domviol/enewsletter/vol12/expert1.html

Lee, L. C., Kotch, J. B., & Cox, C. E. (2004). Child maltreatment in families experiencing domestic violence. *Violence & Victims, 19(5)*, 573–591.

Lemon, N. K. D. (1999). The legal system's response to children exposed to domestic violence. *The Future of Children, 9*, 67–83.

Lens, V. (2008). Welfare and work sanctions: Examining discretion on the front lines. *Social Service Review, 82(2)*, 197–222.

Lewandowski, L. A., McFarlane, J., Campbell, J. C., Gary, F., & Barenski, C. (2004). "He killed my mommy!" Murder or attempted murder of a child's mother. *Journal of Family Violence, 19*, 211–220.

Liang, B., Goodman, L., Tummala-Narra, P., & Weintraub, S. (2005). A theoretical framework for understanding help-seeking processes among survivors of intimate partner violence. *American Journal of Community Psychology, 36*, 71–84.

Libal, K., & Parekh, S. (2009). Reframing violence against women as a human rights violation: Evan Stark's *Coercive control. Violence Against Women, 14*, 1477–1489.

Lindhorst, T., Meyers, M., & Casey, E. (2008). Screening for domestic violence in public welfare offices: An analysis of case manager and client interactions. *Violence Against Women, 14(5)*, 5–28.

Lindhorst, T., & Padgett, J. (2005). Disjunctures for women and frontline workers: Implementation of the family violence option. *Social Service Review, 79(3)*, 405–429.

Lindhorst, T., & Tajima, E. (2008). Reconceptualizing and operationalizing context in survey research on intimate partner violence. *Journal of Interpersonal Violence, 23(3)*, 362–388.

Litrownik, A. J., Newton, R., Hunter, W. M., English, D., & Everson, M. D. (2003). Exposure to family violence in young at-risk children: A longitudinal look at the effects of victimization and witnessed physical and psychological aggression. *Journal of Family Violence, 18*, 59–73.

Lockhart, L. L., & Danis, F. (Eds.). (2010). *Domestic violence mosaic: Culturally competent practice with diverse populations.* New York: Columbia University Press.

Lowe, N. (2007). *A statistical analysis of applications made in 2003 under the Hague Convention of 25 October, 1980 on the Civil Aspects of International Child Abduction.* The Hague, NL: Hague Conference on Private International Law.

Lowe, N. (2011). *A statistical analysis of applications made in 2008 under the Hague Convention of 25 October 1980 on the Civil Aspects of International Child Abduction. Part I – global report. Preliminary document No 8 A of May 2011 for the attention of the special commission of June 2011.* The Hague, NL: Hague Conference on Private International Law.

Magnusson, D. (1998). The logic and implications of a person-oriented approach. In R. B. Cairns, L. R. Bergman, & J. Kagan (Eds.), *Methods and models for studying the individual* (pp. 33–64). Thousand Oaks, CA: Sage.

Mahmoody, B., & Hoffer, W. (1987). *Not without my daughter.* New York: St. Martin's.

Margolin, G., & Gordis, E. B. (2004). Children's violence exposure in the family and community. *Current Directions in Psychological Science, 13*, 152–155.

Marshall, C., & Rossman, G. B. (1999). *Designing qualitative research* (3rd ed.). Thousand Oaks, CA: Sage.

Martin, D. (1976). Battered wives. New York: Pocket Books.

Mathews, M. A. (1999). The impact of federal and state laws on children exposed to domestic violence. *Future of Children, 9*, 50–66.

Mbilinyi, L. F., Edleson, J. L., Hagemeister, A. K., & Beeman, S. K. (2007). What happens to children when their mothers are battered? Results from a four city anonymous telephone survey. *Journal of Family Violence, 22*, 309–317.

McCutcheon, A. L. (1987). *Latent class analysis* (Sage University Paper series on Quantitative Applications in the Social Sciences, No. 07-064). Newbury Park, CA: Sage.

McGuigan, W. M., & Pratt, C. C. (2001). The predictive impact of domestic violence on three types of child maltreatment. *Child Abuse & Neglect, 25(7)*, 869–883.

McHugh, M. C., Livingston, N. A., & Ford, A. (2005). A postmodern approach to women's use of violence: Developing multiple and complex conceptualizations. *Psychology of Women Quarterly, 29*, 323–336.

Menjivar, C., & Salcido, O. (2002). Immigrant women and domestic violence: Common experiences in different countries. *Gender and Society, 16(6)*, 898–920.

Mercer, K. (1998). A content analysis of judicial decision-making—how judges use the primary caretaker standard to make a custody determination. *William and Mary Law Review, 5(1)*, 1–149.

Merlino, M., Murray, C., & Richardson, J. (2008). Judicial gatekeeping and the social construction of the admissibility of expert testimony. *Behavioral Sciences and the Law, 26,* 187–206.

Merry, S. (2000). Colonizing Hawai'i: The Cultural Power of Law. Princeton, NJ: Princeton University Press.

Meyer, D. Z., & Avery, L. M. (2009). Excel as a qualitative data analysis tool. *Field Methods, 21,* 91–112.

Miles, M. B., & Huberman, A. M. (1994). *Qualitative data analysis: An expanded sourcebook* (2nd ed.). Thousand Oaks, CA: Sage.

Miller, N. (2004). *Domestic violence: A review of state legislation defining police and prosecution duties and powers.* Alexandria, VA: Institute for Law and Justice.

Miller, S. L., & Smolter, N. L. (2011). "Paper abuse": When all else fails, batterers use procedural stalking. *Violence Against Women, 17,* 637–650.

Moser, C., & Moser, A. (2005). Gender mainstreaming since Beijing: A review of success and limitations in international institutions. *Gender & Development, 13,* 11–22.

Muhr, T. (2005). ATLAS.ti [computer software]. Berlin: Scientific Software Development GmbH.

Muthen, B., & Muthen, L. K. (2000). Integrating person-centered and variable-centered analyses: Growth mixture modeling with latent trajectory classes. *Alcoholism: Clinical and Experimental Research, 24,* 882–891.

National Council of Juvenile and Family Court Judges. (1999). *Effective intervention in domestic violence and child maltreatment: Guidelines for policy and practice (the Greenbook).* Reno, NV: Author.

National Research Council (2006). *Multiple origins, uncertain destinies: Hispanics and the American future.* Panel on Hispanics in the United States. M. Tienda and F. Mitchell (Eds.) Committee on Population, Division of Behavioral and Social Sciences and Education. Washington, DC: National Academies Press.

Northwest Immigrant Rights Project (NWIRP). (2000). U-Visa for victims of domestic violence crimes. Retrieved November 16, 2010, from http://www.nwirp.org/Documents/U-VisaforVictimsofDVCrimes.pdf

O'Hare, U. A. (1999). Realizing human rights for women. Human Rights Quaterly, 21, 364–402.

Ombudsman Foundation (Stichting de Ombudsman). (2002). The Hague convention on child (translated from the original Dutch). Amsterdam: Author. Retrieved November 16, 2010, from http://www.lievebeau.nl/WEB-IMAGES/ombudsman%20onderzoek%20HKOV.pdf

Orloff, L., & Kaguyutan, J. (2001). Offering a helping hand: Legal protections for battered immigrant women: A history of legislative responses. *American University Journal of Gender, Social Policy & the Law, 10(1),* 95–183.

Padilla, M. B., Hirsch, J. S., Muñoz-Laboy, M., Sember, R. E., & Parker, R. G. (Eds.). (2007). *Love and globalization: Transformations of intimacy in the contemporary world*. Nashville, TN: Vanderbilt University Press.

Panchanadeswaran, S., & McCloskey, L. A. (2007). Predicting the timing of women's departure from abusive relationships. *Journal of Interpersonal Violence, 22(1)*, 50–65.

Pedhazur, E. (1997). *Multiple regression in behavioral research: Explanation and prediction* (3rd ed.). New York: Harcourt Brace.

Peled, E. (1998). The experience of living with violence for preadolescent witnesses of woman abuse. *Youth & Society, 29*, 395–430.

Pendleton, G. (2003). Ensuring fairness and justice for noncitizen survivors of domestic violence. *Juvenile and Family Court Journal*, 69–85.

Perez-Vera, E. (1981). *Explanatory report*. Hague Conference on Private International Law, Actes et documents de la Quatorzieme session, Vol. 111. Available online at www.brandeslaw.com

Perilla, J. L. (1999). Domestic violence as a human rights issue: The case of immigrant Latinas. *Hispanic Journal of Behavioral Sciences, 21*, 107–133.

Perry, E., Kulik, C., & Bourhis, A. (2004). The reasonable woman standard: effects on sexual harassment court decisions. *Law and Human Behavior, 28(1)*, 9–27.

Porter, S., & Peace, K. A. (2007). The scars of memory. *Psychological Science, 18*, 435–441.

Postmus, J. L., Severson, M., Berry, M., & Yoo, J. A. (2009). Women's experiences of violence and seeking help. *Violence Against Women, 15*, 852–868.

Preston, J. (2009, July 16). New policy permits asylum for battered women. *New York Times*, p. A1.

Raftery, A. E. (1995). Bayesian model selection in social research. *Sociological Methodology, 25*, 111–164.

Raj, A., & Silverman, J. (2002). Violence against immigrant women: The roles of culture, context, and legal immigrant status on intimate partner violence. *Violence Against Women, 8*, 367–398.

Rao, A. (2006). Making institutions work for women. *Development, 49*, 63–67.

Ravensbergen, J. (2010, December 16). Custody case turns deadly as dad takes off with kids, who are shot as police close in. *The Vancouver Sun*. Available online at www.vancouversun.com

Reunite International (2003). *The outcomes for children returned following an abduction*. Leicester, UK: Author. Retrieved May 9, 2010, from http://www.reunite.org/research.asp

Rhoades, K. A. (2008). Children's responses to interparental conflict: A meta-analysis of their associations with child adjustment. *Child Development, 79*, 1942–1956.

Riessman, C. K. (2008). *Narrative methods for the human sciences*. Thousand Oaks, CA: Sage.

Ritzer, G. (2007). *The globalization of nothing* (2nd ed.). Thousand Oaks, CA: Sage.

Ritzer, G. (2008). *The McDonaldization of society* (5th ed.). Thousand Oaks, CA: New Century Edition.

Rizo, C. F. & Macy, R. J. (2011). Help seeking and barriers of Hispanic partner violence survivors: A systematic review of the literature. *Aggression and Violent Behavior, 16,* 250–264.

Robinson, S. K. (1994). Ten pillars of good lawyering. *Res Gestae, 38,* 33–38.

Roe, E. (1994). *Narrative policy analysis: Theory and practice.* Durham, NC: Duke University Press.

Rossman, B. B. R. (1998). Descarte's error and posttraumatic stress disorder: Cognition and emotion in children who are exposed to parental violence. In G. W. Holden, R. Gefner, & E. N. Jouriles (Eds.), *Children exposed to marital violence: Theory, research, and applied issues* (pp. 223–256). Washington, DC: American Psychological Association.

Rossman, B. B. R., Hughes, H. M., & Rosenberg, M. S. (2000). *Children and interparental violence: The impact of exposure.* Philadelphia: Brunner/Mazel.

Sagatun, I. J., & Barrett, L. (1990). Parental child abduction: The law, family dynamics, and legal system responses. Journal of Criminal Justice, 18, 443–442.

Saldana, J. (2009). The coding manual for qualitative researchers. Thousand Oaks, CA: Sage.

Sandelowski, M. (1997). "To be of use": Enhancing the utility of qualitative research. Nursing Outlook, 45, 125–132.

Sandelowski, M. (2000). Whatever happened to qualitative description? Research in Nursing & Health, 23(4), 334–340.

Sarat, A., & Felstiner, W. (1995). Divorce Lawyers and their clients: Power & meaning in the legal process. New York: Oxford University Press.

Scheeringha, M. S., & Gaensbauer, T. J. (2000). Posttraumatic stress disorder. In C. H. Zeanah Jr. (Ed.), *Handbook of infant mental health* (2nd ed.) (pp. 369–381). New York: Guilford.

Scholte, J. A. (2000). *Globalization: A critical introduction.* New York: St. Martin's.

Schwartz, G. (1978). Estimating the dimension of a model. *Annals of Statistics, 6,* 461–464.

Secretary General of the United Nations. (2006). *In-depth study on all forms of violence against women* (Document A/61/122/Add.1). Available online at www.unhcr.org

Semple, K. (2009, Feb. 25). Court battle over a child strains ties in 2 nations. *New York Times,* p. A21.

Shetty, S., & Edleson, J. L. (2005). Adult domestic violence in cases of international parental child abduction. *Violence Against Women, 11(1),* 115–138.

Short, L. M., McMahon, P. M., Chervin, D. D., Shelley, G. A., Lezin, N., Sloop, K. S., et al. (2000). Survivors' identification of protective factors and early warning signs for intimate partner violence. *Violence Against Women, 6,* 272–285.

Silberman, L. (2000). Gender politics and other issues. *New York University Journal of International Law and Politics, 33,* 221–250.

Silberman, L. (2000). The Hague Convention turns twenty: Gender politics and other issues. *New York Journal of International Law and Politics, 33,* 229–230.

Singh, R. N. (2008). Gendercide. In C. Renzetti and J. L. Edleson (Eds.), *Encyclopedia of Interpersonal Violence* (pp. 291–292). Thousand Oaks, CA: Sage.

Skopp, N. A., McDonald, R., Jouriles, E. N., & Rosenfield, D. (2007). Partner aggression and children's externalizing problems: Maternal and partner warmth as protective factors. *Journal of Family Psychology, 21(3),* 459–467.

Smith, P. H., Smith, J. B., & Earp, J. A. L. (1999). Beyond the measurement trap: A reconstructed conceptualization and measurement of woman battering. *Psychology of Women Quarterly, 23,* 177–193.

Sokoloff, N. (2008). Expanding the intersectional paradigm to better understand domestic violence in immigrant communities. *Critical Criminology, 16(4),* 229–255.

Spilman, S. K. (2006). Child abduction, parents' distress and social support. *Violence and Victims, 21(2),* 149–165.

Stark, E. (2007). *Coercive control: The entrapment of women in personal life.* New York: Oxford University Press.

Stasiulis, D. K., & Bakan, A. B. (2003). *Negotiating citizenship: Migrant women in Canada and the global system.* New York: Palgrave MacMillan.

Stevenson, B., & Wolfers, J. (2006). Bargaining in the shadow of the law: Divorce laws and family distress. *Quarterly Journal of Economics, 121,* 267–288.

Straus, M., Gelles, R. J., & Steinmetz, S. K. (1980). *Behind closed doors: Violence in the American family.* Garden City, NY: Anchor Books.

Tjaden, P., & Thoennes, N. (1998). *Prevalence, incidence and consequences of violence against women: Findings from the National Violence Against Women Survey, NCJ 172837.* Washington, DC: National Institute of Justice and Centers for Disease Control.

Tjaden, P., & Thoennes, N. (2000). *Full report of the prevalence, incidence, and consequences of violence against women* (No. NCJ 183781). Washington, DC: US Department of Justice, Office of Justice Programs. Retrieved September 15, 2002, from http://www.ncjrs.gov/pdffiles1/nij/183781.pdf

Trask, B. S. (2010). *Globalization and families: Accelerated systemic social change.* New York: Springer.

Turner, H. A., Finkelhor, D., & Ormrod, R. (2006). The effect of lifetime victimization on the mental health of children and adolescents. *Social Science & Medicine, 62(1),* 13–27.

Uehara, E. S. (2007). "Disturbing phenomenology" in the pain and engagement narratives of Cambodian American survivors of the killing fields. *Culture, Medicine, and Psychiatry, 31*, 329–358.

United Nations. (1993). Convention on the elimination of violence against women. New York: United Nations General Assembly.

United Nations Department of Economic and Social Affairs, Population Division. (2011). *International migration report 2009: A global assessment.* New York: Author.

United Nations Women. (2011). Violence against women prevalence data: Surveys by country. Available online at www.endvawnow.org

US Department of State. (2010a). *Report on compliance with the Hague Convention on the Civil Aspects of Child Abduction.* Washington, DC: Author

US Department of State. (2010b). Possible solutions: Using the Hague Abduction Convention. Washington, DC: Author. Retrieved November 16, 2010, from http://travel.state.gov/abduction/solutions/hagueconvention/hagueconvention_3854.htm

US Department of State. (2012a). 2011 Outgoing Case Statistics. Washington, DC: Author. Retrieved May 14, 2012, from http://travel.state.gov/pdf/Outgoing_Stats2011.pdf

US Department of State. (2012b). 2011 Outgoing Case Statistics. Washington, DC: Author. Retrieved May 14, 2012, from http://travel.state.gov/pdf/Incoming_Stats2011.pdf

Ventura, L. A., & Davis, G. (2005). Domestic violence: Court case conviction and recidivism. *Violence against Women, 11*, 255–277.

Vest, J. R., Catlin, T. K., Chen, J. J., & Brownson, R. C. (2002). Multi-state analysis of factors associated with intimate partner violence. *American Journal of Preventive Medicine, 22*, 156–164.

Violence Against Women Act of 1994, Pub. L. No. 103-322 (reauthorized in 2000 & 2005).

Vivatvaraphol, T. (2009). Back to basics: Determining a child's habitual residence in international child abduction cases under the Hague Convention. *Fordham Law Review, 77*, 3325–3368.

Vives-Cases, C., Ortiz-Barreda, G., & Gil-Gonzalez, D. (2010). Mapping violence against women laws in the world: An overview of state commitments. *Journal of Epidemiology and Community Health, 64*, 474–475.

Watts, C., & Zimmerman, C. (2002). Violence against women: Global scope and magnitude. *The Lancet, 359*, 1232–1237.

Weiner, M. H. (2000). International child abduction and the escape from domestic violence. *Fordham Law Review, 69*, 593.

Weiner, M. H. (2001). Navigating the road between uniformity and progress: The need for a purposive analysis of the Hague Convention on the Civil Aspects of International Child Abduction. *Columbia Human Rights Law Review, 33(2)*, p. 275–362.

Weiner, M. H. (2003). The potential challenges of transnational litigation for feminists concerned about domestic violence here and abroad. *American University Journal of Gender, Social Policy & the Law, 11,* 749–800.

Weiner, M. H. (2004). Strengthening Article 20. University of San Francisco Law Review, 38, 701–746.

Weiner, M. H. (2008). Intolerable situations and counsel for children: Following Switzerland's example in Hague abduction cases. American University Law Review, 58, 335–403.

Weithorn, L. A. (2001). Protecting children from exposure to domestic violence: The use and abuse of child maltreatment. *Hastings Law Review, 53*(1), 1–156.

West, C. M, Kantor, G. K., & Jasinski, J. L. (1998). Sociodemographic predictors and cultural barriers to help-seeking behavior by Latino and non-Latino white American battered women. *Violence and Victims, 13,* 361–375.

White, J. (1995). What's an opinion for? *University of Chicago Law Review, 62(4),* 1363–1369.

Wolfe, D. A., Crooks, C. V., Lee, V., McIntyre-Smith, A., & Jaffe, P. G. (2003). The effects of children's exposure to domestic violence: A meta-analysis and critique. Clinical Child and Family Psychology Review, 6(3), 171–187.

Wood, S. M. (2004). VAWA's unfinished business: The immigrant women who fall through the cracks. *Duke Journal of Gender Law & Policy, 11,* 141–156.

Wuest, J., & Merritt-Gray, M. (1999). Not going back: Sustaining the separation in the process of leaving abusive relationships. *Violence Against Women, 5(2),* 110–133.

Legal Cases Cited

An asterisk (*) is used to denote cases used in the analysis presented in chapter 7.

Abbott v. Abbott, __S.Ct. __, 2010 WL 1946730

*In re Adan, 544 F.3d 542 (3d Cir. 2008)

*Aldinger v. Segler, 263 F. Supp. 2d 284 (D.P.R. 2003)

* *Antonio v. Bello,* No. Civ.A.1:04-CV-1555-T, 2004 WL 1895126 (N.D. Ga. 2004)

*Antunez-Fernandes v. Connors-Fernandes, 259 F. Supp. 2d 800 (N.D. Iowa 2003)

*Baran v. Beaty, 479 F.Supp. 1257 (S.D. Alabama 2007)

Baxter v. Baxter, 423 F.3d 363 (3rd Cir. 2005)

*Belay v. Getachew, 272 F. Supp. 2d 553 (D. Md. 2003)

*Blondin v. Dubois, 238 F.3d 153 (2nd Cir. 2001)

C v S (minor: abduction: illegitimate child [1990]), 2 All E.R. 961, 965 (Eng.H.L.)

*Ciotola v. Fiocca, 684 N.E.2d 763 (Ohio Com. Pleas 1997)

*Croll v. Croll, 66 F. Supp. 2d 554 (S.D.N.Y.1999)

*Currier v. Currier, 845 F. Supp. 916 (D.N.H. 1994)

Dallemagne v Dallemagne, 440 F. Supp. 2d 1283 (M.D. Fla. 2006)

*Dalmasso v. Dalmasso, 269 Kan. 752 (2000)

*Danaipour v. Danaipour, 386 F.3d 289 (1st Cir. 2004)

*In re D.D., 440 F. Supp. 2d 1283 (M.D. Fla. 2006)

*Edwards v. Edwards, 254 Ga. App. 849 (Ga. Ct. App. 2002)

*Elyashiv v. Elyashiv, 353 F. Supp. 2d 394 (E.D. New York 2005)

*Fabri v. Pritikin-Fabri, 221 F. Supp. 2d 859 (N.D. Ill. 2001)

Friedrich v. Friedrich, 78 F.3d 1060 (6th Cir. 1996)

*Gil v. Rodriguez, 184 F. Supp. 2d 1221 (M.D. Fla. 2002)

*Gonzalez v. Gutierrez, 311 F.3d 942, 949 (9th Circuit 2002)

Harsacky v. Harsacky, 930 S.W.2d 410, 413 (Ky. Ct. App. 1996)

Hasan v. Hasan, 2004 WL 57073 (D. Mass. 2004)

Janakakis-Kostun v. Janakakis, 6 S.W.3d 843 (Ky. Ct. App. 1999)

*Journe v. Journe, 911 F. Supp. 43 (D.P.R. 1995)

*Koc v. Koc, 181 F. Supp. 2d 136 (E.D.N.Y 2001)

In re Leslie, 377 F. Supp. 2d 1232 (S.D. Fla. 2005)

Levesque v. Levesque, 816 F. Supp. 662 (D. Kansas 1993)

*Mendez Lynch v. Mendez Lynch, 220 F. Supp. 2d 1347 (M.D. Fla. 2002)

*Miller v. Miller, 240 F. 3d 392 (4th Cir. 2001)

Mozes v. Mozes, No. 98-56505 (9th Cir. 1999)

*Nunez-Escudero v. Tice-Menley, 58 F. 3d 374 (8th Cir. 1995)

Ostevoll v. Ostevoll, 2000 US Dist. LEXIS 16178 (S.D. Ohio 2000)

Panazatou v. Panazatou, 1997 Conn. Super LEXIS 2627 (1997)

Ponath v. Ponath, 829 F. Supp. 363 (D. Utah 1993)

*Prevot v. Prevot, 855 F. Supp. 915 (W.D. Tenn. 1994)

*Rodriguez v. Rodriguez, 33 F. Supp. 2d 456 (Dist. MD 1999)

*People ex rel. Ron v. Levi, 279 A.D.2d 860 (N.Y.A.D. 2001)

*Salah v. Awes, 629 N.W.2d 99 (Minn. Ct. App. 2001)

Silverman v Silverman, 338 F.3d 886 (8th Cir, 2003)

Simcox v. Simcox, 511 F.3d 594 (6th Cir. 2007).

Tabacchi v. Harrison, NO. 99-C4130, 2000 WL 190576, 13 (N.D. Ill. 2000)

Tsarbopoulos v. Tsarbopoulos, 176 F. Supp. 2d 104 (E.D. Wash. 2001)

Turner v. Frowein, 253 Conn. 312 (2000)

Van De Sande v. Van De Sande, 431 F.3d 567 (7th Cir. 2005)

*Velez v. Mitsak, 89 S.W.3d 73 (Tex. Ct. App. 2002)

*In re Vernor, 94 S.W.3d 201 (Tex. App. 2002)

Viragh v. Foldes, 612 N.E.2d 241, 247 (Mass. 1993).

Walsh v. Walsh, 221 F.3d 204 (1st Cir. 2000)

*Whallon v. Lynn, 230 F.3d 450 (1st Cir. 2000)

*Wipranik v. Superior Court, 63 Cal. App. 4th 315 (1998)

*Wojick v. Wojick, 959 F. Supp. 413 (E.D. Mich. 1997)

Index

Page numbers in italics indicate tables or figures

children: characteristics of returned vs.
remained, 185; Hague Convention's focus
on welfare of, 2, 14–15; judicial comity
among nations as trumping welfare of,
135, 152–54; need for research on Hague
petition effects, 202; right to object to
return, 177; trauma of removal from
mother prior to Hague petition decision,
122. *See also* child abduction; child maltreatment; exposure to domestic violence;
return of child to habitual residence
citizenship: country of as target refuge for
taking parent, 8; habitual residence
as trumping, 7, 56; and institutional
support in other country, 76; mothers
vs. fathers in Hague petition cases,
174–75; and moving to other country,
57n1; overview, 19–20. *See also* immigration status in other country
civil cases, Hague Convention cases in
US as, 8. *See also* lawyering in Hague
petition litigation
coercive control, domestic violence as:
defined, 29–30; economic control, *38,
46–48, 52*; and habitual residence
establishment, 176; Hague Convention's
failure to address, 187; immigration
threat, *38, 48–49, 51,* 86, 91–92; importance in determining grave risk of harm,
145; intentional isolation, *38, 45–46, 51;*
international measurement of, 33–34,
36; and involuntary move to other
country, 58–62; measurement difficulty
with, 53–54; need for legal recognition
of, 195–96; rape as tool of, 50. *See also*
emotional terrorizing
cognitive effects of domestic violence
exposure for children, 109
comity between nations, judicial prioritizing
of, 21, 135, 152–54
consent issue in exceptions to return, 14, 177
Convention on the Elimination of All Forms
of Discrimination against Women
(CEDAW), 19

Copelon, R., 54
court of jurisdiction, women's knowledge of,
128–29, 132–33
criminal kidnapping charges, 7, 96, 127,
128–29, 130–31
Crooks, C. V., 135
cultural issues, gender, and domestic
violence, 15–17, 28, 33–34, 197–98
custody law and recognition of domestic
violence, 7, 110–12, 201

Dallemagne v. Dallemagne (2006), 188
Danaipour v. Danaipour (2004), 180–81
divorce: difficulty in obtaining in other
countries, 74–75; as domestic violence
trigger, 42; as Hague petition trigger, 4,
61; lack of relief from abuse after, 64–65,
83; study participants' status, 37
domestic violence: authors' definition, 36;
child abduction's relationship to, 1–2, 5,
82, 104–6; continuation of after Hague
process, 137–40, 143–44; cultural
acceptance of, 28; defining boundaries
of, 28–32; global context, 2, 16–17,
33–36; as Hague petition case consideration, 11–12, 13, 146, 153–56, 185–86;
incidence of, 33–34, 84, 199; lack of
local support for victims in other
country, *65,* 69–70; need for attention
to research on, 195–96; paradox of
Hague petition's effects, 2, 3–6, 22–23;
policy and practice recommendations,
192–93; redefinition of, 30, *31–32;*
resources for assistance, 207–10; risk
factors for perpetrating, 34, 36; terminology consideration, 3n1; types of
experiences, 37–53. *See also* children;
coercive control; judicial reasoning and
decisions in Hague petition cases
domination. *See* coercive control
Donaldson, R., 104
due process compromise for Hague petition
respondents, 194
Dufort, V., 117

Earp, J. A. L., 29

economic control, *38, 46–48, 52*

Edleson, J. L., 107

Edwards, A., 199

Elyashiv v. Elyashiv (2005), 179, 182

emotional terrorizing: continuation of after Hague petition success, 137; effect on child, 117–19; incidence of, *38, 51, 52*; judges' lack of consideration for, 126, 127; measuring as part of coercive control, 33–34; study participants' experience of, 38–41, 42; threat of harm, 29–30

ending relationship, inability to stop abuse by, 64–65. *See also* divorce

entrapment in coercive control, 30

Eveline, J., 198

evidentiary standards issue, 169, 189, 194

exceptions to return: attorney opinion on use of, 153; and custody law model in US, 111–12; frequency of successful use, 177–78, *178*; judicial reasoning in, 176–78, 188; long-term effects of decision, 141–43; overview of types, 13–15; for psychological harm to child, 135

expert testimony, *128–29*, 132, 159–61, 169, 180–81, 185

exposure to domestic violence, child's: after return to left-behind parent, 23, 192–93; by age, 108; behavioral effects of, 108–9; cognitive effects of, 109; definitional issues, 106–7; expert testimony's role in providing evidence, 161; grave risk of harm criterion, 21, 53, 95–96, 106–10, 119–20, 144–45, 180; Hague Convention's failure to address, 14n7, 95–96; human rights issue, 12, 15, 177; incidence of, 107–8; judicial consideration level, 110–12, 127, 135, 152–54, 188–91, 195–96; mothers' reports on, 112–19; psychological effects of, 109, 115–20, 132, 169–70, 181–82, 196; and rebuttable presumption statutes, 110–11. *See also* grave risk of harm criterion

family abduction, defined, 101. *See also* child abduction

family support for battered women, 48, 76, 89, 91, 98

fathers as primary initiators of Hague petitions, 175. *See also* left-behind parent

federal vs. state jurisdiction choice in US, 161–64, 170–71

Finkelhor, D., 103

Forehand, R., 102

Friedrich v. Friedrich (1996), 177, 188

Garbolino, Hon. JD., 146–47, 150

gay and lesbian families, 9n5, 16, 33n2

gender-based violence. *See* domestic violence

gender inequality and patriarchy: and global cultural contexts, 15–17, 28, 33–34, 197–98; and human rights issue, 19, 199–200; international efforts to address, 17–18; ongoing power inequities in domestic violence, 29; structural lack of support for battered women, 67–69, 73–74, 190

gender mainstreaming, 18, 198

Girdner, L., 105, 106

globalization theory and context, 2, 15–20, 33–36. *See also* transnational context

Goldman, David and Bruna, 9

grave risk of harm criterion: and child's exposure to domestic violence, 21, 53, 95–96, 106–10, 119–20, 144–45, 180; defined, 178; domestic violence potential as, 14, 177, 182; evidentiary standard for, 169, 189, 194; and fatal consequences of return to domestic violence situation, 23; Hague Convention clause on, 7, 12; judicial reasoning factors in, 134–35, 178–85, *179*, 188–89; need for redefinition, 170; psychological damage as fulfilling, 127, 134–35, 146

Greenbook Initiative, 111

Greif, G. L., 103, 105

guardian *ad litem*, 111, 132, 195

habitual residence criterion: complications of ascertaining, 63; definitional issues, 2, 56–57; evidentiary standard for, 169; exception for persistent time away from, 177; Hague Convention's focus on virtues of, 7, 13, 144–45, 147; immigration status disadvantage for taking parent, 56–57, 200; and judicial reasoning in Hague petition cases, 122–27, *128–29*, 130–35, 176, 186–87. *See also* return of child to habitual residence; survival strategy vs. child abduction

Hagemeister, A. K., 107

Hague Conference on Private International Law (HCPIL), 17–18

Hague Convention on Jurisdiction, Applicable Law, Recognition, Enforcement and Co-operation in Respect of Parental Responsibility and Measures for the Protection of Children, 194–95

Hague Convention on the Civil Aspects of International Child Abduction: gender inequality issue for, 197–98; globalization theory and context, 15–20; and human rights definition, 55; overview and implementation, 6–15; projected increase in cases, 22; purpose, 1–3; reasons for studying domestic violence context, 20–23

hardships for mothers and children after Hague petition decisions, 136–41, 192–95. *See also* return of child to habitual residence

Hasanovic, Cassandra, 23

HCPIL (Hague Conference on Private International Law), 17–18

Hegar, R., 103, 105

human rights consideration: defined, 19; evidentiary standard for, 189, 194; and exceptions to return, 12, 15, 177; gender inequality perspective, 19, 199–200; vs. nation-to-nation judicial comity, 135; overview, 18–19; private vs. public sphere

issue for domestic violence, 19, 53–55, 199–200

Hunter, W., 117

ICAAN (International Child Abduction Attorney Network), 149–50

ICARA (International Child Abduction Remedies Act) (1988), 8, 147, 150, 163, 172, 189

immigrants to US. *See* Latinas

immigration status in other country: and habitual residence, 56–57, 200; legal rights issues for taking parent, 200–201; living situation difficulty after Hague petition success, 140–41, 200; and reasons for leaving, 75–76; threats from abuser based on, *38, 48–49, 51,* 86, 91–92

INCADAT (International Child Abduction Database), 147

incoming vs. outgoing case types in US courts, 7, *10,* 10–11, 24–25

institutions, public: challenges in obtaining help in other countries, 65–72, 76, 89, 99–100; and gender inequality, 197–98; human rights responsibility, 19, 53–55, 199–200; intimate relationship brokering role, 17–18

intentional isolation, *38,* 45–46, *51*

intentional physical child abuse, 113–14

International Child Abduction Attorney Network (ICAAN), 149–50

International Child Abduction Database (INCADAT), 147

International Child Abduction Remedies Act (ICARA) (1988), 8, 147, 150, 163, 172, 189

International Social Service, 12–13

intimate partner violence. *See* domestic violence

intimate terrorism vs. situational couple violence, 30

intolerable situation standard, 169, 170, 188

involuntary move to other country, 58–62

Jaffe, P. G., 135
Janvier, R. F., 104
Johnson, M. P., 30
Johnson, R. M., 117
Johnston, J., 105, 106
judicial reasoning and decisions in Hague
petition cases: domestic violence
consideration level, 110–12, 124–27,
135, 144–45, 152–54, 186–91; exceptions to Hague petition, 176–78, 188;
grave risk of harm criterion, 134–35,
178–85, *179*, 188–89; habitual residence
criterion, 122–27, *128–29*, 130–35, 176,
186–87; methods of analysis, 173–74,
183–85, 228–31; nation-to-nation
comity vs. children's interests, 21, 135,
152–54; neglect of research on exposure
to domestic violence, 189–91, 195–96;
parties in Hague Convention disputes,
174–75, 186; petition success rates, 175;
policy and legal practice implications,
189–91, 196; purpose of studying, 172;
US judicial perspective, 110–12, 122–27,
128–29, 130–35, 194. *See also* return of
child to habitual residence
judicial system/police, going to in other
country, 63–69, *65,* 73–75, 83, 89
jurisdiction shopping, 6

Kilpatrick Stockton, LLP, 147
Kotch, J. B., 117

language barriers to obtaining help, 73, 98–99
Latent Class Analysis (LCA), defined, 184,
230–31
Latinas: family and other support in US, 91;
Hague petition and legal process effects,
92–96; immigrant status challenges,
98–100, 200–201; immigration threats,
91–92; introduction, 84–88; participants'
reasons to leave for US, 88–90; *pro bono*
legal representation availability, 134;
resiliency and resourcefulness, 96–98
lawyering, defined, 156–57

lawyering in Hague petition litigation:
assessing domestic violence allegations,
154–56; effort factor for attorneys, 156–61;
evidence retrieval from other country,
157–58, 170; experience factor for
attorneys, 127, *128–29,* 131–32; federal
and state concurrent jurisdiction (US),
161–64, 170–71; helpful lawyer in Latina
case, 93–94; improved practice recommendations, 168–71, 196; introduction,
146–48; judicial comity vs. children's
interests, 152–54; resources for Hague
petition defense, 148–51, 207–10;
undertakings and mirror orders,
164–68, 169
LCA (Latent Class Analysis), defined, 184,
230–31
left-behind parent: assumption as victim of
taking parent, 8; child abduction effects
on, 103–4; child maltreatment after
Hague petition success, 136–37, 144;
defined, 6; exposure of children to
domestic violence, 192–93; fathers vs.
mothers as in actual cases, 186; legal
assistance for, 11, 148–51; use of legal
means to return children, 9–10
legal resources: citizenship issue, 20; judicial
system/police in other country, 63–69,
65, 73–75, 83, 89; Latina women's lack of
in US, 99; for left-behind parents, 11,
148–51; taking parent's challenges in
finding, 11, 23, 149–51, 168, 195; time
frame issue for taking parent, 14, *128–29,*
134, 194
lethality risk, and leaving abusive relationship, 83. *See also* threat to life/to kill
Libal, K., 19
litigation of Hague petition cases. *See*
lawyering in Hague petition litigation
Long, N., 102
Lowe, Nigel, 8

Mahmoody, Betty, 8
marital rape, 28

United Nations Convention on the Rights of the Child, 135

United States: consequences of decision to stay in, 79–81, 141–43; embassy as resource to escape abuse, 65, 71–72, 194; federal and state concurrent jurisdiction, 161–64, 170–71; implementation of Hague Convention, 8–9; incidence of domestic violence in, 199; incoming vs. outgoing case types in, 7, *10*, 10–11, 24–25; judicial decisions in response to Hague petition, 110–12, 122–27, *128–29*, 130–35, 194; lack of information on Hague petition consequences, 5; legal handling of domestic violence, 28–29, 86, 99; Supreme Court on *Abbott v. Abbott* (2010), 20–21, 22; variations in habitual residence definition, 56. *See also* Latinas; lawyering in Hague petition litigation

Universal Declaration of Human Rights, 18–19, 199

U-Visa program, 87, 99

Van De Sande v. Van De Sande (2005), 179

Violence Against Women Act (VAWA) (1994) (US), 28–29, 86, 99

Vivatvaraphol, T., 56

voluntary move to another country, 58

Walsh v. Walsh (2000), 180

Weiner, M. H., 15

Whallon v. Lynn (2000), 188

Winsor, J. R., 117

witnessing of physical abuse of mother by child, 107, 115–17. *See also* exposure to domestic violence

witness testimony, securing, 158–59

Zogg, C., 102